Heroes and Contemporaries

Heroes
and
Contemporaries

JONATHAN AITKEN

continuum
LONDON • NEW YORK

Continuum UK
The Tower Building
11 York Road
London SE1 7NX

Continuum US
80 Maiden Lane
Suite 704
New York, NY 10038

www.continuumbooks.com

First published 2006

British Library Cataloguing-in-Publication Data
A catalogue record for this book is available from the British Library.

ISBN: 0–8264–7833–6 (hb)
ISBN: 0–8264–9441–2 (pb)

Typeset by Kenneth Burnley, Wirral, Cheshire
Printed and bound in Great Britain by MPG Books Ltd, Bodmin, Cornwall

Contents

To Elizabeth

my heroine and contemporary

Preface and Acknowledgements

This book is a collection of biographical portraits featuring remarkable men and women I have known in life's journey. They are in no sense definitive, comprehensive or official portraits. Rather like an amateur photographer, I come at my subjects from an angle. It is the angle of personal knowledge and private glimpses. In each chapter I have tried to keep my own appearances in the portraits to a low level, but in certain scenes and situations I am inevitably present as the narrator, hopefully in a way that does not intrude too heavily.

The choice of my subjects is also amateur but in an alternative meaning of the word. For I like and admire all the individuals I have written about. This means there are no hatchet jobs, but neither is there hagiography. These portraits are frank and honest glimpses of my heroes and heroines.

The main sources of biographical material in each chapter are my own diaries, correspondence and recollections, reinforced by wider research in publications acknowledged in the source notes. In addition I carried out many hours of interviews. Some of my interviewees did not wish to be identified. However, those whom I can gratefully acknowledge for their co-operation include: Lady Wilson of Rievaulx; Lady Antonia Pinter; Lady Annabel Goldsmith; Lady Sarah Aspinall; Taki Theodoracopulos; Mark Thatcher; Pippa Gumbel; Ken Costa; the Reverend Nicky Lee; Jeremy Jennings; Tricia Neill; Sir Frank Williams and Patrick Head.

I am also grateful to Rupert Abbott of Greyfriars College, Oxford, for his invaluable research assistance and to the following secretarial helpers who typed and retyped the manuscript at various stages: Kate Rainbow; Lyndsey Whitcombe; Jackie Cottrell; Andrea Agrell and Helen Kirkpatrick.

Lastly I warmly thank my publisher, Robin Baird-Smith and his colleagues at Continuum for all their encouragement, assistance and superb professional expertise.

Jonathan Aitken
January 2006

CHAPTER 1

Uncle Max,
Lord Beaverbrook

Because of an obscure Aitken family quarrel in the 1930s I did not meet my great uncle, the first Lord Beaverbrook, until the 1960s. But when I was 19 years old, during my first term at Oxford, I wrote to him saying that I was disappointed never to have met my most famous relative. Could he please forget his ancient feuds with my father and grandfather and allow me to come and see him? This chutzpah paid off. The next morning a telegram arrived with the summons: 'Come lunch Sunday, Beaverbrook.'

That Sunday I drove up the imposing mile-and-a-half-long drive of Cherkley Court, Beaverbrook's country house near Leatherhead, I had so much time to spare before lunch that I parked in some shrubbery for a 20-minute wait. The delay gave me a chance to take stock of what I knew about my great uncle. He was the multi-millionaire proprietor of three national newspapers: the *Daily Express,* the *Sunday Express* and the *London Evening Standard,* which in those days sold over 30 million copies a week. He had been a prominent politician, the only Cabinet Minister, apart from his great friend Winston Churchill, to have held office in the coalition governments of both the First and Second World Wars. He was a successful author with nine titles to his name ranging from humorous self-help books (*Don't Trust to Luck* was his great best seller) to weighty tomes of political history. Frequently described as 'a character' – whether good or bad was a matter of debate – Beaverbrook had a reputation for making trouble, being ruthless, giving

1

parties, enjoying the company of beautiful women and wielding hands-on power through his newspapers. So as I rang the Cherkley doorbell my mood was one of fascination and trepidation. It became one of surprise as a camp footman ushered me into the hall and announced in a voice worthy of a pantomine dame: 'The Lord is waiting for you.' Later I discovered that this curious form of address was used by the household staff on the instructions of a Canadian butler unfamiliar with British titles.

As I entered Beaverbrook's study I was surprised by 'The Lord's' appearance. He was small in height, no more than 5′6″ tall, with a stooping gait which made him look tired and shrunken. He had a high, balding forehead whose wizened skin gave him the appearance of a shrivelled prune. Somehow I had expected, even at 82, to meet a figure who radiated power. However, his physical frailty was deceptive. For the energy of Beaverbrook became apparent when he opened his oversized mouth and began speaking in a rasping transatlantic twang.

'Aha, the rising generation,' he said, creasing his features into an impish grin. 'And you're better looking than that father of yours. You've gone to university I hear. Where are you studying?'

'I've just started at Oxford sir,' I replied. 'I'm reading law at Christ Church.'

'Oxford, hmmmm,' said Beaverbrook with a note of disdain in his voice. 'I got my education from the university of hard knocks.'

'And you did very well there,' piped up the voice of a thin, olive-skinned lady who had just come into the room. She was introduced to me as Lady Dunn. I had read about her in *Private Eye*, which labelled her 'Lord Beaverbrook's permanent house guest'.

We sat down to lunch as a threesome and I soon found myself being grilled on all manner of subjects. 'Do ya read any books at Oxford?' asked Beaverbrook. 'I've just been reading a biography of you by Tom Driberg,' I replied in an attempt to ingratiate myself. It failed. 'That's bad. That's a bad, bad book,' replied the subject of it. 'You should read the review of it published in the *Daily Express*. The headline was: "Lord Beaverbrook – an inaccurate biography".'

I resisted the temptation to ask who had written the headline.

After lunch, there was an amusing illustration of where the power lay in this department of the *Daily Express*. We were having coffee in Beaverbrook's study when a Reuter's ticker tape machine whirred into life, printing out a fresh item of news. My Uncle Max, evidently an insatiable news junkie, tore the item off the machine and read it. Then his face puckered into laughter. 'Aha, we can make some mischief with this,' he said, picking up the telephone that connected him directly to the *Daily Express*. 'Who's in charge of the clattering train today?' he asked, apparently his usual way of enquiring who was the duty editor. A Mr Wood came on the line. 'Mr Wood, have you seen this story about four soldiers from the British Army of the Rhine killed near Berlin when their jeep was struck by lightning?' asked his proprietor. The editor had not seen it, reasonably enough since it had only come across the ticker tape a few seconds earlier. 'Mr Wood I advise you, as the editor of the *Daily Express*, to keep up with the news,' said Beaverbrook winking at me. 'When ya do catch up with this story I recommend a headline. It will help the policy of the *Daily Express* which, I remind ya, is against the Government's attempt to drag us into the Common Market. The headline I commend to you is: 'BRITISH SOLDIERS SLAIN IN GERMAN (big eye-talics) THUNDERSTORM!'

At that Beaverbrook let out his own thunderclap of laughter and put down the phone. Then he asked me: 'Are you for or against the Common Market?'

'I'm against it sir.'

'Good boy! But that father of yours is all for it. He never stops making speeches in the House of Commons saying he's for it.'

'I know. But we disagree on that.'

'Good. So you have some independence of mind then,' said Beaverbrook, tailing off into an ancient grievance, 'that makes you a better man than your father. He's a party man. A whips office man.'

Thinking it was about time I stuck up for my father, I paid him one or two filial compliments. This started an argument about the political merits of Sir William Aitken MP. It ended in Beaverbrook saying, somewhat unfairly, 'Ho, yuss, I can see Oxford is teaching you how to speak well. But a son should speak well of his father – even

3

when he's in the wrong. That's the fourth commandment, "Honour thy father and mother." How is your mother by the way? She's a beautiful woman. The one good thing that father of yours did was to marry your mother!'

'As the son of both of them I can agree with you on that, sir,' I replied, which made Beaverbrook laugh. Soon after that he told me to call him Uncle Max instead of sir. As we finished coffee he asked me if I smoked cigarettes. On hearing I did not, he said approvingly: 'That shows wisdom in a young man. If you must have vices, don't let them be petty ones.'

When it was time to go he insisted on escorting me to the front door. His last words to me, standing in the cavernous porch of Cherkley, were: 'If you're thinking of a political career always remember that politics is the best of lives and the worst of lives.'

Two days later, before I had written my own letter of thanks for the lunch, I received a note from Mr A. G. Millar, an executive at the *Daily Express*. It read, 'Lord Beaverbrook has asked me to thank you for coming to lunch at Cherkley. He enjoyed your visit. He hopes you will come again. In the meantime he has asked me to send you the enclosed cheque for fifty pounds to help you with your travel expenses and your expenses at Oxford.'

Fifty pounds in 1961 was the equivalent of about £750 in today's money. So I lived like a king for the rest of the term.

A few weeks later I was invited back to Cherkley. This time I was in trouble for reasons I had not anticipated. 'Before we go in to lunch I must speak to you about blasphemy,' said Beaverbrook sternly. I knew what he had in mind. A satirical undergraduate magazine called *Oxford Circus* had put on its cover a picture of Rembrandt's *Madonna and Child* with a speech bubble coming out of the Madonna's mouth saying: 'Isn't he divine?' In 1961 this was considered a joke too far by the University proctors who reprimanded the editor, Noel Picarda, fined him five pounds, and banned the offending issue. The episode was reported in the gossip columns of the national newspapers. Although I had nothing to do with the cover, my name was mentioned in the reports because I featured on the masthead of the magazine as its Union correspondent. The reports of this trivial incident had not escaped the eagle eye of my newspaper-addicted great-uncle, who had managed to acquire a copy of the offending edition of *Oxford Circus*. This he now waved in my direction letting off a fusillade of 'oh-dear-oh-dear-oh-dear-oh-dears,' ending with the question: 'Do ya believe in God, Jonathan?' On getting an affirmative answer he became less stern, eventually conceding that my offence was one of bad judgement rather than blasphemy. If I was going into politics I must be very careful not to offend the religious sensitivities of the voters, he warned me. His admonishment ended '. . . and always remember what the Bible says. "The fear of the Lord is the beginning of wisdom".'

At that precise moment I had more fear of the Lord Beaverbrook than of any higher authority. But his solemnity melted away and we had a lunch that was particularly enjoyable because I led him back, with student questions, to the political dramas of the First World War, on which he had written a classic work of eye-witness history, *Men and Power 1917–1918*. Beaverbrook retold one or two anecdotes of the period with great gusto. Then he said to me: 'If you're so interested in Lloyd George [he pronounced the name as Lard Garge], perhaps you'd like to listen to me dictating some revisions to my new book on him.'

Beaverbrook the dictator (of history books) was a theatrical character. He stood upright on a raised platform behind a piece of furniture that was somewhere between a Victorian schoolmaster's desk and a church lectern. Gripping it tightly with one hand, and turning over sheaves of handwritten notes and typed drafts with the other, he addressed the assembled company of me and two secretaries as if we were a large public meeting of the hard-of-hearing. His style was one of staccato sentences, building up to muscular perorations and sweeping judgements. 'Gibbon with Canadian fireworks,' I wrote in my diary. One Gibbonian similarity was that Beaverbrook loved footnotes which introduced humorous details connected to the main narrative. On that first afternoon when I listened to him dictating, he was composing a sonorous judgement on Sir Austen Chamberlain, the leader of the Conservative party in the 1920s. In the middle of a purple passage about Chamberlain's views on Tariff Reform, Beaverbrook suddenly switched into what he called 'Parenthesis –

Footnote' and told a story about Sir Austen Chamberlain dining with a society hostess, Mrs Ronnie Greville. During the dinner she noticed that her butler was inebriated. So she scribbled a note which read: 'You are drunk – leave the room at once,' and handed it to him. Instead of obeying this command from his employer, the butler put the note on a silver salver and swayed his way unsteadily (Beaverbrook imitated the lurchings and swayings of the drunken butler, with his hand in the air bearing aloft an imaginary silver salver) to the top of the table. There the guest of honour, Sir Austen Chamberlain, was in full flow to the assembled company.

As the butler put the salver before him, Sir Austen, recognizing the handwriting of his hostess, screwed in his monocle to read her note. He was so startled by her message that his monocle fell out. 'It was the only recorded occasion when this Tory bird of paradise was shocked into silence,' concluded Beaverbrook.

As I laughed, a question was asked by the author. 'Should it be a footnote or should it be in the main body of the text? Whaddya think?' my Uncle Max demanded. Mentally tossing a coin, I opted for the main body of the text. There it went and there it stayed, my only contribution to what is perhaps Beaverbrook's finest book, *The Decline and Fall of Lloyd George,* scripturally subtitled: *And Great was the Fall Thereof.*

Scriptural quotations, from the King James Version of the Bible, were scattered freely throughout Beaverbrook's conversations with me. He was much given to offering pearls of wisdom in this form, such as: 'Cast your bread upon the waters and it will return to you in a few days', when I asked for his advice on how to sell advertising space for a student magazine. On one occasion he enquired if I knew the parable of the prodigal son, adding gloomily, 'When I was your age I was an even wuss character than the original prodigal son.' This must have been quite an achievement in the sleepy Canadian town of Newcastle, New Brunswick, where his father the Revd William Aitken was the Minister of the Presbyterian church. 'Neither his strap nor his sermons could change my ways,' continued Beaverbrook's version of the parable of the Aitken son. 'I continued in riotous living until my twenty-first birthday. At the end of my birthday party I got drunk and my friends got drunk, so drunk that they threw me into a boat. I hit my head so hard on the bottom of that boat that I was knocked unconscious,' he said, 'but when I came round I found that my whole attitude to life had changed. A lot of bad habits got knocked out of me and a lot of good habits got knocked into me. It was a turning point. From then on I became a hard worker, a great reader, and a maker of money.'

Like many of Beaverbrook's anecdotes about his early years, this one should be taken with a pinch of salt. As my relationship with my Uncle Max developed, he seemed to enjoy telling me stories of his family life, most of which involved various relatives of mine. However, when I relayed them to older members of the Aitken clan, particularly to my Great Aunt Gyp, Beaverbrook's sister, these stories, including the account of the head-banging in the boat, were greeted with a considerable degree of scepticism. 'Max loves to embroider his yarns,' declared Aunt Gyp, who enjoyed rubbishing various Beaverbrook apocrypha, such as the tale of how the Revd William's household was so poor that the 7-year-old Max had to go barefoot to school. When I asked the 82-year-old Max about the truth of this story, he grinned and said that it was 'another version of the same' – apparently a frequent rubric in the Scottish Psalter denoting an alternative tune.

Two legacies of the young Max Aitken's upbringing as a son of the manse were much in evidence in the Lord Beaverbrook I was getting to know. The first was a prodigious memory. The second was a fear of death.

Beaverbrook's extraordinary memory was trained by his father who insisted that all his children should learn psalms and passages of scripture by heart. Having acquired this discipline in the service of God, the young Max was soon using it in the service of Mammon, for he deployed his powers of recall to master the details of balance sheets and figures for takeover bids. The gift helped him to become a successful financier and later, after emigrating to England in 1910, a successful politician. He once astonished me by reciting at least three minutes' worth of a 1915 speech by Lloyd George which crescendoed in a peroration about 'the great white pinnacle of sacrifice, pointing like a rugged finger to heaven'. After I had expressed my amazement at his perfect recollection of the speech, Beaverbrook said: '"Genius is memory". That's what Thomas Carlyle said. And he's right.'

By this time I was getting invited to Cherkley quite often, sometimes for fascinating lunches and dinners full of eminent people of whom the greatest was Sir Winston Churchill and the rudest his son Randolph (see the next two chapters). As a host Beaverbrook was generous and charming. His parties were fun because he so much enjoyed stirring up rows, loving the sparks that flew when left-of-centre journalists such as Michael Foot, Emlyn Hughes, George Gale and Hugh Cudlipp dined at the same table as such Conservative political figures as Lord Rosebery, Julian Amery, Hugh Fraser and Iain Macleod. Sometimes on these occasions Beaverbrook could be quite a bully. I recall one embarrassing evening when a then little-known London solicitor, Arnold Goodman, was given a terrible dressing down for his failure to extract an apology from the BBC in response to an eccentric complaint from his client, Lady Dunn, that broadcasting a Tom Lehrer song, 'Poisoning Pigeons in the Park', was an outrage against human decency and animal rights. After the assembled party had been made to listen to a recording of this light-hearted ditty, the unfortunate Arnold Goodman was cruelly berated for his inadequacy in not persuading the BBC to take Lehrer off the air. The attack was made primarily by Lady Dunn who seemed to have an obsession with protecting the lives of pigeons, but Beaver-brook backed her up, shouting: 'Don't pay his fees!' and: 'Get yourself a proper lawyer!'

The same cruel streak was sometimes apparent in Beaverbrook's dealings with his staff. 'Drat that Vines!' he would yell in the direction of his hardworking but terrified private secretary, Colin Vines, who was often cursed for no discernible reason. Even Beaverbrook's son, Max Aitken, did not escape the lash of his father's tongue. One morning when I had been an overnight guest at Cherkley I was summoned to the study to hear Max (then the Joint Managing Director of the *Daily Express*) being given a ferocious rocket for not being able to answer detailed questions on the paper's advertising sales. 'The trouble with you is that you're always away yachting [pronounced yatting] when ya should be working,' bellowed Beaver-brook, whose only motive in bringing me in to hear this diatribe must have been to inflict additional humiliation on his son.

Beaverbrook had a legendary temper which exploded more ir-rationally in old age because of gout and other infirmities. In his eighty-third year these took a turn for the worse when he was diagnosed with cancer of the prostate. The bad news was given to him by his doctor, Sir Daniel Davies. On a summer afternoon in July 1962 Davies called to report the results of his tests. 'How long have I got?' asked Beaverbrook. Instead of giving his patient a direct reply the doctor walked over to the window of the big drawing room and gazed out across the rolling landscape of the Cherkley estate for what Beaverbrook called 'a diabolically long 30 seconds'. Eventually Sir Daniel Davies turned round and declaimed a verse of poetry in a funereal voice:

> Dear God, you were a little unkind
> To make these hills and dales
> So beautiful
> And the days of the shepherd
> So few.

'Oh Uncle Max, I'm so sorry,' was my reaction when he told me this poignant story several weeks later. Perhaps I should have guessed from his theatrical account of the episode that there might be a twist in the tale.

'So now I'm just a poor old man,' he continued in tones of morose self-pity. I was on the point of taking out my handkerchief when Beaverbrook sat bolt upright in his chair and bellowed: 'BUT I'M NOT DEAD YET!' Then, with joyful triumph, he told me that he had been so appalled by Sir Daniel Davies's death sentence that he had sought a second opinion from the greatest prostate cancer specialist in the world who came over from Paris. This French consultant had poured scorn on the British medical reports, calling them '*un sac à puce*' (a bag of fleas). So Sir Daniel's diagnosis and his poem were 'all moonshine'.

'And d'ya know what the lesson from this is?' asked my apparently revitalised Uncle Max. 'It's a lesson I commend to you. It is: Always dispute the umpire's decision!'

For a time Beaverbrook did seem to be in better health, although in fact the medical reality of his condition had been correctly diagnosed on this side of the Channel. Perhaps his cancer was in remission. Or perhaps he was temporarily invigorated by the four remaining interests in his life to which he gave his full attention. These were: the reviews of his last two books; his marriage to Lady Dunn; his newspapers' reporting of the Tory leadership crisis; and the making of his will. Having a ring-side seat at these sagas gave me several fascinating insights into the character of the ailing Lord Beaverbrook.

1963 was a year in which Beaverbrook's publishers brought out two of his books. One was *The Decline and Fall of Lloyd George*, an eyewitness account of one of the great dramas of twentieth-century British politics. The other was *The Divine Propagandist*, a slender volume of amateur theology. The first was acclaimed by heavyweight historians. The second was panned by more cynical commentators.

After a lifetime of dishing out editorial praise and censure on other people in the columns of his newspapers, I would have guessed that my Uncle Max might be inclined to treat these two impostors with some nonchalance if either of them came his way in the books pages of rival publications. Not so. Beaverbrook the author was child-like to the point of ecstasy in his delight at good reviews, and thin-skinned to the point of paranoia when he received bad ones. On a weekend visit to Cherkley soon after the publication of *The Decline and Fall of Lloyd George,* a file of its reviews was produced by a secretary. I was required to read them aloud to my Uncle Max even though, to judge by the underlinings and annotations of the dog-eared clippings, he was already familiar with them. When guests arrived for dinner I was back in action again as a reader of the reviews. The performance (punctuated by avuncular stage directions such as: 'Slowly, Jonathan! The next paragraph is good') was repeated again for the benefit of the Sunday lunch guests. There was one particularly fulsome review by Lady Violet Bonham Carter which I must have read out at least four times to various guests. Lady

Violet's laudatory comments on the book were followed by applause – led by the author himself.

Beaverbrook's elation at the praise showered on *The Decline and Fall of Lloyd George* caused him to talk enthusiastically about his next two literary projects, *The Age of Baldwin* and *The Power of Churchill*. He said to me: 'If I am remembered at all in 50 years' time it will be for my books, not for my newspapers or my time as a Minister.' This pride in the acclaim given to his work as a historian evaporated in the face of the vilification he received for his first appearance in print as a theologian. For *The Divine Propagandist* had a rough reception. Beaverbrook took the slings and arrows of outrageous reviewers personally. He was deeply hurt that his 77-page attempt 'to present the story of Jesus as it appears to worldly men of my generation' should have been greeted with ridicule. He was literally in tears after I read aloud to him a scathing review in the *New Statesman*, headlined 'CHRIST!' by Malcolm Muggeridge. This was such an uncharacteristic reaction that I asked my great uncle why he minded Muggeridge's barbs so much. Instead of answering my question he asked me one of his own: 'Are you afraid of dying?'

It was a bizarre enquiry to put to a 21-year-old. The more I thought about it the more I suspected that my Uncle Max was interrogating himself. From this and other clues I began to wonder if *The Divine Propagandist* could be Beaverbrook's attempt to get his accounts straight with his maker.

The Divine Propagandist received at least one good review. It appeared under the byline 'A. G. Artis' in a student magazine, *Oxford Tory*, of which I happened to be the editor. Beaverbrook was well pleased by the complimentary opinions of Mr Artis whom he praised in a letter to me as a 'most thoughtful and perceptive reviewer'. The letter ended: 'Kindly send me Mr Artis's address so that I may write and thank him for his comments.'

Beaverbrook's request was a problem. For A. G. Artis was a pseudonym derived from an anagram of *Ars Gratia*. The real reviewer was me. Eventually I felt obliged to confess this to my Uncle Max who, at first, was cross ('so you're a devious boy – eh?') and then rather pleased. For I managed to convince him, first, that a favourable notice by a junior Aitken of the senior Aitken's book would have been discounted by the readers of *Oxford Tory* and, secondly, that my positive view of *The Divine Propagandist* was genuine.

Deep down Beaverbrook was a lonely and insecure man who craved affection and applause. He longed to be respected and liked for himself, not for his power and money. In some small way I may have helped to fill this insecurity gap. For although I was far from averse to receiving over-generous reimbursements of my so-called travel expenses, my enthusiasm for visiting Cherkley was not financially motivated. I was fascinated by the very subjects that fascinated my great-uncle – politics, journalism, history and the latest gossip. Also, in some subliminal way, I was perhaps more interested than I then knew in the study of God, a major preoccupation of Beaverbrook in his final years. My review of *The Divine Propagandist* created a bond between us which grew as he talked with passion about his father, the Revd William, and his sermons. 'As I boy I thought my father was an old fool. I did not pay enough attention to him,' he told me. 'But now, in the evening of my days, I recognize that my father was a far greater man than me. If I had to choose between being a cabinet minister, a millionaire or an evangelist I would now choose to be an evangelist. It is the evangelist who has the greatest capacity for doing good.'

I was not deeply interested in my Uncle Max's spiritual ruminations but I listened to them with attentiveness because they were part of a growing old man–young man rapport between us. This rapport manifested itself in numerous small ways (such as handwritten letters, inscribed books, recommendations for reading, advice on the speeches I was making in the Oxford Union) and in one big way. I was the only member of the family Beaverbrook told in advance of his intention to marry Lady Dunn. In retrospect I think he singled me out for this confidence in order to annoy his children, Max and Janet, who were both opposed to this much-rumoured match. But at the time I was flattered to be told in confidence, on 28 May 1963, that the Dunn–Beaverbrook nuptials would be taking place ten days later. The reasons for the marriage seemed curious. When we were alone together in his study after dinner my Uncle Max embarked on a rambling encomium of Lady Dunn's youth (she was 53 to his 84), her beauty, her courage and her wealth.

'Do ya realize she's worth 80 – eight, zero – million dollars?' he asked rhetorically. 'And d'ya realize she is using her great fortune to develop many fine projects for my Foundation at the University of New Brunswick … now hear this. I commend to you this advice, Jonathan: Never be afraid to marry a rich woman!'

This pearl of avuncular wisdom was the first real clue to me that a wedding might be in the offing. Somewhat to my Uncle Max's discomfiture, or so it seemed, I congratulated him enthusiastically. I also asked him what had been the decisive factor in persuading him to take the plunge. Nervously he insisted that I must swear never to divulge this deep secret to Janet or to Max. Then, in a conspiratorial whisper he said the answer to my question was: 'A promise. I pledged my troth to her before God a long time ago.' Raising his voice he declaimed two lines of a poem by Robert Frost:

> For I have promises to keep
> And miles to go before I sleep.

It was a moving but baffling explanation for re-marriage in his eighty-fifth year.

Beaverbrook had just over 12 months' worth of miles to go. His health was visibly failing but he rallied for one last rumbustious saga of intrigue and infighting – the Tory leadership crisis of 1963.

Beaverbrook was an expert in the making and unmaking of Prime Ministers. He had been the decisive influence in pushing Asquith out of the doors of No. 10 Downing Street in 1916 and ushering in the Premiership of Lloyd George. Without Beaverbrook's machinations to break up the coalition government in 1922 it is improbable that Lloyd George would have fallen, and impossible for Bonar Law (a Beaverbrook protégé) to become the new Prime Minister. It is also arguable that if it had not been for the stalwart financial, editorial and personal support Beaverbrook gave Winston Churchill throughout the 1930s, England's greatest statesman might not have been ready to take the helm in 1940. With this history of power-broking, it was inevitable that Beaverbrook should throw himself and his newspapers into the fray with gusto when a totally unexpected battle erupted in October

1963 for the leadership of the Conservative party and the Prime Min-
istership of Britain.

Early on in that battle the *Sunday Times* reported that, when the
editor of the *Sunday Express* had consulted his proprietor as to which
of the Tory contenders should be supported, Beaverbrook had
responded by singing down the telephone: 'Sow the seeds of discontent,' to the tune of 'Polly Put the Kettle On'. The morning this gossip
column story appeared Beaverbrook called me in Oxford to ask me if
I had read it.

'It is not so. It makes me sound mad. It is a most inaccurate piece
of reporting,' he protested, somewhat unconvincingly. I tut-tutted to
him sympathetically over the telephone but under my breath I said:
'*Se non e vero e bene trovato.*' (If it's not true it's well founded.) For I
already knew that my great-uncle was frustrated by his lack of inside
knowledge of the Tory leadership crisis. It seemed likely that his
musical advice about sowing seeds of discontent was simply his way
of covering up his uncharacteristic political ignorance.

By a strange quirk of coincidences I was more in the know than
Beaverbrook was about the twists and turns in the Conservative
leadership crisis of 1963. All that summer I had been employed by
my godfather, The Rt Hon Selwyn Lloyd MP, as his gofer, chauffeur
and amateur private secretary. In this role I accompanied my boss
to the Tory party conference in October 1963. It turned out to be
the most exciting week of my 21-year-old life because it exploded
into a US Presidential-style leadership convention. Instead of the
usual bromides and banalities from the platform in the opening
session of the conference, the hall was electrified by an announcement that Harold Macmillan had been taken into hospital and
would be resigning as Prime Minister. From then on, Blackpool
became Oberammergau, as a passion play of political infighting
unfolded scene by scene before a transfixed audience of party
workers and journalists.

Knowing how much my Uncle Max loved keeping up with the
news, I made it my business to telephone him every evening from my
hotel room in Blackpool. I gave him many tit-bits of gossip about the
conference which he passed on to his editors, usually with instruc-

tions that I should be paid ten or twenty pounds for providing such 'excellent information'. These colourful details, many of which ended up in the Londoner's Diary column of the *Evening Standard*, were nothing to the big secret I became privy to before the Conservative party decamped from Blackpool. For while the conference delegates and the newspapers (especially the *Daily Express)* were whipping up a frenzy of excitement over the two-horse leadership race between R. A. Butler and Quintin Hailsham, behind closed doors the magic circle of decision-makers had decided that they would prefer to back a dark horse – the Fourteenth Earl of Home.

Selwyn Lloyd was a key figure in this king-making process. He carried great weight in the party as a former Foreign Secretary, Chancellor of the Exchequer and chairman of a current inquiry into Central Office reorganization. He disliked Butler, mistrusted Hailsham and had a high regard for Alec Home who had been his successor at the Foreign Office. He persuaded other key figures of his view that Home was the man to back, among them Martyn Redmayne, the Chief Whip, and John Morrison, the chairman of the 1922 Committee. With the support of these and other grandees a Home bandwagon began quietly rolling. Ten days later it rolled all the way to 10 Downing Street.

At the time when Beaverbrook telephoned me about what he had or had not sung about the Tory leadership crisis to the tune of 'Polly Put the Kettle On', he had no idea that Alec Home might be moving into pole position. In the eyes of most political observers the Fourteenth Earl of Home appeared to be a complete non-starter, not least because he had downplayed his own chances in an artfully self-deprecating speech towards the end of the conference. So my Uncle Max was underwhelmed by my thesis. Indeed as I persisted with it he became angry, saying: 'That sea air in Blackpool's infected your brain. Ya talking balls.' He may, however, have been more intrigued than he let on for, 24 hours later, he asked me to come and stay the night with him to tell him more about Blackpool.

From the moment I arrived at Cherkley, the Tory leadership crisis was the number one topic of conversation. By this time I had gleaned more intelligence from Selwyn Lloyd about the growing support for

Home. I thought my reinforced thesis sounded impressive but Uncle Max remained unconvinced. He thought Home would be an anachronism. He kept talking about Curzon in 1923 and how his membership of the House of Lords made it necessary for King George V to send for Stanley Baldwin, Beaverbrook's arch-enemy.

'Butler could be worse than Baldwin,' I observed with the omniscience of youth.

'Worse than Baldwin!' exclaimed Beaverbrook. 'That's bad. That's terrible. We'll have to do something about that.'

Then he picked up the telephone to the *Daily Express* and asked to be put through to Mr Marks.

'Mr Marks I have here in my study at Cherkley a bright young man,' the conversation began. He is the President of the Oxford University Conservative Association. He tells me that the new Prime Minister is gonna be the Earl of Home. Whaddya say about that?'

Derek Marks, the political editor of the *Daily Express,* told his proprietor in vernacular language that Oxford was the home of lost causes. Beaverbrook repeated this to me. Then he said, 'Mr Marks, I hear what you say. But now I would like you to hear what the boy says. He is not a stupid boy. And he has his ear to the ground in high places. So hearken to him. He is coming on the line. His name is Jonathan Aitken.'

I was put on the line to the political editor of the *Daily Express*, who became more polite in his tone after the mention of my surname. However, he remained impolite about my view that Lord Home would become the next Prime Minister.

'Did ya change Marks's mind?' asked Beaverbrook when the conversation had finished. 'No,' I said, 'but he's thinking about it.' 'Think no more,' was my great-uncle's command. 'Lord Home is a bad bet.' I stuck to my guns, adding somewhat incautiously that I thought Home was such a good bet that I had put my money where my mouth was – with a bookmaker in Oxford. 'Whaaat?' cried Beaverbrook, throwing his hands into the air with melodramatic indignation. 'You mean you can bet on Prime Ministers like you can bet on hosses? What's the world coming to?'

He then delivered a lecture on the folly of gambling. Apparently it was the only activity on which my great-uncle had ever lost money.

He embarked on a long ramble about his disastrous investments in horseracing, which had included buying a house in Newmarket. 'Racing people are thieves of the worst type,' was the conclusion of the ramble. 'The only thing that wasn't stolen from me was that house. At least before I quit racing I renamed it Calvin House. It's the only house overlooking the Newmarket gallops named after a great Protestant reformer.'

After a further denunciation of the evils of betting, I was asked a question: 'What odds did ya get on Lord Home?' inquired Beaverbrook, evidently suppressing his Calvinistic conscience in the interests of journalistic curiosity. 'Eleven to one,' I replied, adding in response to further questioning that I had staked forty pounds on the bet. 'Good God!' said Uncle Max. 'That will bring ya four hundred and forty pounds if ya win. That's a fortune for a young boy!' For a moment he frowned in mock disapproval. Then he broke into a cackle of laughter, saying 'I could have got much better odds on Bonar Law if the bookmakers had let me place a bet on him in 1922.'

During lunch a footman wheeled a telephone up to the table. On the line was Randolph Churchill who was writing an article for the *Evening Standard* on the Tory leadership drama. According to his sources, Hailsham was now sure of winning the Premiership.

'Well, I've 'eard different,' said Beaverbrook in imitation cockney. 'In fact I've heard from the boy wonder of Oxford that Lord Home is going to be carried into No. 10 by an army of Tory backwoodsmen. Jonathan is so sure of himself that he's run off to his bookmakers and bet four hundred and forty pounds on Lord Home.'

The noise of an explosion emanated from the other end of the telephone. 'Randolph says *he's* put a monkey [£500] on Hailsham and that you're a complete, bloody fool,' reported Uncle Max, purring with pleasure at having stirred up this conflict between his informants. I had come to know Randolph Churchill as a result of meeting him two years earlier at Cherkley. So I was not surprised to get an earful of abuse when the receiver was passed over to me, although the abuse ended in an invitation to join him at White's for dinner. But that's another story for a later chapter.

The saga of the Tory leadership battle ended in vindication for Oxford as the home of accurate information. Although the unfancied runner I had tipped remained the darkest of dark horses until the final stages, eventually the magic circle delivered the keys of No. 10 Downing Street to Lord Home. Meanwhile, down at Cherkley, the proprietor of the *Daily Express* kept nagging away at Mr Marks and other editors about the rumours on Home's prospects.

In the nick of time the paper picked up the scent and ran it ahead of the competition under the headline: 'HOME IS HOME AND DRY'. So the *Express* had a good scoop for which I was sent a cheque for one hundred pounds. With that, and my winnings from the bookies, I was once again living like a king.

I had two more conversations with my great uncle about money. The first concerned his will. After staying overnight at Cherkley in the spring of 1964 I was breakfasting in the morning room when Mr Mead, the butler, murmured into my ear: 'The Lord would like to see you in his study right away.' Mr Mead added a second murmur as he escorted me along the corridor: 'The Lord seems to be in a very good mood this morning.'

This forecast proved correct. My Uncle Max was positively radiant. Sitting bolt upright in his chair with his legs up on an adjacent blue ottoman he was sparkling with *joie de vivre* as he invited me to take a seat beside him, waving a sheaf of typewritten pages in my direction. 'I've been making my will,' he began. 'And I've been thinking about you, Jonathan. You're a very good boy. A very good boy indeed.'

This promising beginning got even better. My Uncle Max was on some sort of a high as he praised me to the skies. He thought I had shown fine potential as a debater over dinner the night before when I had been locked into a lively argument with Michael Foot. Then a file was produced containing some student magazine articles I had sent him. Beaverbrook read out one or two sentences from them and praised my abilities as a journalist. 'However, you must improve your style,' he added. 'Read Kinglake. Start with *Eothen*. Kinglake is the author who has shaped my style of writing.' After that we moved on to politics, where my career prospects received excessive flattery.

At this point Beaverbrook returned to the subject of his will. He was making it now and he had been thinking of me as he wrote it, he said. But, just as my heart and wallet were beginning to swell with excited anticipation, an unwelcome caveat was entered into the monologue. 'Inherited money can be a curse for a young man,' he declared. In lugubrious tones he mentioned several people, especially members of his family, who had allegedly been spoilt by too much money given them at too young an age. 'So as I was thinking of you when making my will, I decided to pay you a great compliment,' said Beaverbrook with a wickedly expansive grin. 'I'm going to do the greatest thing I can for you. The greatest thing of all. I'm not going to leave you any money. Not a cent!' Alas, he was true to his word.

The last time I saw my great uncle was on his eighty-fifth birthday. This was celebrated by a spectacular party given in his honour by Lord Thomson of Fleet, the owner of Times Newspapers. On the night of 25 May 1964 a glittering guest list worthy of the book title *Men and Power* assembled for this dinner in the Dorchester Hotel. Within the family there had been considerable doubt prior to the event as to whether the guest of honour would ever make it. For Beaverbrook's health was failing badly during the weeks before his birthday. He was bedridden for all but a few hours each day, slipping in and out of consciousness. Realizing that he might be too ill to attend his own festivities, he tape recorded a speech to be played to the guests at the Dorchester in his absence. It was a pale shadow of the address he eventually delivered in person.

The reserves of willpower that Beaverbrook drew upon to rise from his sick bed and attend the dinner must have been enormous. But when he got to his feet to respond to the toasts, power and energy surged into his voice. He delivered a tour de force of a speech with captivating charm and coruscating wit. 'All my life I have been an apprentice,' he began, as he thundered down the memory lanes of his variegated careers in business, politics, authorship and journalism, with jokes, teases and flashes of zest.

To those of us who knew how close Beaverbrook had been to death's door in the days running up to his eighty-fifth birthday, the vigour of his 20-minute speech seemed little short of miraculous. But then came a poignant peroration.

'Well, now I am in the first day of my eighty-sixth year. I do not feel very different from my eighty-fifth year. But this is my final word. It is time for me to become an apprentice once more. I have not settled in which direction. But somewhere, sometime soon.'

Many people in the 650-strong audience, including me, were close to tears. But we hid our feelings by singing 'For He's a Jolly Good Fellow', followed by 'Land of Hope and Glory'. On the way out I was one of the multitude who congratulated the guest of honour on his speech. As I shook my great-uncle's hand he asked me to wait on one side for a moment. Ostensibly this was to take part in a family photograph, followed by the agreeable tradition Beaverbrook had invented of giving presents to his relatives on his own birthday. As we all knew it would be the last such occasion, there was a sad and valedictory atmosphere in the room. Yet, when he handed me an envelope containing a handsome cheque, his voice was as strong and cheerful as it had been in his speech.

'Don't go off again to that bookmaker of yours with this, will ya?' he chuckled. 'For there's no gambling like a career in politics. Are you still sure that's what you want to do with your life?' 'Yes – definitely,' I replied. 'Well as I've told ya before, politics is the best of lives and the worst of lives. But enjoy it, and make sure you stir up lots of mischief.'

Thirteen days later Beaverbrook died. I cherish his memory. Perhaps I may have followed his last words of advice rather too well. Yet without the influence of my Uncle Max I would have had a far duller, narrower life. He remains one of my greatest heroes.

CHAPTER 2

Sir Winston Churchill

Winston Churchill was a hero of titanic proportions to me in my schoolboy years. His picture hung in my bedroom. His effigy was on my tea mug. His voice reverberated around our house because on my gramophone I was so often playing the LP records of his war speeches. This permanent state of homage meant that I was forever quoting Churchill's phrases, imitating his mannerisms and worshipping at the shrine of his greatness. I doubt whether any contemporary football fan's admiration for their modern sporting hero could equal the veneration I felt for my political hero. For me, Winston Churchill was and still remains the greatest British statesman of all time.

The idea of meeting my hero, at least when I was a young boy, was a dream far beyond the horizons of my imagination. Yet in the fullness of time I had three encounters with the great man. The first was a passing handshake at a historic ceremony in Westminster Hall on his eightieth birthday. The second was a magical dinner party conversation with him about political oratory. On the third occasion I was rudely asked to leave his house in circumstances of enormous embarrassment.

On the 30 November 1954, the day of Winston Churchill's eightieth birthday, both Houses of Parliament assembled in Westminster Hall to present him with gifts and formal addresses of congratulations. I was present, quite possibly the youngest person at 12 years old, in the 2,500-strong audience. I was there because my father, a backbench Tory MP, had been allocated two tickets for the ceremony. As my mother was feeling unwell that morning, I went in her place. To this day I remember walking through the gates of Palace Yard in a state of high excitement.

My morning began and ended with memorable handshakes. The first one caused a row. As we were entering Westminster Hall in a crush of bodies, my father found himself alongside Nye Bevan, whom he knew well. So he said: 'Nye, may I introduce my son Jonathan?' and to me: 'Jonathan, this is Mr Aneurin Bevan.' Nye Bevan, who was at that time regarded as a fiery left winger who might soon succeed Clement Attlee as Leader of the Labour party, put out his right hand. I put mine firmly behind my back. The only explanation for this appalling rudeness was that my schoolboy's political zealotry had led me to regard all socialists as mortal enemies. My father was horrified. He gave me a whack on the back of my legs with his walking stick and ordered me to shake hands. As I reluctantly obeyed this paternal order Nye Bevan was much amused.

'Proper little Tory boy you've got here, Bill,' he chuckled.

As a result of my bad behaviour, the first two or three minutes after taking my seat at the Churchill ceremony were filled with an enormous ticking-off from my father. But once this was over, I took stock of my surroundings with awe and wonder. The magnificent tenth-century walls and rafters of Westminster Hall looked to me like the throne room of an Emperor's palace. It was an impression heightened by the arrival of various colourfully robed and bewigged personages on the platform such as the Lord Chancellor and the Speaker of the House of Commons. Once these and other famous figures like Mr Attlee were in their seats, a hush fell over the assembly. It was an eerily expectant silence broken only by a Guardsman thumping out a repetitive refrain on his big drum: 'da-da-da-DUM'. As every schoolboy in those days knew, this was the morse code signal for 'V', the victory symbol that was part of the Churchill legend.

The legend himself strode into Westminster Hall on the stroke of 11. In the flesh he looked identical to the figure I had idolized from his many portraits and photographs. He had a spotted bow-tie that seemed to jut out in symmetry with his protruding chin. He was wearing a frock coat, striped trousers and black waistcoat adorned by a thick gold watch chain that he twirled between his thumb and index finger. His baby-faced features were creased in smiles of recognition and rejoicing as he acknowledged the tumultuous applause. Still Prime Minister, still in the plenitude of his powers and sounding just as vigorous in voice as he did on my LP records of his war speeches, here a mere 80 feet away from me on the steps of Westminster Hall stood the Winston Churchill of my dreams.

Over fifty years on from this historic ceremony I can still remember several key ingredients of it. One was the warmth of the love and admiration of the huge audience. Another was the number of good jokes by the supporting speakers. I recall Mr Attlee declaring that he had come not to bury Caesar, but to praise him, adding: 'Caesar indeed, for you have not only waged war but you have written your own commentaries upon it.' To a schoolboy wrestling with Caesar's Gallic War in the classroom, this seemed a most felicitous compliment.

Churchill's speech had everything. Even I could tell he was underwhelmed by the House of Commons' gift of a Graham Sutherland portrait from his caustic inflexion of the words: 'It seems to me a most interesting example of modern art.' I could feel from the emotion throbbing in his voice that he was close to being overwhelmed by the outpourings of gratitude of his fellow Parliamentarians. And I loved the theatrical performer in him when he came to his peroration: 'It was the nation that had the lion's heart. I had the luck to be called upon to give – the roar.'

Churchill's imitation of the lion's roar brought the whole of Westminster Hall to its feet in cheers. A few seconds later the great man came off the platform and walked down the central aisle that parted 250 rows of chairs in Westminster Hall. I can remember Winston Churchill's progress down that aisle as if it were yesterday. Everyone was clapping and stamping and cheering him with a fervour that threw post-war British reserve to the winds. Vanished in the heat of the moment were the traditional postures of steadiness on parade, understatement of emotion and stiffness of upper lips. Churchill's upper lip had certainly softened for he was openly weeping. I had never before seen a man blub (as we called it at school) but here was the Prime Minister and wartime leader with rivulets of tears pouring down his cheeks. Overcome with emotion I started to cry myself.

I was in an aisle seat about a quarter of the way down Westminster Hall. This gave me an excellent view of the platform and suddenly a full close-up view of my hero. He was shaking hands every row or two of his journey and when he approached our section his eye caught mine, possibly because I was a small and incongruous figure in my grey flannel school uniform. A second later his catch of the eye turned into a shake of the hand. It was a strong handshake with a powerful squeeze to it and a special look for me, or so I imagined, from those watery yet happy eyes. I was on cloud nine. 'He shook my hand. Winston Churchill shook my hand,' I told my father several times over in ecstasies of excitement, even though he had perfectly well seen the handshake for himself. 'I'm not going to wash for a week!' I announced to my mother when we got home, proudly holding aloft my sacred Churchillified palm. School matron soon put an end to that boast, but neither soap, water nor the passage of time has erased the memory of seeing, hearing and shaking hands with Winston Churchill on his eightieth birthday.

My second encounter with Winston Churchill came eight years later in 1962 when staying at Cherkley, the home of my great-uncle, Lord Beaverbrook. I drove down from Oxford without any sense of anticipation since no one had told me that my hero was coming to dinner. When I was given this news, together with the information that I would be sitting next to Sir Winston, my excitement was dampened by a health warning: 'Chaarchill's a sick old man,' warned my Uncle Max. 'You'll have to work hard to get anything out of him. But ya never quite know. He's like a lighthouse. Long cycles of darkness but then, suddenly, a few short flashes of the old brilliance can light up the horizon.' As things turned out, this was a remarkably accurate forecast of the evening's events, although we had to endure some long and painful hours of darkness before reaching the light.

In advance of Sir Winston's arrival, I noticed that my Uncle Max was as jumpy as the proverbial cat on hot bricks. He kept sending instructions to the kitchen via the butler about the importance of keeping the meat rare, the vegetables undercooked and the gravy hot. Then there were worries about whether or not the Pol Roger champagne would be over chilled, under chilled or just right. 'Chaarchill in his prime liked to say he was always the better and never the worse for Pol Roger – even when he'd drunk two bottles of it,' said Beaverbrook with a puckish grin. Then he reverted to the role of over-anxious host, insisting that the champagne should be sampled before the guest of honour's arrival to double check its temperature.

The party was a small one. Apart from Beaverbrook and Churchill, the only other guests were Renée McColl, the chief foreign correspondent of the *Daily Express*, George Malcolm Thomson, the chief leader writer of the *Express,* Lady Dunn and myself. As Lady Dunn was a teetotaller, and Beaverbrook was abstaining on doctor's orders, the champagne tasting duties fell to me, Thomson and McColl. We voted it 'perfect' but my Uncle Max, after putting his hand on the bottle, declared it too cold. 'Warm it up,' was his order to a startled footman who scurried away to perform this unusual duty. The butler at this time was stationed outside the house, keeping watch for the lights of Churchill's car at the end of the drive. When they appeared, Beaverbrook left us in the drawing room to greet his principal guest at the front door. It sounded a noisy arrival with much clanking, banging and raised voices. Later it emerged that Sir Winston's wheelchair had got stuck between the doors on the porch.

When he was wheeled into the drawing room by an attendant accompanied by a male nurse, Churchill's eyes gazed out of his cherubically pink face with alert curiosity but his body was crumpled into his blue siren suit in the posture of an invalid. However, his handshake had some firmness to it and he nodded at the various introductions, although he did not make any verbal acknowledgement of them. His disconcerting stares and silences during the next few minutes seemed to indicate that the great man was not entirely with us. However, this impression was corrected when he perked up as the Pol Roger was poured out. For, once his glass was filled, Churchill raised it, saying: 'To love, peace and health, and honest friends.'

The words of this toast meant nothing to me but Beaverbrook seized on them as proof that his guest of honour was on good form.

'Ah, you've still got your fine memory for verse, Winston,' he said. 'That was Kipling before he compared me to an harlot.' A lengthy explanation of this remark followed. Apparently Rudyard Kipling had been a regular visitor to Cherkley in the 1920s and had written a poem for the visitors' book. This red leather volume was brought in by the butler. George Malcolm Thomson was handed it with instructions to read Kipling's composition aloud. As he declaimed the final stanza, Churchill was stirred into beating time on the side of his wheelchair, mouthing the words in silent accompaniment until reaching the final line, which he echoed *con brio*.

> Beneath your roof at Cherkley Court
> Oh long, long may the record run
> And you enjoy until it ends
> The four best gifts beneath the sun
> *Love, Peace and Health, and Honest Friends*

Everyone applauded Sir Winston's powers of recollection, which were displayed again a few moments later. My Uncle Max told the story of how Kipling had betrayed him by switching his allegiance to his cousin, Stanley Baldwin, at the time of a critical by-election in 1931 in which Beaverbrook's Empire Free Trade candidate was the challenger to Baldwin's Conservative party candidate Duff Cooper. Towards the end of the campaign, Baldwin had lashed out against Beaverbrook, accusing him and his newspapers of 'seeking power without responsibility – the privilege of the harlot throughout the ages'. Apparently the unkindest cut of all, according to Beaverbrook, was that 'the words came from the mouth of Baldwin but they were written by the pen of Kipling. And they were just enough to let the Conservatives pip us at the post – a grievous blow to the cause of Empire Free Trade.'

Sir Winston decided to set the record straight. 'No, Max. You were shoundly beaten,' he growled. 'Duff romped home with a majority of over five thousand.'

This remarkably accurate recollection of the votes cast in the St George's by-election 31 years earlier was, alas, the last hurrah of Churchill's memory for the next couple of hours. For, soon after these exchanges, the great man's chin slumped towards his chest and he was incommunicado for the rest of the pre-dinner drinks. When we went into the dining room I was seated next to my hero but I might as well have been adjacent to a sedated vegetable. Prodded by my Uncle Max I tried every imaginable conversational gambit, such as: 'How do you think the Macmillan government is doing, sir?' 'Do you think the Profumo crisis will do the Conservatives lasting damage, sir?' And even: 'Are you enjoying your soup, sir?' The fact that I was reduced to asking Sir Winston Churchill a question equivalent to 'likee soupee?' showed the measure of my desperation.

I continued to deploy my conversational gambits at irregular intervals throughout the meal but answers came there none. The only consolation was that the two trusty retainers from the *Daily Express*, both of whom had endured such evenings with Churchill before, fared no better in their attempts to rouse some interest from him. However, he ate and drank quite heartily with some assistance from his male nurse and appeared to be enjoying himself in his own world of oblivion, cut off from the rest of us. Almost the only indication that he was on the same planet came over the coffee when he turned his rheumy eyes towards me and asked in slow, slurred sentences:

'Where were you at school?'

'Eton, sir.'

'Were you often swished?'

'No sir.'

'Pity!'

I felt crushed. My hero had demeaned me as if I were still a schoolboy who deserved to be caned more often. I retreated into wounded silence, worrying that I had somehow offended the former Prime Minister. But my Uncle Max, who perhaps sensed that Churchill was emerging from a conversational coma, urged me on.

'Try again – louder!' he commanded.

Plucking up my courage I raised my voice and shouted into Sir Winston's right ear: 'Sir, I was reading an interesting article about you recently in *The Spectator* by Henry Fairlie.'

The old man seemed to perk up. 'What did it shay?' he enquired.

Improvising wildly, for I could only just remember Fairlie's piece, I offered a paraphrase along the lines that the greatness of Churchill lay in his oratory. There was a silence as the subject of this compliment pondered upon it. Then he raised his head and gave me an enormous smile. ''Fraid its ballsh,' he said. 'I was never an orator.'

I tried to protest at this absurd modesty but suddenly the dark lighthouse became powerfully illuminated and a younger Churchill started speaking in a torrent of vigorous words, sweeping aside my objections.

'No, my boy. I was never a true orator,' he began. 'For when I rose to speak I always prepared meticulously. So afraid was I of making a slovenly speech that I often over prepared.' Churchill took a sip of brandy and with sparkling eyes continued: 'When I was a young Member I polished my words so thoroughly that I could not bring myself to jettison a single sentence of my prepared speech, even when circumstances demanded it . . . I remember a terrible occasion when I attacked the Government for announcing a policy that they had been expected to announce, but that they did not announce. So when A. J. Balfour came to wind up the debate . . .'

He paused to ask: 'My boy, have you ever heard of A. J. Balfour?'

'Yes, sir,' I gabbled quickly, fearful of slowing the flow of reminiscence. I need not have worried for Churchill was now in full flood. 'When Balfour wound up he turned on me, saying: "The honourable member has fired his guns down the road up which the enemy has not yet come." And I felt very shmall . . .' Everyone around the table laughed. The appreciation encouraged further memories: 'And even when I was Prime Minister, with all the apparatus of that office behind me, my speeches sometimes smelt too much of the midnight oil,' he continued. 'I remember when my private secretary once caught me pacing up and down the garden of No. 10 saying over and over again: "Mr Speaker, I had not intended to intervene in this debate but . . ."'

Pulling himself up in his chair to address his host, Churchill went on: 'You will remember, Max, in 1940, how many drafts and redrafts were needed before I was satisfied that my speeches could be delivered to the House of Commons or on the BBC. Those speeches performed their task but they were not oratory. I was never a bird on the unpinioned wing.'

Turning back to me, Sir Winston concluded his summary of the art of the true orator with a crescendo of comparisons. 'You see, my boy, when I got up to speak I always knew pre-schisely,' he gave a fierce drawl to the final word, 'where every noun and adjective was going to go, where every subjunctive would go, and how every piece of punctuation would bed into my speech. By contrast, the best Parliamentary orators like Lloyd George, F. E. Smith, Healy the Irishman, or even that shit Bevan ... when they rose to speak they did not know where they would begin, they did not know how they would end, and they certainly did not know what they would say in the middle. For their phrases were dictated by some inner God within. That, my boy, is oratory.'

After this peroration, in which the names of his selected orators were declaimed on a rising scale of decibels falling away to a mystical murmur when he delivered the phrase, 'some inner God within', Churchill's head drooped back on to his chest and he fell back into dumb oblivion. His dinner table companions also fell into a reverential silence, which was eventually broken by Beaverbrook, once he was sure that his guest was fast asleep: 'That was quite something,' he pronounced. 'D'ya know what Winston liked to say about his own conversation? He said "we are all worms but I do believe that I am a glow worm." Tonight we heard him glow.'

I was aglow that night long after Sir Winston went home. Inspired by the thought that I had caught one of the last, fleeting glimpses of the great statesman in full flow, I burned a little midnight oil of my own, writing an account of the evening in my diary. Then, as now, my words on the page do not begin to do justice to the words that poured out of Churchill's lips. For he had a compelling charisma that I have never seen or heard approached by anyone else in a lifetime of observing political leaders.

The third and last time I met Sir Winston Churchill was not just an anti-climax. It was one of my life's most embarrassing moments. The morning of this unhappy day began gloriously over breakfast in Oxford. My host was Randolph Churchill. The previous evening he had been addressing the Union on the resolution: 'Freedom from the Press is preferable to Freedom of the Press'. I was the undergraduate opposer and Randolph was the guest speaker on my side of the motion. Over a breakfast post mortem, we analysed the debate in a mood of mutual admiration, warmly congratulating each other on our speeches, our jokes and our victory by an overwhelming majority. A bottle of champagne was ordered to fortify our good spirits. In this agreeable atmosphere I missed my first lecture and Randolph missed his train to London. When he realized what time it was he flew into a tantrum. Amidst many obscenities he revealed that he had a lunch date with his father and mother who would be angry with him for missing it. Then a solution occurred to him. 'Could you drive me up to town in your motor car?' he asked. 'I'll telephone my mother and ask her to fit you in for lunch.'

The prospect of lunching with Sir Winston and Lady Churchill seemed far more attractive than any amount of law lectures. So I accepted immediately. Soon afterwards Randolph and I were on the road in my battered mini. In those pre-motorway days, the journey from Oxford to London lasted a good two hours and took us past a large number of roadside pubs. Randolph was an alcoholic. He craved his drink at the best of times and on this particular morning he was unconscionably nervous at the prospect of seeing his parents, with whom he had a difficult relationship. So ignoring my protests that we were already running late, he insisted on stopping 'just for a quick one' at hostelries in Beaconsfield, Hounslow and Acton. The inevitable result of these pauses for refreshment was that our progress became slower and slower. Eventually we arrived for our 1 o'clock lunch date at a quarter to 2.

As soon as we entered No. 28 Hyde Park Gate it was apparent that a chill of disapproval was pervading the Churchill home. The butler intimated it by saying in frigid tones that everyone was worrying about where we had got to. Lady Churchill was more outspoken. She let fly as soon as we entered the drawing room, berating Randolph and, by implication, me, for being 'inconsiderate and downright rude'. While this maternal diatribe was in progress, Randolph kissed his father on the forehead and introduced me. As I shook hands with Sir Winston it was obvious from his vacant stare that he had not the slightest interest in his lunch guest. However, according to Lady

Churchill's continuing commentary, he was very interested in his lunch and very cross that it was going to be served to him so late.

Instead of placating his parents with a few soft words of apology, Randolph became belligerent. Raising his voice, he protested that he couldn't help the bloody traffic and told his mother to stop making such a bloody fuss. His aggression made Lady Churchill furious. She pushed her son away as he tried to kiss her, declaring in a piercing voice: 'You've been drinking. You stink of drink!' It was an accusation which made Randolph furious too, and he began roaring less than truthful denials at his mother.

Sir Winston, for all his frailties of body and mind, could not miss what was happening. He started to show signs of acute displeasure. First his pale white features turned red. Then his blue-siren-suited right leg began making kicking movements in the air. Finally he rattled his two walking sticks together in angry disapproval.

Encircled by three ill-humoured Churchills, I made one feeble attempt to defuse the situation by whispering to Randolph: 'Why don't you say we are sorry for being so late?' My suggestion was not well received. 'Shut up!' he bellowed. 'Why don't you bugger off!'

Taking this as an announcement that my invitation had been cancelled I began making my excuses. When I told Lady Churchill that I ought to be going the tone in which she replied 'I understand' was so icy that I could see she really meant 'Good!' So I shook hands again with Sir Winston and beat a hasty retreat. It was an ignominious and lunchless exit but I consoled myself with the thought that I had perhaps caught an unusual glimpse of the Churchillian temperament. It was one I saw much more often as my relationship with Randolph Churchill developed.

CHAPTER 3

Randolph Churchill

Randolph Churchill squandered many of the talents he inherited from his father. Succumbing at an early age to the demons of alcoholism, he became notorious for his explosions of bad temper and bad behaviour. Yet in the last few years of his life he mellowed. Retiring in his early fifties for health reasons to a country house in Suffolk, he reinvented himself as a hard-working political journalist, historian and author. In 1961 his life was transformed by his appointment as the official biographer of Sir Winston Churchill, and by the critical acclaim for his first volume of this momentous project.

Despite the formidable workload that his work as a biographer demanded, Randolph found time for a variety of wider activities, such as 'quickie' books, pamphlets, columns, articles and eccentric political campaigns. He enjoyed giving encouragement to a younger circle of writers and politicians, of which I was one. As a result of becoming Randolph's friend and Suffolk neighbour, my memories of him are much kinder, funnier and more favourable than the judgements of his older contemporaries. For even though our relationship included furious rows, embarrassing upheavals, appalling scenes and a passionate but lunatic campaign on his part to get me selected as the MP for his local constituency nine months *before* my twenty-first birthday, I remember Randolph with great fascination, qualified admiration and special gratitude for enhancing my early life.

I first met Randolph in the whirlwind of one of his tantrums. Along with some forty or so other guests, we were dining at Cherkley, the home of my great-uncle, Lord Beaverbrook. Suddenly the convivial atmosphere of the party was shattered by a volcanic eruption. From my end of the table it was far from clear what was happening or why. All I could see was that Mr Randolph Churchill had risen to his feet and was shouting insults at Mr Hugh Cudlipp, the editor-in-chief of the *Daily Mirror*. Mr Cudlipp shouted back. This duel of dinosaurs grew worse when the supremo of the *Mirror* hurled his napkin across the table, striking Randolph on the chest. Randolph's roars increased by several decibels. White with anger, he knocked his chair backwards with a kick so violet that it crashed to the ground. In the space created by the fallen chair, Randolph swivelled on his heel and stalked out of the room, leaving behind him a company of guests frozen into silence by the ferocity of the fury we had just witnessed.

Although Randolph had made most of the noise and aggression in this exit scene, my Uncle Max displayed a surprising sympathy towards his departed guest. In the hiatus that followed he reproached Hugh Cudlipp, saying: 'You shouldn't have provoked him, Hugh. Speaking ill of his father always unleashes the furies in him. You shoulda known better.'

Although Cudlipp defended his role in the altercation, I could tell that Beaverbrook was upset by what had happened. A few minutes later he beckoned me over and said: 'Jonathan, you're a young diplomat. You know how to pour oil on troubled waters. Go find Mr Churchill and persuade him to come back and join us for the rest of dinner.' This was a tall order but I could hardly say no. Once I got outside the dining room I was informed by the butler that Mr Churchill had retired to his bedroom. So I knocked on his door, which was flung open by a still furious Randolph. 'Who the hell are you and what the hell do you want?' he yelled. I explained that we had been introduced before dinner and that I too was staying at Cherkley as an overnight guest. This information temporarily cooled his temper. 'Well then, go downstairs and bring me up a whisky and soda, will you?' he asked.

The whisky improved matters. We started to talk. I told Randolph that I was particularly pleased to meet him because my family lived in a Suffolk village just a few miles further up the A12 from his Suffolk village. 'So we are both country bumpkins!' he explained. 'You must come over to lunch.' I said I would be delighted to come over to lunch but that my first task was to persuade him to come back to dinner. This launched Randolph into a further orbit of anti-Cudlipp obscenities. But when I told him what my Uncle Max had said about the incident, Randolph seemed mollified. Eventually he accompanied me back to the dining room. At the last moment he insisted on occupying my seat at the dinner table so that he would not be placed opposite Hugh Cudlipp. Honour was satisfied by this rearrangement and tranquillity reigned for the rest of the evening. My Uncle Max was inordinately pleased. 'A Chaarchill in a rage is a dangerous beast of the jungle,' he declared. 'You did well to corral him.'

A week or two later Randolph corralled me. A letter from him arrived with an invitation to lunch. It contained the line: 'I cannot promise that the menu will be as good as the one at Cherkley but we country bumpkins know a thing or two about good grub.' Encouraged by this gastronomic promise I drove from my parents' home in Playford, near Ipswich, to Randolph's home in East Bergholt, near Manningtree. Arriving well ahead of time I stopped at a pub in the village and asked for directions to Mr Churchill's house. 'So you're going to visit the Beast of Bergholt, are you?' said one of the locals propping up the bar. 'Why do you call him that?' I asked. 'Because he's a bloody bastard, who's bloody rude to everyone, and who doesn't pay his bloody bills to small village tradesmen,' was the vehement retort. After that description I almost expected to be greeted by a monster with horns and a tail as I rang the doorbell of Stour, an elegant Georgian mansion nestling in the shadow of the church. But the Randolph sitting by a crackling log fire in his drawing room was in a hospitable and affable mood.

'Have a Bull Shot!' he urged, introducing me to his favourite summertime libation of consommé and vodka. 'It will put you on your mettle when you meet the young gentlemen from my factory.'

The factory turned out to be the work rooms where the research for the multi-volume official biography of Sir Winston Churchill was being carried out. Randolph took me on a guided tour of his plant and machinery for the project. There were fireproof strong rooms, packed with steel filing cabinets containing several tons of original letters and documents. There was a massive reference library including half-a-century's work of bound volumes of Hansard, the official daily report of Parliament. A secretariat, presided over by 22-year old Miss Barbara Twigg, toiled away at their typewriters and photocopiers. As for the young gentlemen, who were also toiling away amidst sheaves and bundles of files, they were given the command: 'Truce and Luncheon! At which we will introduce our guests to both kinds of lovely grub.'

My first lunch at Stour was a delicious meal, far above the pay grade of a country bumpkin. It included gulls' eggs; lobster with home-made mayonnaise; new potatoes straight from the garden; summer pudding; and a superb cheese board. Randolph, however, ate little of it. He merely toyed with the delicacies on his plate, preferring to fortify himself with several refills of Bull Shot. So it was left to me and the young gentlemen to appreciate the excellence of the cuisine, which was by no means the only excellence on display that afternoon.

'The first opinion of a ruler is based on the quality of the men he has around him,' wrote Machiavelli in *The Prince*. Applying the same test to a biographer, I soon formed a high opinion of Randolph based on my first impressions of the quality of his researchers. This was not just the effect of Bull Shot which had been handed me with my host's warning: 'This is a drink which should compel you get your vowels right.' It was also that the 'young gentlemen' I met that day at Stour included Martin Gilbert, then a rising star among Oxford dons; Michael Wolff, who later became Director General of Conservative Central Office; Franklin Gannon Jnr, subsequently a White House aide who became the chief researcher for Richard Nixon's memoirs; and Andrew Kerr, who progressed to a career as a television producer. All of them were made to sing for their metaphorical suppers because, during and after lunch, they had to read out examples of Randolph's other kind of 'lovely grub'. Away from the kitchen this phrase, in the lexicon of Stour, meant a nugget of biographer's gold, mined from the archives of Churchillian papers. Randolph explained that the theme of his magnum opus was to be: 'He shall be his own biographer.' This put a heavy premium on excavating treasures of Winston Churchill's own writing in letters or other documents which would illuminate every episode of his career. So far as I could judge, the young gentlemen were doing a brilliant job in unearthing gems of the Churchill genius. I was dazzled by the great man's descriptive powers as I listened, on that first afternoon, to Churchill's accounts of various dramatic scenes he had witnessed as a subaltern during the Boer War.

After a couple of hours or so of truly wonderful readings from young Winston's letters on that conflict, Randolph declared: 'The Boers can become boer-ing. Let's go for a walk.' So he led me off on a circuit of Stour's 12 acres of lawns, woodlands and herbaceous borders. Until this moment I had formed an impression that Randolph was predominantly a metropolitan man. For a start his fingers were brown from nicotine rather than green from gardening, while his personality seemed far more at home in the bars of White's and El Vino's than in the fields of Constable Country. Yet Randolph was full of surprises. That afternoon he amazed me, as we strolled round his property, with his horticultural expertise of flowers and shrubs, whose Latin names tripped authoritatively off his tongue. I also remember his intense interest when he learned that my mother was growing a certain kind of lily in her garden. 'Can I come over and take a cutting?' he asked with boyish enthusiasm.

After Randolph the gardener I was introduced to Randolph the lover. As the shadows lengthened over Stour we were joined by a beautiful woman, Natalie Bevan, who shimmered across the lawn like a graceful gazelle in high heels, bearing a bottle of Pol Roger. Randolph kissed her lovingly and accepted the gift graciously – but only for a moment. On feeling the temperature of the bottle he became ungracious. 'Warm champagne, Natalie? You are my post-mistress,' he barked. This public declaration of their relationship astonished me. However, Natalie's husband, walking a few paces behind his wife, seemed completely unfazed by it. This was just as well as Randolph and Natalie vanished up the staircase of the house for the next hour or so, leaving me, Commander Bobby Bevan and the senior young gentleman on duty, Michael Wolff, to our own devices. When Bobby Bevan was out of the room I wondered aloud to Michael Wolff how on earth Randolph got away with it. 'Oh Bobby's completely on side,' said Michael, nonchalantly. 'He often brings Natalie over here for a *cinq à sept*.' It all seemed highly unconventional, at least to me at the sheltered age of 20, but on this and many subsequent visits I found much to enjoy in the iconoclastic lifestyle of Stour and its mercurial owner.

Despite all the hustle and bustle of the factory, the young gentlemen, the Bevans and the biography, Randolph was a lonely figure in rural Suffolk. He enjoyed congenial company and he got too little of it, particularly during the late-night hours when he did some of his best thinking and writing. It was not everyone's taste to sit round a blazing log fire (always at full blast even in the height of summer) listening to new or revised paragraphs of the biography being dictated after midnight to the long-suffering Miss Twigg. However, I was a willing audience and often motored over to Stour in response to Randolph's call, 'How about a nightcap?' The progress of the Churchill biography fascinated me, not least because the author, like his father, was a master of the English language. Not only did Randolph possess a majestic vocabulary; he deployed it with a musician's ear for rhythms and cadences. 'That sentence doesn't scan . . . it is beating to the sound of an unsteady drum . . . I must conclude this chapter with a fanfare of trombones and trumpets,' was typical of the stern judgements he would pass on his own work as he scrumpled up draft upon draft of the same paragraph, hurling them into the flames of the log fire. Then he would buzz for Miss Twigg, pour himself another whisky and totter over to Disraeli's writing desk (a gift from his father, of which he was inordinately proud) in order to dictate and re-dictate the passage over and over again.

Although Randolph's consumption of alcohol was prodigious (two bottles of whisky a day was the estimate given in the filial biography written by his son Winston) and often had disastrous effects on his health and his temper, the late-night dictating sessions did not seem to be unduly affected by it. Somehow Randolph got a second wind in the small hours of the morning which brought both industry and inspiration. I soon lost count of the number of times I heard him declaim these lines by Henry Longfellow:

The heights by great men reached and kept
Were not attained by sudden flight,
But they, while their companions slept,
Were toiling upward in the night.

Not every night at Stour was toilsomely productive. Like most members of Randolph's circle, I quickly learned how to ignore his outbursts of mere irascibility. But some of his waves of anger were so tidal in their ferocity that they created a storm that could not be ridden out. Randolph on the crest of such a wave was, as my Uncle Max had said, 'a dangerous beast of the jungle'. The worst night that I can remember when the dangerous beast was on the rampage concerned the episode of his review for the *Sunday Times* of my first book.

Randolph gave me great encouragement in my earliest fumbling steps as a writer. At the time of my first appearance in hard covers with *A Short Walk on the Campus,* co-authored in 1964 with a fellow 22-year-old Oxford undergraduate, Michael Beloff, Randolph read the proofs, made suggestions and declared that he liked the book so much that the would review it for the *Sunday Times*. This was an exciting bonus. On the Saturday night before the review appeared, Randolph telephoned to say: 'My piece is definitely in tomorrow's paper. Would you like to come over for a nightcap and read it?' So I drove to Stour with eager anticipation, and read the typescript of the highly favourable review with great delight. But after thanking my literary benefactor effusively, I felt obliged to mention that he had been unfair in one sentence. For his review had, *en passant,* chided the authors for 'schoolboy inaccuracy'. It went on: 'For example, they say that the Rosenbergs were electrocuted. They were hanged.'

Hesitantly I pointed out to Randolph that the US atomic spies, Julius and Ethel Rosenberg, really had been executed by the electric chair rather than by the hangman's noose. This information was initially unwelcome. In a series of bad-tempered snarls I was accused of 'not knowing the facts', 'not being able to take criticism', and 'being bloody ungrateful'. But when I did not retreat in the face of these onslaughts, Randolph began to get worried as to which of us had been

38

inaccurate. He commenced his fact-checking at an exalted level: 'Get me Bobby Kennedy,' he commanded the young gentleman on duty that evening at Stour as the night telephonist. 'The Attorney General of the United States ought to know the facts.' Observing my surprise at such superior channels of research, Randolph declared: 'I always do business at the top!' Thankfully, the Kennedy at the top of the US Department of Justice was not available in Washington on a Saturday afternoon. 'Get me Harry Luce then,' was the next order. The owner and editor-in-chief of *Time* magazine was not around either but a startled secretary had the presence of mind to say: 'I can put you through to the morgue, Mr Churchill.' The morgue, or library of press cuttings at *Time*, yielded up the confirmation that the Rosenbergs had definitely met their deaths by electrocution, not by hanging.

On receiving this news, Randolph went into convulsions of rage. It is no exaggeration to say that he went berserk; yelling, screaming and stomping up and down his drawing room in an explosion of obscenities. I was alarmed and not a little frightened. However, my fears were mild compared to the terror experienced by the object of his wrath. He was Franklin Gannon Jnr, Randolph's American 'young gentleman' who had the misfortune to be on duty that evening. His crime was not his performance as a night telephone operator (he had done rather well in getting through to the secretaries of Henry R. Luce and Robert F. Kennedy) but his failure as a book review researcher. For it was Gannon who had supplied his master with the erroneous information about the Rosenbergs' method of execution.

If Randolph could have laid his hands on a rope or an electric chair in the middle of his fury, he might have tried to execute Frank Gannon on the spot. But instead of summary execution, the punishment was summary dismissal. The trembling Gannon was sacked on the spot and told: 'You will get out of my house tonight! Now! At once – if not sooner!' As the browbeaten young American retreated upstairs to pack his bags I was pressed into service as the replacement telephone operator. Randolph was determined to correct the mistake in his review before a million copies of the *Sunday Times* arrived on the doorsteps of its readers. 'They could easily stop the presses and make a quick plate change,' he said. Having no wish to see the favourable review of *A Short Walk on the Campus* obliterated in this way, I advised sticking to the status quo. I was bawled out for my pains and told: 'Get me Lord Thomson! His home number is in my book.' Fortunately the proprietor of the *Sunday Times* was fast asleep in bed, according to his housekeeper. The paper's editor, Frank Giles, could not be raised either, nor could its literary editor. Eventually Randolph spoke to the night editor. Although underwhelmed by the Churchillian exhortation, 'Hold the book page!', he agreed to investigate further. When he did so, he found no mention of the Rosenberg execution in Randolph's review. Further nocturnal inquiries revealed that the piece had been too long. Half a paragraph had been cut by the subs, and it was the one complaining about the author's non-inaccuracy. 'Phew!' said Randolph, 'our luck's in'.

It seemed a good moment to mention that Frank Gannon's luck was still out. So I pleaded the case for his reinstatement, or at least the case for sleeping on his dismissal, since eviction into the cold night air of East Bergholt at 1 o'clock in the morning seemed cruel and unusual punishment. Grumpily, Randolph relented. 'It's difficult to find good young Americans for this job,' he muttered, telling a shell-shocked Gannon to unpack his bags and stay.

Americans loomed large in Randolph's life. I made three trips with him to Washington DC where he always stayed at the Halle Hilton. This was his name for 3001 Dent Place, the ten-bedroom Georgetown Mansion owned by Miss Kay Halle, who had been his fiancée in the early 1930s. The engagement had been broken off at the insistence of Randolph's parents, who were horrified at the idea of their son getting married at the age of 20. Kay Halle, however, continued to adore her English suitor. Thirty or so years after their brief betrothal she told me: 'I am at my happiest when Randolph is staying in my house.' This was true love indeed, for her ex-fiancé could be the house guest from hell.

Randolph would arrive at the Halle Hilton with a mountain of luggage and an entourage of friends, several of whom he expected to be put up in the house. He made demands for a ceaseless flow of drinks parties, lunches and dinners in his honour and gave no firm date for his departure. Kay Halle rose to these challenges as a true heroine of hospitality. She was a Georgetown hostess with a carefully constructed network of alliances in the media and on the Democratic side of politics. When John F. Kennedy was elected President, Kay became one of the social stars of Camelot. Her table was often filled with luminaries from the Administration such as Robert McNamara, Dean Rusk, Fred Holborn, J. K. Galbraith and Bobby Kennedy. Other regular guests included media heavyweights like Scotty Reston and Arthur Krock of the *New York Times*; the syndicated columnists Joe and Stewart Alsop; Eric Sevareid of CBS; and fellow hostesses Kay Graham, owner of the *Washington Post* or Alice Roosevelt Longworth, the daughter of President Theodore Roosevelt. At a dinner party attended by Washington insiders of this calibre, an English visitor might be well advised to listen carefully and speak cautiously. Not Randolph. He crashed in and out of conversations like the proverbial bull in the china shop. Sometimes he added a buzz of electricity to the proceedings. More often he exploded like a hand-grenade into boorish aggression and drunken bad manners. I recall an evening at the Halle Hilton when he gave such grievous offence that Joe Alsop walked out in disgust. The row had started in a trivial conversation about a best-selling book of that era, *How to Win Friends and Influence People*. Joe Alsop took his coat, muttering darkly: 'If Randolph ever writes his autobiography it should be called "How to Lose Friends and Influence Nobody".'

One set of Randolph's friendships that never lost their mutual warmth was with the Kennedys. He loved both JFK and RFK. For months after the assassination of the President on 22 November 1963, Randolph could barely speak of his slain hero without being overcome with emotion. It was the proudest moment of his life when, in 1966, Bobby Kennedy invited him to write the official biography of John F. Kennedy, as soon as he had completed what he always called 'The Great Work' on Sir Winston. Alas, neither project reached fulfilment owing to Randolph's early death.

One of the last conversations Randolph had with President Kennedy was on the 8 October 1963 in the Oval Office. The day before, when staying with Kay Halle, Randolph had a strange premonition that all was not well with the British Prime Minister, Harold

Macmillan. In an attempt to seek reassurance for her curiously agitated houseguest, Kay put a call through to Macmillan's son-in-law, Julian Amery. He told Randolph the still secret news that Macmillan was going to announce his resignation the following day, having just been diagnosed as suffering from cancer of the prostate. Never one to sit on important news, Randolph telephoned Evelyn Lincoln, the President's secretary, and was immediately put through to JFK. After they had both expressed their shock and concern for 'Uncle Harold', Randolph startled the President by asking him how he could 'face the thought of having to deal with that little shit Harold Wilson'. The amused answer from the Oval Office was that the President of the United States could work with any Prime Minister of Great Britain.

A few hours after his telephone call to President Kennedy, Randolph flew to London and on to Blackpool, where the Conservative party conference had been electrified by the news of Macmillan's imminent resignation. From that moment onwards the proceedings bore a striking resemblance to a US Presidential election convention. Lord Hailsham threw his hat into the ring with a dramatic announcement that he would disclaim his peerage. R. A. Butler, the apparent frontrunner, tried to strengthen his hold on the succession by making the traditional leader's speech at the end of the conference. Other possible contenders, such as Reginald Maudling and Iain Macleod, had their prospects excitably canvassed by supporters, opponents and journalists. Into this bubbling cauldron of intrigue and excitement plunged the late-arriving Randolph Churchill, determined to stir and shake the pot until it cooked up the result he wanted.

I was attending the conference and will never forget the scenes Randolph created on the afternoon and evening of Friday the 11 October in the Imperial Hotel. *The Times* reported his impact with the sentence: 'Mr Churchill's arrival was like Hurricane Flora hitting Blackpool instead of Cuba.' Randolph's first broadside was an onslaught on Rab Butler. The First Secretary of State and Deputy Prime Minister was in his suite working on the speech he would be delivering to the conference the following morning. His concentration was disturbed by thunderous knocks on the door which he opened to reveal Randolph looking, Rab said afterwards, 'rather like the Pearly King, festooned in silver buttons over his suit'. These buttons were 'Q' badges, denoting Randolph's enthusiasm for the cause of Quintin Hailsham. 'Rab, I've come to tell you that you haven't a cat in hell's chance,' declared the unwelcome caller. 'Quintin's got it in the bag. Why don't you withdraw now?' Mr Butler politely declined the suggestion and the offer of a Q badge. 'But surely you know which way the wind is blowing?' Randolph persisted. 'You've seen all those telegrams, haven't you?' Since over 60 of the telegrams sent to the Deputy Prime Minister had originated from East Bergholt, where Randolph's young gentlemen had been made to sit up all night dictating them, they were a less than convincing manifestation of party opinion, despite many ingeniously invented signatories such as Manningtree Conservative Women and Ipswich Young Conservatives.

Having failed to persuade Rab Butler to defect from his own camp to Hailsham's, Randolph set up shop in the bar of the Imperial Hotel and distributed his stock of Q badges to all and sundry. Although there were many enthusiastic recipients, 'no' was not to be taken for an answer from those who refused. For they were quite literally buttonholed by Randolph who, personally and compulsorily, stuck his badges on to their lapels. As he had forgotten to attach any adhesive to the back of the Q's, this was a cumbersome operation involving several pins and many arguments. One rather large Tory grandee who resisted Randolph's advances by pushing him away was the Lord Chancellor, Lord Dilhorne. However, Hailsham's supporters had the last laugh a few minutes later when Randolph crept up behind the Lord Chancellor when he was leaning over the bar buying drinks. Equipped with safety pin at the ready, Randolph surreptitiously affixed a Q badge to Lord Dilhome's ample hindquarters. Unfortunately a lack of Churchillian steadiness with the safety pin led to the hindquarters as well as the trousers getting punctured. The Lord Chancellor's shouts of pain and his assailant's cackles of laughter added greatly to the merriment of the spectators.

Randolph's antics soon attracted the interest of the television cameras. When interviewed on the BBC, he talked up Hailsham's chances with vigorous enthusiasm. Asked by Robin Day whether he thought Lord Home could emerge as a dark horse, Randolph dismissed the idea with the contemptuous words: 'that's a lot of rot'. I was one of a handful of people at Blackpool who knew that the rumours of the Earl of Home becoming the next Prime Minister were far from being a lot of rot. For in my nepotistic role as private secretary to my godfather, Selwyn Lloyd, I had become aware of his and other people's king-making activities. Within what was later known as the magic circle of the Tory hierarchy, Home was turning into the clear favourite. However, I did not immediately share my inside knowledge with Randolph, even though we did share one or two drinks at Blackpool.

Two days later I was down at Cherkley, trying to persuade my great-uncle Lord Beaverbrook that Home was coming up fast on the rails in the Prime Ministerial stakes. In the middle of that conversation, Randolph telephoned with his assessment that Hailsham was going to be an easy winner of the race. In his mischievous way, my Uncle Max promptly connected his two diametrically opposed sources on the same line. Although Randolph ridiculed my views, I thought I could detect a note of insecurity in his voice. What had particularly bothered him was that I was so confident of the authenticity of my tips from the Selwyn Lloyd stable that I had put a large bet on Home. Randolph did not seem quite so confident about the five hundred pounds (approximately £7,000 in today's money) he had wagered on Hailsham. So the telephone call ended not in more disagreement but in an invitation to join him for dinner that evening at White's.

'The trouble with this club is that it has let in far too many château-bottled shits,' boomed my host as we met at the bar of White's. 'Meaning yourself, Randolph?' enquired a fellow member. When we had settled down after the row that exchange produced, I was grilled far more intensively than the Dover soles we were eating about the reliability of my political information. It was not an easy meal. Randolph drank far too much and became angry far too often. But towards the end of the evening he vanished into a telephone booth, from which he emerged saying: 'You haven't convinced me. But I have taken precautions. As I can't afford to lose a monkey [five hundred pounds], I've put a ton on bloody Alec at 6–1. So I've hedged my bets.' As events soon showed, it was a wise move. Six months later Randolph published a quickie paperback, *The Fight for the Tory Leadership*. It was a bestseller. My copy bore the delightful inscription: 'To Jonathan – who saved my bacon.'

One of the paradoxes of Randolph was that beneath his outer carapace of bombast and arrogance there lay a sensitive soul of great kindness. However, his acts of generosity could be mixed blessings, as an earlier episode in our friendship demonstrated. Returning to my rooms in Oxford on a Monday afternoon after a long week-end away in Scotland during the autumn of 1962, I was greeted by my landlady who seemed to be quaking with anxiety: 'Where have you been?' she asked. 'Since last Friday morning I've had 11 telephone calls at all hours of the day and night from Mr Randolph Churchill. He's very angry at not being able to speak to you. I think these telegrams must be from him too.' She was right. The stack of six telegrams, in chrono-logical order, began: RING ME SOONEST RANDOLPH. They rose steadily on an ascending scale of peremptory imperatives such as: YOU MUST CALL ME URGENTLY, and VITAL REPEAT VITAL YOU CALL TONIGHT, until the last one, which said: YOU ARE THROWING AWAY THE CHANCE OF A LIFETIME IF YOU DON'T REPLY. RING AS A MATTER OF EXTREME REPEAT EXTREME URGENCY – RANDOLPH.

I wondered what on earth all this could be about as I dialled East Bergholt 356. After receiving the expected blowing-up for my irre-sponsible behaviour, Randolph calmed down and announced that he'd done bloody well and got me an interview the day after tomorrow. 'Interview for what?' I asked. 'Interview for the Sudbury and Woodbridge constituency, you BF . . . I told you I'd throw my weight behind you to take over from Lord Clam.' My mind reeled as I recalled a night of hard drinking some weeks earlier. Lord Clam of Claydon was Randolph's nickname for the recently ennobled Lord Blakenham, whose insistence on 'clamming up' whenever he received a journalistic enquiry from his neighbour at Stour about what was going on in the Cabinet caused much Churchillian frustration. Until a few weeks earlier Lord Blakenham had been the Rt Hon John Hare, MP, Minister of Labour and Member of Parliament for Sudbury and Woodbridge. His elevation to the House of Lords meant that there would be a by-election in the constituency where Randolph and I lived. At the time of the announcement of Hare's peerage we had joked (or so I thought) over our respective nightcaps about the chances of my being elected as the new MP for the area. 'We could run you as the local-boy-makes-good candidate,' chuckled Randolph. 'That would be a jolly wheeze.'

In the cold light of the following morning I had completely forgotten about the jolly wheeze. But now it was back on Randolph's agenda, as a cause he was championing with total seriousness. For as soon as he discovered that the Sudbury and Woodbridge Conservative Association was about to begin its selection process, Stour and its entourage of young gentlemen and secretaries was transformed into a campaign office with the cry of 'Aitken's the One'.

Sir Martin Gilbert, who later succeeded Randolph as Sir Winston Churchill's official biographer, wrote an amusing eye-witness account of this quixotic campaign in his memoir: *In Search of Churchill*. According to Gilbert, 'For a while this episode absorbed all Randolph's energies . . . he dictated a magisterial letter to the constituency chairman extolling the young Aitken's qualifications as a Parliamentarian. We "ghosts" were put to work manning the telephone as Randolph put through mellifluous calls to members of the selection committee, some of whom were audibly terrified when they were told (sometimes by me), "I have Mr Randolph Churchill on the line".'

Meanwhile in my rooms at Oxford I was getting terrified too as Randolph described what he called his 'battle plan' to win the nomination for me. As he went down the list of Sudbury and Woodbridge worthies to whom he had spoken, checking them off like a canvasser into 'yes', 'no', 'doubtful' and 'leaning your way' categories, he ended with an announcement that he had secured an appointment for me to be interviewed by the selection committee at 7 o'clock on Wednesday evening. I started to panic. 'Randolph, I'm terribly grateful to you but I don't think I can go on with this,' I said as my mind started to reel with nightmares of angry Oxford tutors, upset parents and mocking contemporaries. 'Whaat . . . don't be so bloody wet!' roared the voice on the end of the telephone in full Beast of Bergholt mode. 'But there are some real practical difficulties,' I protested as soon as I could get a word in edgeways. 'You see I am only just 20 and you have to be 21 to be elected to Parliament.'

'Why the hell didn't you say so before,' bellowed Randolph, slamming down the receiver just as I was beginning to point out that he had neither asked me for my age nor for my consent before launching his battle plan. At least the abrupt termination of this conversation meant that the campaign to turn me into an MP was now ended – or so I thought. But well after midnight when I was fast asleep my phone rang with a jubilant Randolph on the line. 'Problem solved. You are still on your way to Westminster as the future MP for Sudbury and Woodbridge,' he declared. 'I managed to track Sir Barnett Cocks down at home. He very decently got out of bed, checked his reference books, and Bob's your uncle, he's given us the solution.' 'Who is Sir Barnett Cocks?' I asked, unable to place the name among the local knights and baronets of East Suffolk. 'He's the Chief Clerk of the House of Commons, you dunderhead,' said Randolph genially. 'Clerk to the Parliaments is his official title I think. Anyway, he's the fellah who wears a wig, sits at the table in front of the Speaker and knows the rules.' 'This is the person you just got out of bed to ask about me becoming MP for Sudbury and Woodbridge?' I asked, wondering if I was still dreaming. 'Wake up!' shouted Randolph. 'Do you or do you not want to know the good news brought to you by the Clerk to the Parliaments, Sir Barnett Cocks, no less.'

Whether or not I wanted to hear it, Randolph was going to give me the news anyway. The essence of it was a surprising lesson in Constitutional history. I was told that under the British Constitution it is entirely legal for anyone to stand for Parliament and to be elected to Parliament at the age of 20 or even younger. All that the law says is that no one can take their seat in the House of Commons until they have reached the age of 21. 'Sir Barnett found a couple of precedents in the eighteenth century and one in the nineteenth century for Members of Parliament who'd been elected when they were under 21 and just had to wait a bit to take their seats,' boomed Randolph. 'No reason why you can't do the same.' I absorbed this information about ancient Constitutional precedents and voiced a more up-to-date objection. 'I don't think the electors of Sudbury and Woodbridge will like the idea of voting in an MP who can't represent them in Parliament for the best part of a year,' I said. 'Oh don't talk such rot,' retorted Randolph. 'These country bumpkins will be perfectly happy to wait until you take your seat.' Realizing that this was a dialogue of the deaf, I ended the conversation politely, went back to sleep and set off the next morning for my usual routine of lectures. By the time I returned to my college at lunchtime, another flurry of telegrams awaited me at the Porter's Lodge. HAVE FIXED CHAIRMAN, RANDOLPH, said one. BANDWAGON WELL AND TRULY ROLLING CALL ME URGENTLY, RANDOLPH, commanded another.

By the time I telephoned Randolph he had despatched another magisterial epistle to the Chairman of the Sudbury and Woodbridge Conservative Association. It addressed the problem of my being too young to take a seat in Parliament. After summarizing the advice and Constitutional precedents supplied by Sir Barnett Cocks, the letter drew a comparison (in my favour!) between the careers of J. Aitken, the 20-year-old undergraduate, and William Pitt the younger, the 24-year-old Prime Minister. There then followed a lengthy quotation from one of Pitt's speeches, which began: 'Mr Speaker, the atrocious crime of being a young man I can neither attempt to palliate nor to deny ...' Extracts from a Winston Churchill speech *circa* 1929 with the message: 'Let youth seize the helm', were also deployed. Randolph said the Chairman had agreed to photocopy his letter and distribute it to all members of the selection committee.

As I listened to the full text of this eccentric effort to boost my non-existent chances of becoming the next MP for Sudbury and Wood-bridge, the remark of a French general witnessing the charge of the Light Brigade came to mind: '*C'est magnifique, mais ce n'est pas la guerre.*' I decided that I must write my own letter to the Chairman withdrawing from the battle. However, before I could put pen to paper, a telephone call came in from the Conservative headquarters in the constituency. A lady with a fruity voice, reminiscent of Joyce Grenfell, said she was ringing to confirm the details of my appointment with the selection committee. I asked whether my age might not be a problem. 'Oh no, I don't think so,' replied the Joyce-Grenfell type.

'Young blood in Parliament would be a jolly good thing.' Between Randolph's jolly good wheeze and Joyce Grenfell's 'jolly good thing', I felt I was walking into a political version of *Alice in Wonderland*.

Incredible though it now sounds some 43 years after the event, I drove over from Oxford to Suffolk the following day and was solemnly interviewed by about 20 members of the Sudbury and Woodbridge Conservative Association. The first question was: 'Mr Aitken, we understand that you are President of the Oxford University Conservative Association. What do you think the young people of Britain would like to hear from the Conservative Party which would help us to win the next General Election?' I cannot now remember what I said in reply but it was greeted with quite a few nods and murmurs of agreement, as were my answers to questions on agriculture, on the Common Market and on law and order, where my recent enrolment as a Special Constable in the East Suffolk County Police seemed to be something of a trump card. Eventually I got a hostile question along the lines of didn't I think it absurd for me to put myself forward at such a preposterously young age? Gratefully I agreed with the questioner. Equally gratefully the Chairman said he thought the selection committee would wish to take Mr Aitken at his word. So that was the end of the adventure.

Paradoxically, Randolph was delighted. He received favourable reports of my interview which he passed on to me the next day in a phone call. 'Mind you, I never thought you'd actually get it,' he declared. 'These country bumpkins round here are just too bloody stupid. But it was jolly good experience for you.'

Interesting experiences were what I gained in abundance as a result of knowing Randolph, even if many of them could be categorized under the definition that says experience is a name that men give to their mistakes. Yet although I saw Randolph make numerous mistakes, I thought his virtues far outweighed his failings. These virtues included kindness, loyalty, generosity, charm, courage and the gift of being a good, if impatient, teacher. On the kindness front, I shall never forget how Randolph pulled me out of the depths of grief after the death of my father, aged 56, of a heart attack soon after my twenty-first birthday. Randolph's methods as a bereavement counsellor were unusual. He chivvied me into doing tasks and duties for him; berated me for handing in work that was 'lacking in sparkle'; and kept exhorting me to 'box on' and to be 'steady on parade'. On one occasion he even bellowed at me: 'Stop wallowing in self-pity – that's for girls!' It may not sound like kindness but he and I knew that it was. I climbed out of my depths far quicker than I would otherwise have done without Randolph's care and friendship.

Loyalty came almost too naturally to Randolph. He loved to champion a friend's cause or corner but he rarely knew when to stop. His biting tongue and unreasoning intolerance towards those who did not share his unstinted support for the friend he was backing sometimes gave offence. But the steadfastness of his loyalty was of a quality. One of his finest hours was his sheltering at Stour of Jack Profumo at the height of his crisis in 1962.

On the rare occasions when he had surplus money in the bank, Randolph was swift to spend it on entertaining his friends or presenting them with gifts. He gave me the most used and most cherished literary treasure on my bookshelves, the fourteen-volume edition of the *Oxford English Dictionary*. He well knew how much I enjoyed looking up unusual words for him in his copy of the greater OED, reading aloud their definitions, derivations and examples of use in early English literature. One day at Stour he said out of the blue: 'I've just had my latest instalment cheque from the Heinemen and the Mifflemen [his nicknames for his publishers, Heinemann and Houghton Mifflin], so I'm giving you your own copy of the OED.' It was an act of enormous generosity and it came complete with an equally generous personal inscription.

Those of us who spent time with Randolph in his years of biographer's seclusion at Stour loved him for his willingness to share his encyclopaedic knowledge of poetry, history and political anecdotes. He had a richly stocked mind and a near-photographic memory which enabled him to recite great swathes of Macaulay, Tennyson, Belloc, Gibbon, Kipling and Betjeman. He bubbled with epigrams, quotations, one-liners, stories and good jokes. There was also a teaching talent in Randolph, for he was a stickler for accuracy as he opened the eyes and ears of his young gentlemen to the gems of literature and history which had inspired him. Above all he relished the art of conversation. ('It should be full of zest, running from "gay to grave, from lively to severe", as Congreve puts it,' he once told me.) If you could keep up with Randolph's drinking, you could simultaneously drink at the wells of his knowledge and mastery of the English language. I took deep draughts from them which have inspired much of my own reading and writing ever since.

Charm is not a word automatically associated with Randolph Churchill, for his noisy arrogance and bullying manner made him many more enemies than friends. Yet he had charm in abundance when he was inclined to use it. He could be amusing, attractive, romantic, chivalrous, gentle and sensitive. I remember those gifts far more clearly than his demons and curses.

No-one ever doubted Randolph's courage. He had proved it physically in war and he never stopped demonstrating it morally in his frequent clashes with the many high personages with whom he crossed swords, among them newspaper proprietors, judges, QCs, Ministers, editors and other powerful figures. The only time I ever saw him appear to lose his nerve was in the days immediately before the reviewers pronounced their judgements on the first volume of his great work. At that time he became visibly nervous, tremulously musing about his fears of failure. Such fears were misplaced. The book was greeted with almost universal praise. Randolph the biographer was acclaimed as a huge success. This was a novel experience for him. He enjoyed saying that his reviews ruined Noel Coward's *bon mot*: 'Dear Randolph – so unspoilt by failure.'

Alas, Randolph's hour of triumph was soon to be spoiled by the approach of death. He had a lung cancer operation in 1964 which he announced had removed a benign tumour. This prompted Evelyn Waugh to jest: 'Trust those damn fool doctors to cut out of Randolph the only part of him that was *not* malignant.' I had my doubts about the accuracy of the diagnosis when I visited the patient in the Brompton Hospital. Although he was as defiant as ever, the pallor of his complexion and the hollows of his sunken cheeks seemed to be telling a different story.

Even though Randolph recovered well enough to finish an equally acclaimed second volume of his father's biography, his life soon became a struggle with mortality. The last time I saw him at Stour, some ten days before he died, on 6 June 1967, his skin was as white and transparent as thin parchment. But he brushed away all talk about his health. With a complete absence of self-pity, he said he was finding it hard to marshal his thoughts about the 'Life of Jack' (John F. Kennedy) and that his daily quota of words for the third volume of his father's life was becoming 'hard going'. We drank a couple of beers sitting on the terrace enjoying the spectacular views of the Vale of Dedham. Then he insisted on shuffling to the front door and seeing me off with a valedictory cry of 'Box On!' Randolph Churchill does not fit the conventional definition of a hero but his strengths and weaknesses were on a heroic scale that made him quite unlike anyone else I have ever met in my life.

CHAPTER 4

Lord Longford

'He is a traitor to his class. I won't have him in my house and that's that!' These words, almost spat at me by the most powerful political hostess in the world I then thought was important, were an unpleasant surprise which caused several problems. However, the enduring result of the episode was the start of a 42-year friendship with Lord Longford.

The hostess imposing this imperious veto on Lord Longford crossing her threshold was Lady Eliot, wife of the Provost of Eton, Sir Claude Eliot. The year was 1961. I was the 18-year-old President of the Eton College political society. It was a school tradition that our visiting speakers were entertained to dinner by the Provost. His official residence, the Provost's Lodge, was also the usual venue for the political society's meetings. As the Lodge door was slammed in our distinguished guest's face, I had to cope with the crisis of making new arrangements for him to dine and speak.

This Longford crisis was solved by the Headmaster of Eton, Robert Birley. Unlike Lady Eliot, he was untroubled by feelings of class hostility towards an old Etonian peer who had changed his political allegiance to become a Labour Cabinet minister. Indeed Birley's sympathies for socialism had earned him the nickname of 'Red Robert'. When I told him about the political society's problem he became red-in-the-face Robert.

'This is monstrous,' he said. 'Lord Longford is a most distinguished and courageous man. When he became Minister in charge of the British-occupied zone of Germany in 1945 he stood firm in the face of domestic unpopularity and achieved extraordinary results. Konrad Adenauer regarded him as one of the greatest architects of the post-war reconstruction of the German nation. It will be an honour to have the meeting and the dinner for him in my house.' So the political society gathered in the Headmaster's drawing room to hear a remarkable talk from Lord Longford. In it he described his conversions from Anglicanism to Roman Catholicism, and from Conservative Central Office researcher to Labour Cabinet minister. He offered two controversial visions of the future which he said were 'inevitable' – a united Ireland and a unified Germany. These words of international idealism were punctuated by funny but distinctly feline asides directed towards leading personalities in the Attlee government such as Ernest Bevin and Nye Bevan. After one of these barbs, Longford added that he hoped his joke would not be reported in the Eton College *Chronicle*. His comment ensured that it was. Some parts of his speech were delivered in the self-parodying manner of an absent-minded professor; others in the style of a forceful orator. He ended with a clarion call to the Etonian audience to turn away from our comfortable lives of privilege and to care for poor people and prisoners.

Longford's schoolboy listeners were impressed. However, as we walked back to our houses after the meeting, I recall one earnest sixth former asking: 'Do you think Lord Longford *meant* to be as funny as he was?' Opinions were divided on that point. However, we all felt we had heard a riveting speaker whose concern for underdogs such as starving Germans and suffering prisoners moved several of us.

This Eton episode reflected many of the qualities and characteristics of Frank Longford that were manifested throughout his life. For an outwardly mild man, he retained the capacity to create a surprisingly sharp divide in the public's perceptions of himself and his activities. The brilliance of his mind could be concealed by the vagueness of his demeanour. One moment he could be gentle, kind and self-deprecating; the next he could be stubborn, steely and self-willed to the point of intellectual arrogance. The private impression of personal modesty was contradicted by a public enthusiasm for appearing in the headlines. So there were complexes and paradoxes within Lord Longford that made him such an unusual and fascinating public figure.

The paradoxes began showing up with colourful variety later in the 1960s. By the end of that decade I had become a Fleet Street journalist and, like many of my contemporaries, I was often writing news and diary stories about Longford. The first ones I can remember came in 1968, when he rescued his political career from obscurity by resigning as Leader of the House of Lords. His departure from Harold Wilson's Cabinet won him a blaze of sympathetic headlines because Longford had quit over a genuine issue of principle – the Government reneging on its promise to raise the school-leaving age to 16. Out of office, he gained bigger headlines but less sympathy for his next two causes. They were a campaign for an early release from prison of the Moors murderer, Myra Hindley, and a report demanding tougher laws against pornography. In the first role he was vilified and in the second, ridiculed. Sometimes he had to endure both experiences, as in Evelyn Waugh's comment: 'If Frank ever became Home Secretary we should all be murdered in our beds by sexual maniacs.'

Longford's reputation came close to being murdered during his crusade against pornography. Dubbed 'Lord Porn' by the tabloids, he unwisely courted publicity for his investigative visits to sex shops in Copenhagen and bookstores in Soho. These made him a famous but farcical national figure. Although he never publicly admitted his mistakes in this crusade, when reflecting on it in a conversation with me in 1999, he said: 'I probably got the balance wrong . . . there was too much fuss.' This may have been the nearest he came to an expression of regret for this episode in his life. In any event, the Longford Report of Pornography achieved nothing. After its publication, it was significant that the author never again returned to the subject.

Despite having tasted the mixed blessings of celebrity during his incarnation as Lord Porn, Longford remained over-eager to please both his friends and his foes in the media. His attitude to their attentions was perhaps best summarised by the phrase, 'backing away into the limelight'. This was apparent in the next arena that brought him into prominence: the world of books and publishing. However, most of the literary fame that came his way was vicarious, a situation that was partly, but not entirely, to his liking.

In 1969 the Chelsea bookshop Truslove and Hanson put on a window display of the best-selling titles published by members of the Longford family. The books included: *Victoria RI,* by Elizabeth Longford; *Mary Queen of Scots*, by Antonia Fraser; *The Boer War,* by Thomas Pakenham; and *All Things Nice,* by Rachel Billington. As part of this promotion, Elizabeth Longford did a book-signing event in the shop. Her husband turned up to support her. Initially unrecognized, he approached a shop assistant, and enquired: 'Why have you left my book out of the window?' 'What is its title?' asked the assistant. 'Humility, by Lord Longford,' was the reply. It was a story he enjoyed telling against himself.

The success of 'The Literary Longfords' led to plans for an ITV documentary with that title. Filming was scheduled for the summer of 1969 with all members of the family participating, including Longford's youngest daughter, 23-year-old Catherine Pakenham, who was a trainee journalist in her first job on the *Sunday Telegraph Magazine*. On the day before filming was due to begin, when Catherine was driving down from Essex to attend a meeting with the producer and director of the documentary, she was tragically killed in a car accident. As I was the producer of this documentary-that-never-was, I felt intimately involved in the tragedy, which naturally resulted in the filming being cancelled. I thought the cancellation had been well communicated around the family. Apparently not, in the case of Lord Longford. The day after his daughter's death he showed up at the appointed time and place for his interview, expressing surprise that the camera crew had been stood down.

Longford's bizarre short-term reaction was obviously due to his traumatic shock. He had learned of the tragedy in a particularly distressing way just a few hours earlier when a reporter from the *Evening Standard* telephoned to ask for his reaction to the loss of Catherine. As Longford knew nothing about her death until this call, its effect on him was devastating. Alone in his London flat he tried to break the news to Elizabeth who was visiting Poland. Unfortunately she could not hear what he was saying, owing to a faulty connection in Warsaw.

Eventually he got through to the wife of the British Ambassador, who passed on the terrible message to Elizabeth. Broken in his lonely grief by the loss of Catherine, her death was a seminal event in Longford's life, resulting in a long-term deepening of his spirituality as he wrestled with that most difficult of Christian conundrums: Why does God allow suffering?

An even more seminal experience on Longford's spiritual journey had been his conversion to Catholicism 29 years earlier. There were many influences on that event of which the most important was the Jesuit Master of Campion Hall, Oxford, Father Martin D'Arcy. He had been giving Longford informal spiritual instruction and pastoral care during several months of emotional difficulties which amounted to a mid-life crisis. The main cause of the crisis was Longford's inability to come to terms with life in the army, for which he had volunteered in 1939 as a private soldier. At odds with the culture of a battalion preparing to go to war, he was also at odds with his wife Elizabeth because his searchings for religion clashed with her agnosticism, which included a particular antipathy towards Roman Catholicism.

In the midst of these pressures, Longford woke up one Saturday morning 'filled with overwhelming religious certainty'. That same evening, 14 June, he visited the Greyfriars community of Franciscans in Oxford. There he was received in the Catholic Church, staying overnight and taking mass the following morning as a full communicant. Then he went home to Elizabeth and broke the news of his conversion to her.

In retrospect it seems extraordinary that Longford should have taken what was probably the most momentous decision of his life without telling his wife. It was not surprising that Elizabeth felt hurt and betrayed. It took months, if not years, before her wounds healed. Antonia Fraser, the Longfords' eldest daughter, tells a story of a tense incident in the family one Sunday morning a few weeks after her father's conversion. As Longford came into the house after mass, 'my mother said: "Beat the Orange drum, children. Go on, beat the Orange drum." So I said "What do you mean?" I'd imagined a very beautiful, enormous, orange drum. And she said, "Oh, well Dada's been to church, beat the Orange drum!" Then I think she got quite embarrassed. But it was significant; a very hostile kind of behaviour from my mother who unqualifiedly adored my father.'

Elizabeth's adoration of her husband triumphed over her hostility towards his new-found faith. Six years later she too became a Catholic. Both Longfords were shaken to the core of their emotional and spiritual beings by Catherine's death. Outwardly Elizabeth's grief was worsened by religious doubt and feelings of helplessness, whereas Frank inwardly derived great comfort from his acceptance of God's will, serene in his confidence that Catherine had joined the angels in heaven. Yet in the months after her funeral Longford began to worry whether he could ever have found it possible to forgive the lorry driver (also killed in the accident) who was alleged to be responsible for the collision with Catherine's car. 'When I realized how difficult that act of forgiveness might have been for me, I began to wonder whether I had sinned by being insensitive to victims of crime who could not accept my Christian point of view, that even the worst of sinners deserve forgiveness,' he told me in 1999. 'My failings of obedience towards God's teachings on forgiveness at that time made me feel convicted of sin. I went through my own small equivalent of St John of the Cross's long, dark night of the soul.'

While these spiritual wrestlings were taking place, Longford was increasingly busy in the House of Lords and in the world of book publishing. In 1970 he became Chairman of Sidgwick and Jackson, then a small and undistinguished firm of publishers. Some members of his family nicknamed the company 'Dredgewicks' because everywhere Longford went he was always trying to 'dredge up' new authors. However, within seven years the turnover and profits of Sidgwick and Jackson had quadrupled and its chairman had been named as one of six 'great English publishers' by the *Sunday Times*. This was largely due to Longford's ability to 'dredge' or recruit best-selling writers, among them Shirley Conran, author of *Superwoman*, and Ted Heath, whose books on *Sailing* and *Music* each achieved sales of over 100,000 copies in hardback. Longford, whose relations with Heath remained distant, enjoyed the joke that the rarest copies of these two volumes were those that had not been autographed by the former Prime Minister.

Longford was an assiduous attendee at the House of Lords, which he entered in 1945 as Lord Pakenham, a hereditary peerage of first creation given him by the incoming Prime Minister, Clement Attlee. This title was superseded when he inherited the Earldom of Longford on his brother's death in 1961. It was an Irish peerage that brought with it the English barony of Silchester. When all hereditary seats in the House of Lords were abolished in 1999, Tony Blair created Longford a life peerage at the age of 93, making him the only member of the Upper House to have sat there under four different types of peerage.

For all this multiplicity of titles, Longford showed great single-mindedness of purpose in the House of Lords, for most of his work there became focused on society's most despised outcasts, particularly prisoners. Late in life he attributed this passion to his own experience as a despised outcast. He entered this category, at least by his own estimate, when he was invalided out of the army in May 1940 after suffering a nervous breakdown. 'I saw it as the greatest humiliation of my life – a terrible failure from which part of me has never quite recovered,' Longford told me. 'You see my father had been killed at Gallipoli. Several other members of my family had been distinguished army officers and military heroes. But I simply could not cope with army life. It wasn't that I was a coward, although unpleasant people did call me that once or twice. I didn't apply for my discharge. It was given to me by two medical boards. I just went to pieces, mentally and physically in a sort of total collapse. So I've known what it means to be in the depths of brokenness and despair. I think that's where the impetus for my love of prisoners comes from.'

Longford's love of prisoners was rooted in the teachings of the gospels, particularly the parable of the sheep and the goats, which exhorts the faithful to make visits to prisons. One Sunday morning in the early 1940s he heard this passage read at mass. It prompted him to visit a distant acquaintance, a solicitor who was doing time in Oxford prison for embezzling his clients' money. When he came face to face with the solicitor in the jail environment of noise, overcrowding and humiliation Longford was overwhelmed with such compassion that he choked up and was unable to speak for several minutes.

This was the start of a steadily growing programme of visits to prisoners in all parts of the country. In HMP Wakefield in 1957 Longford met a particularly notorious prisoner, Christopher Craig, who had shot and killed a police officer in the course of an armed robbery. Craig's companion on the night of the robbery had been Derek Bentley who, although already arrested, had shouted, 'Let him have it Chris!' just before the fatal shot was fired. Whether these words shouted across the rooftop meant 'give him the gun!' or 'kill him!' was a matter of intense argument in court, but at the end of the trial the jury found both defendants guilty of murder. As he was only 17 years old Craig could not be sentenced to death but Bentley, although mentally retarded, was hanged as an accomplice to the murder.

After many meetings with Craig, Longford became impressed by his contrition and by the changes in his character. Having entered prison as a violent, dyslexic, illiterate and disturbed teenager, Craig by his mid-twenties had become a model prisoner, acquiring good educational skills and accredited qualifications as an electrical fitter. So in co-operation with Craig's family, Longford lobbied the Home Office for the young man's early release. This was granted in 1962. In 1965 Craig invited his benefactor to his wedding. By this time Longford was in the Cabinet so he sought clearance from No. 10 to attend the marriage service. It was refused. 'To this day it is still much on my conscience that I gave way to Harold Wilson and skipped the wedding,' Longford told me 35 years after the event. 'I tried to soften the blow by giving him and his fiancée dinner the night before they got married. I kept on seeing Christopher and I kept on campaigning for Derek Bentley to receive a posthumous pardon – which, thank God, he did in 1997, 45 years after his execution.'

This story of the Craig–Bentley *cause célèbre* and Longford's role in it says much about his persistence as a campaigner for prisoners he believes have been wrongly treated or convicted. But were his activities in this field also influenced by his love of publicity? This is a charge that was frequently levelled against Longford for he was often in the headlines for befriending such notorious prisoners as Christopher Craig, George Blake, the Russian spy, Michael Davies, the Clapham Common murderer, and the Moors murderers, Myra Hindley and Ian Brady.

Although Longford may have become interested in these and other well-known prisoners because of the huge press coverage they and their crimes received, such cases should be seen in proportion alongside his far larger numbers of unsung and unpublicised prison visits. For Longford was a regular caller at most of Britain's jails for 60 years of his life between the years 1943 and 2003. In those decades he visited, at a conservative estimate, at least 500 prisoners. Of these, no more than 25 or 30 of his visits were ever reported in the media. This means that around 95 per cent of his work as a prison visitor was carried out in obscurity. On that basis it seems fair to acquit Longford of the charge of publicity-seeking in his prison activities.

One group of people who talked favourably about Lord Longford's compassion for prisoners were uniformed officers in the prison service. I encountered this phenomenon myself during my own prison sentence in 1999–2000. Indeed I shall never forget Lord Longford's first visit to me in HMP Belmarsh in June 1999. It began when a Senior Officer (SO) unlocked my cell door and said, 'Aitken you've got a visit. Come with me.' 'Oh sorry, I didn't see it up on the noticeboard,' I said, hastily pulling on a clean shirt and sweater. 'No, it wasn't up on the board,' said the SO. 'In fact your visitor's been making a bit of a nuisance of himself at the gate. He's been camping there for the last two hours. I only just managed to stop the gate officers from calling the police to remove him as an unknown vagrant.'

My mind reeled. 'Who on earth is he?' I asked. 'Lord Longford,' said the SO, 'and I've decided to use my discretion to allow him in as a special visitor. Mind you, I'm not doing this as a favour to you, and don't you forget it. I'm doing it because I've got a lot of respect for the old boy. When I was a young officer starting at Strangeways he used to come all the way up to Manchester to visit the worst of the worst and the lowest of the low, if you get my meaning. Then when I was in Gartree, same again. Same again in the Scrubs.'

By now I was being escorted through long corridors and several locked gates towards the visiting hall. The SO was one of that wise, humane and experienced breed of ex-military prison officers of whom I met many during my sentence. 'If you've been in this job for as long as I have,' he was saying, 'you know that even the untouchables – perhaps especially the untouchables – need to feel the warmth of human kindness. And that's what Lord Longford's been doing for the last 40 years or so to my certain knowledge; so he's the last man on earth I'm going to turn away. He's in his nineties now and he looks it, but he's still going strong. A very special gentleman in my book.'

Unfortunately some of the officers on duty at the visiting hall were not reading from the same book as the SO when it came to their handling of the Earl of Longford. He had made himself a nuisance; he had beaten the system; so both he and the prisoner he was visiting were going to be given a hard time – that seemed to be their attitude. The hard time they gave me was marginal. I was searched much more aggressively than on any subsequent visit, issued with a bright orange bib to tie around my neck, and brusquely directed to a numbered seat behind a wooden barrier on the far left of the visiting hall. After waiting in this aircraft-hangar-sized room for several minutes, watching some 250 other prisoners enjoying their visits, I became aware of an altercation somewhere behind the entrance doors. As they swung open, above the hubbub I heard the familiar voice of Frank Longford protesting, 'But unless I have my sticks I really can't walk that far.'

This protest evidently failed, because when Frank slowly shuffled his way into the visitors' arena he was without his sticks. They had been confiscated, he explained later, 'by a rather officious young man who had the curious idea in his head that you could use them as an offensive weapon'. This idea was not on my agenda, but rules are rules in Belmarsh. So Frank had to wobble his stickless way towards me, teetering and tottering in unsupported lurches of such fragility that his progress was agonizing to watch. He advanced about halfway across the hall before his 94-year-old legs gave way. As he crashed to the ground, four or five officers stationed at strategic points of vigilance around the perimeter rushed to his rescue. The scene put me in mind of Humpty Dumpty, particularly when Frank's bald head had to be propped up by all the Queen's men as they lifted him off the floor. For a moment I was worried about injuries to my visitor, but I realized he was unharmed when I heard that piercing Longford voice telling the officers, 'I warned you I'd be more trouble without my sticks!'

Frank visited me four times during the seven months I spent in prison. We had deep conversations on all these occasions, but our personal and spiritual intimacies were often leavened by humour. On the first occasion he came to see me in HMP Standford Hill, he enjoyed telling me the story of his journey. Arriving at the local train station, he hailed a cab and asked to be taken to his destination. 'Money upfront,' demanded the taxi driver. Longford said he was unfamiliar with this expression. The driver forcefully explained that so many of his fares to Standford Hill had 'done a runner' on arriving at the prison that he now insisted on cash in advance for journeys there. Longford protested that at his age he could not run anywhere. The driver remained adamant, saying he had been tricked by elderly gentlemen with walking sticks before. There was an impasse, for Frank could be stubborn. After some discussion, the cab eventually took him to the prison gates, with the fare being paid in the normal way at the end of the journey.

'What did you say to the driver that changed his mind?' I asked as he told me the story. 'Oh, I just mentioned my last three appointments before coming to see you.' 'What were your last three appointments?' 'Well, since you ask, they were the Garter ceremony at Windsor, a reception in the House of Lords for ministers who served in Clem Attlee's government, and dinner with the Queen Mother.'

This was beyond parody but, even so, the three appointments told their own tale of what a busy and varied life Longford was still leading in his ninety-fifth year.

The Garter ceremony at Windsor Castle was an annual event Longford loved. He had become a Knight Companion of Britain's most ancient order of chivalry in 1972 – the year in which he launched his anti-pornography campaign. Whispers from court circles hinted that the honour might have been delayed if it had been known that the new knight was about to tilt his lance and charge off on a self-appointed mission to rescue damsels in undress. However, the Garter was already in the post by the time the tabloids were in overdrive on 'Lord Porn', so Longford's installation as a Knight Companion went ahead as planned.

For the last 12 years of his life, he was the senior knight of the order, a position which entitled him to sit on the right of the Queen at Garter lunches. At the 1999 ceremony Longford was bold enough to ask his Sovereign: 'Tell me, Ma'am, is it true what the press are saying about Charles and Camilla?' To which the Queen replied, 'Well, they do seem to need each other.' This private acknowledgement came years before there was any sort of public acceptance of the relationship by Buckingham Palace.

For all his enjoyment of royal parties and pageantry, Longford did not care whether or not he was socially accepted by the British establishment. His priority was always for the underdogs of society. Never in his life did he turn away from a disgraced or despondent sufferer. When he heard from his daughter Antonia that Jack Profumo was languishing in miserable loneliness after his fall (in sharp contrast to his wife Valerie, who was being taken out by many friends) Longford invited him to lunch. In an unworldly touch, Frank suggested the Savoy Grill. It was left to Profumo to point out that this was not an ideally discreet venue for a meal with someone hiding from the paparazzi. When they did lunch in more private surroundings, Longford was touched by Profumo's penitence. Their relationship developed into a deep friendship and resulted in Longford guiding Profumo to Toynbee Hall where he dedicated his life to welfare work in the East End.

Another fallen politician whose rehabilitation received a helping hand from Longford was Richard Nixon. When he, initially in a mood of considerable nervousness, made his first visit to Britain in 1978, four years after resigning from the Presidency of the USA, he was surprised but pleased when a handwritten note arrived in his suite at Claridges from Longford asking him to lunch in the House of Lords. This invitation, thanks to the generosity of Charles Forte, was expanded into a dinner for 200 Nixon well-wishers at the Hyde Park Hotel. Longford, who took the chair at this event, told Nixon: 'Many who have made worse mistakes than yours have risen again to play an influential role in national and international affairs. May this be true of you in your future years as an elder statesman.'

This was music to Richard Nixon's ears, for at that time he was a long way from being rehabilitated in the eyes of his fellow countrymen from the scandals of Watergate. Later Longford wrote a short book on Nixon, praising the Thirty-seventh President for his foreign policy achievements and minimising his domestic transgressions. It was all part of the Longford pattern of rushing out to extend the hand of friendship and support to those suffering from the agonies of public disgrace.

An earlier outcast rescued by Longford was Peter Wildeblood. In the 1950s, when homosexuality was still a criminal offence, Wildeblood, Lord Montagu of Beaulieu, and a third man, were jailed for their gay relationships. Longford visited Wildeblood regularly in Wormwood Scrubs, befriended him after his release and made him one of the founders (along with himself and Edward Montagu) of the New Bridge Society. It flourishes to this day as a much-respected charitable organization caring for the welfare of ex-prisoners. However, when it began in 1955 it was so closely associated with the 'three musketeers', as the three young men who had been jailed for minor homosexual offences were known, that senior Home Office officials regarded New Bridge as a suspicious group of gay men looking after other gay men. Someone argued that this could not be true because Lord Longford had eight children. 'Oh that's just good cover,' retorted a Deputy Secretary at the Home Office.

Longford never covered up his attitude to homosexuality, which was one of strong moral disapproval. However, his antipathy to what he called 'that dreadful sin' did not prevent him from steadfastly supporting the campaign inside and outside Parliament for the implementation of the Wolfenden Report, which recommended decriminalizing homosexuality between consenting adults. This controversial legislation had to be initiated in the House of Lords, Longford told an amused public meeting in Oxford, 'because elected MPs are too worried about protecting their seats'.

Longford often used the Lords as a platform for furthering his agenda of compassionate and Christian causes. On one occasion he achieved the rare distinction of being booed by his fellow peers for a speech of uncharacteristic insensitivity in which he attacked supporters of abortion law reform. Usually he was a master of the style required in their Lordships' house, using wit, scholarship and practical knowledge to make speeches of considerable effectiveness. In 1955 he launched the first-ever Lords debate on prison conditions. Subsequently he was a member of a Parliamentary committee whose report, *Crime – A Challenge*, recommended the introduction of the parole system and a programme of aftercare for prisoners. He developed his groundbreaking ideas on penal reform in several influential books, among them *Causes of Crime* (1958); *The Idea of Punishment* (1961); *Young Offenders* (1991); and *Prisoner or Patient?* (1992). The last dealt with the treatment of the rising number of prison inmates suffering from mental disorders. This was a subject dear to Longford's heart for poignant reasons, namely the mental disorders of his son, Paddy Pakenham, with whom he set up a charitable trust to help prisoners with similar conditions.

Paddy was the third and most vulnerable of the Longfords' eight children. Like his father, he knew the occasional angst of being a second son in an aristocratic family where primogeniture prevailed. 'I am but one sperm away from the castle,' he would wistfully say. Also, like his father, he suffered a nervous breakdown while serving in the army. In Paddy's case, this was the harbinger of disruptive mood swings and outbreaks of manic depression which assailed him throughout his life. Eventually they brought a premature end to his flourishing career at the bar. They also caused his involvement in numerous tragi-comic disturbances that required him to be rescued from bars, bookmakers, police stations and A&E wings of hospitals. The rescuer was usually his father who showed Paddy special love and treated him as a favourite son. An endearing story about their relationship is told of the time when Longford was Chairman of the National Bank and Paddy, off on one of his 'highs', was losing money at the roulette tables in Le Touquet. At such moments of exuberance it was not uncommon for Paddy to ennoble himself. On this occasion he telephoned the National Bank's head office in Dublin. 'This is Lord Longford speaking,' he began. 'I would like Pounds 1,000 to be sent at once to the Credit Lyonnais.' Unfortunately for Paddy his father happened to be visiting the bank's Dublin office that day so the switchboard operator connected the caller to the chairman. The two 'Lord Longfords' spoke to each other. A sum smaller than the one requested was later transferred to Le Touquet as settlement for Paddy's gambling debts.

As a father, Longford was loving but often distant. In common with many men of his time, he remained aloof from much of the family fray. He never visited any of his children at school, and the idea of helping with the washing-up or any other domestic chores did not occur to him. Elizabeth enjoyed telling the story of how in the early days of their marriage she was surprised to see her husband leaving his shoes outside the bedroom door at night, apparently in expectation that they would be cleaned by the following morning. She had to point out that there was no cleaner other than herself in the house.

Such unworldliness often surfaced in the Longford home. Apart from his brief stint as a bank chairman, he was never a large earner. The modest attendance allowance he received from the House of Lords was always a vital ingredient in his slender income. So life was frugal at Bernhurst, the Sussex country house he inherited from an aunt. Making ends meet was a task he delegated to Elizabeth, whose success as a best-selling author was an immense help to the family budget, as was the money she inherited from family relatives.

For all his vagueness and unworldliness Longford was fiercely competitive, with a mind and a memory which could have taken him to the top of the academic world, had he decided to remain in it. He got a first in Modern Greats at Oxford in 1927, coming second in the honours list of firsts, several places above his closest friend and rival, Hugh Gaitskell. He had two spells as an Oxford don but in both periods he could hardly wait to escape to his higher vocations of politics and prisoners. He displayed his prodigious memory in feats such as learning Hansard by heart, not only in his own day as a Parliamentarian but also in bygone ages, as he could recite many of Gladstone's speeches word-perfectly. He could do similar recitals of Test and County Cricket scoreboards, for his love of that game led him to memorize the entire contents of Wisden for many years. Cricket was only one of the sports he enjoyed. He also played soccer and rugby well and won youthful prizes as a sprinter on the athletics track. He remained a keen jogger well into his eighties.

Such accomplishments nurtured Longford's competitive spirit but they were diversions compared to the supreme passion of his life – his Catholic faith. He took this far further than his exemplary spiritual disciplines of prayer, bible reading, confession and regular attendance at mass. Whenever political pressures (some might say political common sense) came into conflict with the doctrines of his church, Catholicism always won. So from opposing all forms of contraception to publicly kissing the ring of a German cardinal when he was the British Minister of the Crown in charge of occupied Germany, Longford was willing to embrace secular absurdity to comply with religious obedience. His formidable intellect, which he used so effectively to question many established political nostrums of the state, was never used at all to question the doctrinal nostrums of his church. It would be hard to imagine a more zealous, faithful and obedient convert to Catholicism than Frank Longford.

His unquestioning fidelity to the most conservative teachings of his church on matters of personal morality sometimes led Longford into tensions within his own family. These became acute when he saw four of his offspring's marriages end in divorce. According to the sternest tenets of Catholic doctrine, their divorces, and their subsequent re-marriages, were mortal sins. This troubled Longford greatly but he came to terms with these conflicts between love of his faith and love of his family after many vacillations and contradictions. For example, when his eldest daughter, Antonia, separated from her husband, Hugh Fraser, to live with and later marry the playwright, Harold Pinter, Longford at first became uncharacteristically judgemental. For a time there was an estrangement between father and daughter. It was not helped by the paternal comment, 'Oh well, all theatre people are homos.' Later Longford attempted to come down on the side of tolerance by saying, 'Oh well, all theatre people are bohemians.' To this Antonia replied, 'Well you can't have it both ways.' Eventually Longford seemed to accept that his adult children in their forties had a right to make up their own minds on divorce and re-marriage. So bowing to the inevitable he welcomed all his children's new marriage partners and returned to a state of familial if not spiritual grace by restoring his fatherly love.

The power of Longford's love for Elizabeth and their huge family (eight children, 26 grandchildren, 25 great grandchildren) was matched by the staying power of his compassion for prisoners. 'Hate the sin and love the sinner,' was his motto. To honour it he defied the conventions of his class and the infirmities of his old age. Well into his nineties, his iron will took him on journeys behind iron bars to jails throughout the country. I was by no means the only prisoner on Longford's visiting list in the last years of his life. Another was a former Catholic priest serving a 14-year term for paedophile offences. A second was a schoolmaster 'doing a five' for buggery. A third was a murderer who had killed his own children. A fourth was an embezzler who had left his disabled wards penniless through fraud. All of us were unlovable people in the eyes of the world, but not to Lord Longford.

On his last two visits to me in HMP Standford Hill, Longford was accompanied by his closest friend, Andrew McCooey. Their unpublicized partnership was an important element in both their lives. McCooey was a Kent solicitor (in 2001 he was elevated to the judiciary as a Recorder of the Crown Court) who specialized in voluntary work for British prisoners incarcerated in foreign jails. Working closely as a team, Longford and McCooey achieved extraordinary successes in winning reprieves for Britons under sentence of death for drug offences in overseas jurisdictions. They also won early releases for men and women who had been excessively sentenced or wrongly convicted. This part of Longford's work with prisoners went almost completely unreported in the media.

Andrew McCooey was Myra Hindley's solicitor. His client had been visited once a week since 1970 by Longford, who was often accompanied by his wife Elizabeth. 'I think the starting point for Frank's visits to Myra was his belief that nobody, however terrible their crime, is below the reach of God's grace,' said McCooey. 'Their relationship grew when he learned that Myra was a lapsed Catholic who had returned to her faith after full confession and penitence. Also I think Frank felt a bit of a hero for taking her on. The bigger the flak, the more he dug in his heels. One day when the media were giving him a hard time, I asked him whether he regretted his association with her.

"Not at all," he replied. "My support for Myra is one thing I won't have to worry about on the day of judgement.'"

Myra Hindley's judgement on Longford was less generous, at least towards the end of their association. In the mid-1990s, when her campaign to be released from her life sentence was gathering momentum, Hindley abruptly decided to stop receiving visits from Longford on the grounds that he had become too controversial and perhaps too counterproductive a supporter of her cause. After nearly a quarter of a century of befriending her, this rejection hurt Longford. But he took the decision on the chin, even adding a little spiritual balm to his wounds when he said, 'Myra has long ago repented of her dreadful crimes. She is at peace with God and that is what really matters. It does not matter at all who helps her to find peace with the world by securing her release.'

Some people found Longford's advocacy for Myra Hindley naive to the point of insensitivity. He himself came to understand that school of thought which emanated from the families of the victims of the Moors murderers. However, he rejected it, saying that only God could see into the souls of sinners.

If such talk was foolish it was holy foolishness. Certainly there were many occasions in his life when Longford was made to look a fool as a result of being tricked by prisoners, deceived by politicians and ridiculed by journalists. Yet none of these disappointments reduced his commitment and enthusiasm for the causes to which he dedicated his life. Nothing diminished his Christian convictions or tarnished the aura of holiness he brought to his work. Both as a politician and as 'that prison person' (a label he acquired in the 1950s), Longford honoured his vocation to the rejected so well and for so long that he came to be regarded almost as a saintly figure – especially in the eyes of those who knew, as he himself knew, what it feels like to fall from grace to brokenness.

The last time I saw Frank Longford was in July 2001. It was a month in which he had delivered his last speech in the House of Lords (characteristically on prisons) and a few days later had collapsed with pneumonia. Sitting upright in an armchair in his West London nursing home, he looked alarmingly frail and weighed down by every one of his 95 years. However, his mind was sharp and his voice clear. As usual, we talked about faith. He told me he was reading a chapter a day of St Luke's gospel. So we read one together containing the parable of the talents, which ends with the words: 'Well done thou good and faithful servant.' As I was able to tell him at the time, there could be no better epitaph for his own life, which came to a peaceful end twelve days afterwards.

CHAPTER 5

Harold Wilson

'Minister, might it not be a little . . . er . . . unwise . . . to have a portrait of Harold Wilson on your walls?' These words were murmured by my private secretary on the day when, as a newly appointed Minister of State for Defence, I visited the Government Art Collection to select some suitable paintings to decorate my Whitehall office.

The curator had laid out various items he thought might be decoratively appropriate for a Defence Minister. They included battle scenes from the Peninsular War, portraits of Nelson, a bronze statuette of General Gordon and sketches of the Trooping of the Colour. Instead, I asked to look at paintings of political leaders. They were an unimpressive lot, largely because long-serving ministers and ambassadors had already bagged the best of the collection. However, tucked away in a corner, I saw a picture that sent my artistic spirits soaring. It was Ruskin Spear's portrait of Harold Wilson, painted in 1975 when he was beginning his second term as Prime Minister. Pipe in hand, quizzical smile playing on his lips, he looked as though he had just thought up a quip with which to goad Ted Heath at Prime Minister's Question Time in the House of Commons. This was a Harold Wilson I well remembered. So, despite the reservations of my private secretary, the portrait was given a place of prominence in my fifth floor office at the Ministry of Defence.

Harold Wilson had fascinated me for many years. Because I grew up in a political family, even as a schoolboy I had been kept surprisingly well informed about the internecine feuds within the disintegrating Labour government of 1950–1951. I knew that Wilson had been described in a *Daily Express* headline as 'the youngest Cabinet minister since William Pitt'. Less flatteringly I remember the epithet 'Nye's little dog' sticking to him because, to the delight of my Tory MP father and his colleagues, Wilson had allegedly precipitated the fall of the Labour government by resigning with Nye Bevan from Attlee's Cabinet in 1951.

Ten years later, as an Oxford undergraduate, I met Harold Wilson – still a demonized figure in the eyes of many Tories – in the Randolph Hotel. He was Labour's Shadow Chancellor, enjoying a drink in the bar after addressing the Oxford University Labour Club. By coincidence the actual Chancellor of the Exchequer, Selwyn Lloyd, was in the same bar, having just addressed the Oxford University Conservative Association. The two Parliamentary adversaries forgot their differences and had a remarkably congenial nightcap together. I was invited to join them because I was Selwyn Lloyd's godson. At the end of the evening Selwyn said to me, 'Harold's got a great sense of humour and a brilliant mind but he'll never lead the Labour party. The brothers think he's as slippery as an eel.'

That was a misjudgement, for Harold Wilson was elected Leader of his party in 1963. The next two years were the most successful of his career. Indeed there has probably never been a more effective Leader of the Opposition than Wilson in 1963–1964. I watched him at relatively close quarters in this period for, by then in my early twenties, I was working in the back rooms of Conservative party politics as a part-time political secretary to Selwyn Lloyd. He was Leader of the House of Commons and the closest Cabinet colleague to the new Prime Minister, Sir Alec Douglas-Home. My job was to draft speeches for both of them, designed to attract 'the youth vote'. I was singularly unsuccessful at this task. For as the 1964 election approached it became increasingly clear that the youth vote had already been captured by Harold Wilson. He was younger, wittier, more technocratic and more in touch with the rising generation than the opponent he caricatured as 'the Fourteenth Earl of Home'. With Labour pulling ahead in the polls and the mood at Conservative Central Office becoming despondent, I was despatched on an undercover mission: 'Do your best to look like an uncommitted voter. Go to one or two of Wilson's election meetings. And come back and tell us if the little man has an Achilles heel,' were my instructions.

Instead of discovering weaknesses in the Leader of the Opposition's armour, I could only report on his enormous strengths. For Wilson was master of one of the great art forms of election campaigning that was still alive and well in the 1960s – dominating a big crowd at a public meeting.

The first election rally where I saw Harold Wilson at the top of his oratorical form was in Ipswich. It was an open-air event with free access to all comers, including several hecklers. To the delight of the 2,000-strong crowd, Wilson took his opponents head on from the start, declaring himself amazed at the discovery of 'a human species I thought was extinct – the Tory working man'.

Examples of *homo laboriens Toriensis* present that afternoon were no match for the Leader of the Opposition in command of the microphone. Interrupters were crushed like ants under a giant's heel. After a succession of such squashings, Wilson took a sip from a glass of water. The pause allowed the shout, 'Getting tired, are you?' Back came the instant riposte: 'No, it's the Tories who are tired – and ever since Profumo we know what's been tiring them!'

After more such knockabout, all but one of the hecklers had been ridiculed into silence. The sole survivor was weaving his way, somewhat unsteadily, around the crowd, bellowing his insults from a variety of different vantage points. Wilson watched the peripatetic troublemaker with amused detachment until pouncing on him with the scornful cry: 'Hamlet, Act I, Scene V: "Well said old mole, canst work i' th' earth so fast?"'

After the rubbishing of hecklers came the rubbishing of Tory ministers. My boss, Selwyn Lloyd, came under fire for the wage restraint policy known as 'the pay pause', which he had introduced as Chancellor. It had been relaxed by the new Prime Minister. 'Oh well, the one thing the Tories can plan is an election boom,' said Wilson. 'Old Celluloid puts the brakes on the economy then the Fourteenth Earl puts his foot on the accelerator. They make a fine couple. I call 'em Stop-Go and Son.'

Other flashes of invective included describing Quintin Hogg as 'The Minister of Science with a broken computer' and deriding the new Chancellor, Reginald Maudling, for 'setting up his own Aunt Sallys and then getting knocked down by them'. A Labour government would sweep away such 'yesterday's men'. Instead, a new Britain with equal opportunities for all would be 'forged in the white heat of the technological revolution'. It was rousing election rhetoric and even Conservative Central Office's secret agent could scarce forbear to cheer the Labour Leader for providing such wonderful entertainment.

On the basis of my observations of Harold Wilson at his meetings in the 1964 campaign, I thought that he would win the election easily. In fact he only just squeaked home with a hairline majority in Parliament of three seats. Before he could go to the Palace he had to wait for the result in Meriden, a Conservative-held seat in Warwickshire with an outsize electorate of 93,000 voters. Eventually after two recounts it went Labour by 396 votes. Six months later, at the ripe old age of 22, I was surprised to be selected as the Conservative Parliamentary candidate for this constituency, which was by then classified as a key marginal.

Because of the slenderness of his 1964 majority, everyone knew that Harold Wilson would have to call an early election. It was an article of faith among many over-optimistic Tories that a Labour government would make such a mess of its first few months in power that the electorate would reverse its decision at the earliest opportunity. The opposite happened. Wilson immediately showed himself to be an energetic and capable Prime Minister. His handling of the Rhodesia crisis was skilful, enhancing the public's perception of him as an international leader by his authoritative broadcast after the Ian Smith government in Salisbury declared UDI (Unilateral Declaration of Independence). With his ratings in the opinion polls moving well ahead of the new Conservative leader, Ted Heath, Wilson called an election for the 31 March 1966. As the campaign started the Conservative candidate for Meriden (the tenth most marginal seat in the country) was one of many Tory hopefuls who knew they hadn't a hope.

Harold Wilson and Ted Heath both made election stops in Meriden. Wilson's visit was in the nature of a royal progress. His decision to come to the area at all was due to what the press kept calling 'The West Midlands factor'. This was an alleged regional swing against Labour, which the local polls said would bring several marginals, including Meriden, back to the Conservatives. The main cause of this swing was said to be rising anxiety in and around Birmingham about the level of immigration. Since this was not a significant issue in Meriden I had expected the Prime Minister to avoid mentioning it during his visit or, possibly, to deliver some calming bromide on the subject. Far from it. Wilson's language on the hustings was vitriolic as he accused the neighbouring Tory MP for Smethwick of exploiting racial fears and denounced him as 'a Parliamentary leper'. He was almost as scathing about Conservative MPs, 'whose Neolithic Imperial instincts make them cling like limpets to the ruins of Rhodesian white supremacy'. This style of invective was unusual from a sitting Prime Minister 40 years ago.

Harold Wilson won the 1966 General Election by a landslide, increasing his Parliamentary majority from three seats to 97. In Meriden, the West Midlands factor proved a mirage, for the Labour majority of 396 that the opinion pollsters had predicted I would overturn actually rose tenfold to over 4,000.

After that defeat I began a new life as a Fleet Street journalist. Some of my reporting duties took me to Washington DC where I covered the first White House summit in 1969 between the new US President, Richard Nixon, and the well-established UK Prime Minister, Harold Wilson.

The relationship between Wilson and Nixon was a fascinating one, which could perhaps be attributed to 'the attraction of opposites'. I discovered many more insights into this relationship than ever appeared in the British press during the course of my long friendship with Nixon. Like most Labour politicians of his era, Harold Wilson had an instinctive aversion to Richard Nixon, whom he expected to lose the 1968 Presidential election. Indeed, so confident was Wilson of the outcome to this contest that several months in advance of it, he asked the Democratic contender, Vice President Hubert Humphrey, whom he would like to work with as President in the post of British Ambassador to Washington. In September 1968, two months before the US election, Wilson appointed as Ambassador-designate John Freeman, the former editor of the *New Statesman*, who was a personal friend of Hubert Humphrey. After Humphrey lost the election, President-elect Nixon was not best pleased to learn the reasons for Harold Wilson's selection of Ambassador-designate Freeman. Nixon let it be known through intermediaries that he hoped the British Prime Minister would reconsider the appointment. The cause of this tension was Nixon's elephantine memory, which enabled him to recall a 1962 *New Statesman* article in which Freeman described him as 'a man of no principle whatsoever except a willingness to sacrifice everything in the cause of Dick Nixon'. The article had concluded with the view that Nixon's defeat for the Governorship of California in 1962 had been 'a victory for decency in public life'.

In spite of the new President's umbrage at this ancient article, Harold Wilson refused to consider changing the appointment. This caused more umbrage in Washington, not only from Nixon but from former President Dwight D. Eisenhower, who said that a Freeman ambassadorship would be an insult to Nixon personally and also to the Presidency as an institution. Fired up by this counsel from his old chief, given two weeks before Nixon was due to make the first overseas visit of his administration to London, word came to No. 10 from the White House that the new President would boycott the Prime Minister's dinner in his honour unless Freeman was removed from the guest list. A diplomatic tizzy ensued, causing much heartache to the US Ambassador in London, David Bruce, who was unable to persuade either the President to change his mind or the Prime Minister to change his invitations. Just as the diplomatic tizzy was on the verge of becoming a diplomatic row, Nixon blinked first. Even so, the episode seemed likely to cast a chill over the Prime Minister's dinner. But Nixon loved to surprise. In his toast after the meal he poured charm over Wilson's choice as British Ambassador, saying that American newspapers had written far worse things about him than the *New Statesman*. 'Some say there's a new Nixon,' he went on, 'and they wonder if there's a new Freeman. I would like to think that's all behind us. After all, he's the new diplomat and I'm the new statesman.' As warm applause greeted this conciliatory bouquet, Harold Wilson scribbled a note on the back of the President's menu card: 'That was one of the kindest and most generous acts I have known in a quarter of a century of politics. Just proves my point. You can't guarantee being born a lord. It is possible – you've shown it – to be born a gentleman.'

Nixon, who was unaccustomed to receiving such gracious compliments about his gentlemanly antecedents, took a shine to Harold Wilson from that moment onwards. The conservative Republican President and the left-of-centre Labour Prime Minister made the Anglo-American alliance work far more smoothly than it did after Ted Heath replaced Wilson at No. 10 following the 1970 election. In a conversation with me in 1978, Nixon compared the change in his relations with the two British leaders to the seasonal climate changes between spring and autumn:

> For all my affinity for Ted Heath's politics I could never get on any sort of wavelength with Ted Heath personally. There was a kind of autumnal chill about him, whereas Wilson brought with him a warm human dimension that felt like spring sunshine. I liked his humour, his openness, his frankness. Of course we never got into that kinda touchy-feely stuff that world leaders put on nowadays, but because we were both centrists and realists, Harold and I became buddies – real buddies.

Harold Wilson demonstrated his reciprocal feelings of buddiness for Richard Nixon after the 37th President of the USA was forced to resign over Watergate. In the months following that resignation, the bombardment of vilification from Nixon's political and media opponents made him the most despised hate-figure in America. Much of that obloquy prevailed on this side of the Atlantic towards 'the disgraced ex-President', as the press labelled him. So when Nixon decided to make his first post-resignation overseas visit to Britain (ostensibly to speak at the Oxford Union), the news of his imminent arrival produced some surprisingly hostile reactions in high places. The Foreign Secretary of the day, David Owen, asked his officials for advice on whether the former President could be declared *persona non grata* and refused entry. All government ministers received instructions from No. 10 Downing Street to refuse invitations to the Speaker's reception for Nixon. Among former Prime Ministers, Harold Macmillan declined an invitation to this party, saying 'I just couldn't face it . . . I was too fond of Jack.'

Harold Wilson, by contrast, said he would be delighted to welcome Nixon. Although the former Labour Prime Minister was not well off, he spared no expense to welcome the former President. A private suite in the Dorchester, beautiful flowers, the finest food and wine (of which Nixon, apparently something of an expert on Bordeaux vintages, was highly appreciative), and the most jovial of greetings set the scene. Apart from the two principals, the only guests were Wilson's long-standing personal secretary, Lady Falkender, and myself. Lady Falkender and I were almost completely silent throughout the meal as the elder statesmen roamed through recent political history with a glorious panoply of reminiscences. When the brandy came round, Nixon observed: 'Well, Harold, you and I are two surviving members of a small club. We have held real power but now we're out.' 'Down but not out,' interjected Wilson, who at this time was regarded as something of a political pariah by his own Labour party. 'Right, right, we'll show 'em,' continued Nixon, 'but what I really want to know from my fellow club member is how do you fill your days? Do you read? Do you write? Are you preparing some great testament?' Wilson seemed to find this a difficult question. After much puffing on his pipe he eventually replied: 'As a matter of fact, Dick, I'm spending a lot of time on Gilbert and Sullivan.'

Nixon nodded seriously as if to convey the impression that he thought this an entirely suitable occupation for a world statesman. 'I'm quite a Gilbert and Sullivan buff myself' was his unexpected comment. 'In my college days I was one of the stage managers for a couple of productions – *Pinafore* and *Pirates of Penzance*.' Not to be outdone, Wilson countered: 'As a matter of fact I'm word-perfect on both of them myself.' He explained that as a lifelong Gilbert and Sullivan enthusiast he was campaigning to save the D'Oyly Carte Opera Company, which owned the copyrights. A few moments later he decided to prove his musical expertise with a demonstration.

> *When I was a lad I served a term*
> *As office boy to an Attorney's firm,*

piped up the former British Prime Minister.

> *I cleaned the windows and I swept the floor,*
> *And I polished up the handle of the big front door,*

carolled the former President of the USA.

> *I polished up that handle so carefullee*
> *That now I am the ruler of the Queen's Navee,*

the singing statesmen warbled together in passable unison, beating time on the table. They were off – for at least four verses of 'When I was a Lad'. As they reached the final refrain,

> *Stick close to your desks and never go to sea*
> *And you all may be rulers of the Queen's Navee,*

the enthralled audience of Lady Falkender, myself and a Dorchester waiter burst into rapturous applause for this unique Anglo-American duet. 'Harold sure knows how to make a party go,' said Nixon as he left the Dorchester at 1.30 am.

The story of this dinner party reflected certain human qualities in Harold Wilson which were not always visible when he was at the height of his career. They were his kindness, his loyalty, his sense of humour, his enjoyment of good wine and brandy, and his prodigious memory. These qualities were well displayed in the next episode of my association with him which included a visit to the Isles of Scilly, and a business venture that came close to making him chairman of a major ITV company.

To understand some of the deeper dimensions of Harold Wilson, it was useful to have seen him enjoying the relaxed life in the place he regarded as home – St Mary's, the largest island in the Scillies. Ever since his parents had moved to Cornwall in their retirement, Harold had been fascinated by this archipelago of rocky islets 30 miles off Penzance. He had planed to honeymoon there with his bride, Mary, after their wedding in January 1940 but wartime travel restrictions made that journey impossible. However, the couple started visiting St Mary's for annual bucket-and-spade holidays at the Star Castle Hotel with their two small sons from 1952 onwards. In 1959 the Wilsons bought a plot of freehold land in the heart of Hugh Town and built an unpretentious three-bedroom, rectangular bungalow which they called 'Lowenva'. For Mary this haven was the fulfilment of her poetic dreams while for Harold it became his escapist hideaway from the pressures of No. 10. He also found the islands a creative environment for political thinking. One of the most original achievements for which he is remembered to this day – the creation of the Open University – came to him while he was walking round the coastline of St Mary's in the early 1960s.

When I visited Harold at his home there soon after his retirement as Prime Minister, it was clear that the locals had adopted him as one of their own. Just about every fisherman, shopkeeper and passer-by greeted him with unfeigned warmth as we walked around the town. He reciprocated their affection. Much of his conversation consisted of lyrical enthusiasm for all things Scillonian, from the seals and seabirds of the outer islands, to the smugglers' songs and shanties sung by the boatmen who propped up the bar in his local – the Mermaid pub on St Mary's Quay.

One of the best picnics I ever had in my life was with Harold Wilson in the Scillies. He found a boatman who navigated through swirling currents and rocky inlets to drop us off at a remote beach on an outer island – Bread and Cheese Cove on St Martin's. Until we were picked up again four hours later we did not see another human being. So the four of us (Harold, Mary, Marcia Falkender and I) luxuriated in the lonely splendour of blue skies, translucent sea and golden beaches. 'It's hard to believe that we're still in the United Kingdom,' said Harold as we toasted the far horizons of the Atlantic in Moet et Chandon champagne.

Before and after the toasts there was business to be discussed. My mission on that visit to the Scillies was to persuade Harold Wilson to come out of retirement and to become Chairman of a bid for the Yorkshire Television franchise. The Labour MP for Grimsby, Austin Mitchell, and I (both former presenters of the YTV regional news programme *Calendar*) were submitting the bid to the Independent Broadcasting Authority on behalf of a co-operative of YTV employees, led by the shop stewards of the ACTT trade union. This improbable coalition of Socialist workers and Tory capitalists needed all the skills of a former Labour Prime Minister to hold together in unity behind its bid document. Wilson played this leadership role with gusto. He was cheered to the echo when he came to address the union members in Leeds, but he was not quite so sure-footed when he did the rounds to raise money in the City of London. I cherish the memory of his meeting with a group of merchant bankers headed by the legendary Walter Salomon, Chairman of Rea Brothers.

'How are you going to defeat the union's inevitable demands for excessive pay, Sir Harold?' asked Salomon, in his guttural mid-European accent. Wilson gave an answer in the evasive. It would have been appreciated in the House of Commons but it did not find favour in the City. Struggling to find common ground with the men of money, Wilson asked them for their ideas on handling pay claims. 'Personally I would bomb ze unions,' declared Walter Salomon. 'Sounds like that Tory independent nuclear deterrent, Skybolt,' retorted Wilson. 'It won't work.'

Our bid did not work either, even though it included a bravura performance from Chairman Harold at the decisive IBA meeting, which happened to be chaired by his former Cabinet appointee, George Thomson. But despite our commercial failure, for me there were personal compensations – as I continued to see Wilson in the years following our abortive efforts to win the Yorkshire Television franchise. These encounters took place in the bar of the House of Lords and, on one occasion (to the astonishment of my fellow Tory MPs), in the smoking room of the House of Commons. Despite failing health Harold was always good company. 'Are you buying champagne again Acorn?' he would say, using the nickname he had given me at our St Martin's picnic on the Isles of Scilly. I usually did.

For all his bonhomie over drinks in the Palace of Westminster there was a sadness in Harold Wilson during his years of retirement. Towards the end of his life the sadness became extremely painful when he developed a creeping form of dementia. But long before that cruel disease cast its shadow over him there were times when Wilson seemed to be haunted by other even more nebulous ghosts. The most disturbing of these were the strange conspiracy theories which lingered on for years after his unexpected retirement as Prime Minister in April 1976. The essence of these theories was that Harold Wilson had been forced into an abrupt resignation because of some deep, dark secret known only to the security services.

It was no secret that a rogue element of right-wing officers in MI5 behaved as though they were out to get Wilson in the last years of his Premiership. He himself suspected the security services of dirty tricks against him and gave a somewhat lurid interview about his fears to the *Observer* journalists, Barrie Penrose and Roger Courtiour. Although dismissed at the time of publication as ex-Prime Ministerial paranoia, the basic story was largely confirmed 11 years later when a former MI5 officer, Peter Wright, brought out his book, *Spycatcher,* in 1987. Wright made it clear that he and a small group within MI5 believed that Harold Wilson was a Soviet mole or double agent. This group's suspicions were so strong that they kept a dossier on their target even while he was Prime Minister and they leaked much of its contents to journalists after he left office. But how did such a conspiracy theory ever come to be taken seriously? Was there any credible evidence to support it?

I can offer some of the answers to these questions. This is because, in the late 1970s, I came to know the deputy director of the CIA, James Jesus Angleton, whose debriefings of a Soviet defector were the source of the conspiracy theory used to smear Wilson. Angleton in turn introduced me to Arthur Martin, a senior MI5 officer who had led the investigation of the defector's allegations by Britain's security services. From these sources I gained some unique insights into the secret world's preoccupation with the question: 'Is Harold Wilson a Soviet agent?'

Jim Angleton had been the CIA's deputy director and chief of counter-intelligence from 1954 to 1974. In December 1979 I had lunch with him and an old friend of my late father's, Colonel Charles J. V. Murphy, at the Army and Navy Club in Farragut Square, Washington DC. Both men were interested in a debate that I had attended in the House of Commons a few days earlier. During that debate on Britain's security services, the new Prime Minister, Margaret Thatcher, had confirmed the news, already published in the *Sunday Times*, that the Keeper of the Queen's pictures, Sir Anthony Blunt, was a Soviet agent.

Angleton was a spymaster who exuded mystery and suspense. In appearance he looked as wraith-like as a ghost, with a skeletal face and a hunched, cadaverous body. He talked in elliptical half-sentences that trailed off into ambiguous silences. He seemed to be weighed down between a duty to keep a tight grip on the secrets of his past and a conflicting impulse to loosen up in order to impart knowledge which would reveal vitally important truths to trusted leaders of the present. Several times during that lunch he mused aloud: 'But has your Prime Minister been told the whole truth? The whole truth beyond Blunt?' Eventually Angleton said he had a crucial question to ask me. 'Could you, if necessary, get a letter hand-delivered to Margaret Thatcher herself without it going through all those Prime Ministerial staffers and secretaries?'

'Sure,' I replied with confidence, fortified by the large dry martinis served by the Army and Navy Club. 'Then you're the man I've been looking for,' declared Angleton. 'We must talk.'

We talked well into the afternoon. Jim Angleton explained that he had been in post as the CIA's chief of counter-intelligence at the time of the arrival in Washington of Anatoli Golitsyn, the highest Soviet KGB official ever to defect to the West. Angleton had debriefed Golitsyn personally. Those debriefings had revealed many extraordinary allegations about the Soviet penetration of Britain at all levels, among them the claim that the Director and Deputy Director of MI5 had been secretly working for the KGB. I tried to look stirred rather than shaken as Angleton sipped his fifth martini of the day and added in a sepulchral whisper, 'and the Soviets may have their top agent at an even higher level in the UK'.

'Higher than the head of MI5?' I quavered. 'As high as the head of government,' replied Angleton. For a moment I thought he was alleging that Margaret Thatcher was a KGB agent. That would have been a real clock striking 13 moment. But Angleton by this time was backing down into ambiguity, murmuring non-sequiturs like: 'All started back in 1963 . . . no proof . . . assassination policy an iron rule . . . never have done it without an agent in place . . . nothing firm . . . but too many coincidences . . . Arthur will fill you in.'

Arthur, who Angleton described as 'the finest counter-intelligence specialist I ever worked with in your country', and 'the agent who caught Philby', turned out to be Arthur Martin, a former MI5 officer who, in retirement, was doing a part-time job in the Clerk's department of the House of Commons. As a result of a letter of introduction from Angleton in January 1980, we met for tea in the Pugin room overlooking the Thames. Martin seemed far more cautious and reserved than Angleton, yet was equally pessimistic about the degree of Soviet penetration of Britain's security services. In subsequent discussions he briefed me on his anxieties about MI5, which were sufficiently well corroborated for me to set them down in a letter to the Prime Minister that I arranged to have hand-delivered to her through private channels as Angleton had requested. However, there was not a word in the letter, which Martin had drafted, referring to 'higher' penetration at 'head of government' level.

This subject did come up in my conversations with Arthur Martin who, like Angleton, had taken part in the Golitsyn debriefings. The defector had made some astonishing claims over and above his allegations of high level penetration of MI5. The first was that the KGB had assassinated the Labour leader of the Opposition, Hugh Gaitskell, in 1963. Although it sounded wildly improbable at first hearing, two facts gave it a veneer of possibility. The first was that Gaitskell had died of a mystery illness at the age of only 54. The second was that in the months before his death Gaitskell had been making determined efforts to purge the Labour party of its communists. None of this impinged on Harold Wilson but Golitsyn's second revelation did. For the defector claimed that the KGB had an iron rule about political assassinations. Under 'Moscow rules', they were strictly forbidden unless the heir apparent to the political leader targeted for assassination was a Soviet agent-in-place. So on the basis of these allegations Gaitskell's successor, Harold Wilson, became an object of suspicion to Golitsyn's debriefers at the CIA and MI5.

Soviet defectors were notorious for embellishing the information they disclosed to their Western interrogators. However, Angleton had great faith in Golitsyn. So at the CIA's urgings MI5 took these titbits about KGB assassination policy seriously enough to order an investigation into the bizarre proposition that Hugh Gaitskell had been murdered in order to make it possible for a Soviet agent, in the shape of Harold Wilson, to lead the Labour party. Arthur Martin was the MI5 officer appointed to lead this investigation.

Martin told me that he and his team, which included a medical adviser, interviewed Gaitskell's doctors and nursing staff at the London hospital where the Labour leader died. The cause of his death was a chest infection. The experts believed, on the basis of sputum samples analysed by pathologists subsequently questioned by Martin, that the chest infection was caused by a rare virus which Gaitskell had contracted on a visit to India some months earlier. There was nothing to connect this infection with the virulent streams of staphylococcus killer germs which the KGB were alleged to have on occasion injected into Moscow's political opponents in countries behind the iron curtain. So on medical grounds alone, 'the mystery' of Gaitskell's death did not appear to be a Soviet mystery. Other checks indicated that there were no 'Moscow Rules' governing KGB assassinations, which over the years had been carried out in a variety of widely differing circumstances. So Martin closed the file on this part of Golitsyn's allegations. Unfortunately it did not stay closed because of conflicting suspicions and feudings within MI5.

As part of his inquiry into Gaitskell's 'assassination', Arthur Martin consulted his colleagues within MI5's D branch – the section of counter-subversion specialists. He asked them whether they were aware of any suspicions or fragments of evidence that might support the second part of Golitsyn's conspiracy theory. This was the astounding claim that the Shadow Chancellor, Harold Wilson, was a Soviet agent-in-place. It was to accomplish his promotion to the leadership of the Labour party that Gaitskell had been murdered – so the theory had it.

D branch, whose senior officers included the renegade figure Peter Wright of *Spycatcher* fame, was not well versed in the intricacies of Labour party leadership elections. If they had understood that the party's Deputy Leader, George Brown, not Harold Wilson, had been the strong favourite to win the leadership election after Gaitskell's death that would have demolished the conspiracy theory. Instead the sleuths of D branch took it seriously. They unearthed the suspicious 'evidence' that Wilson during the 1950s had made several visits to Moscow and other Warsaw Pact capitals as part of his consultancy work for a timber company. He also had one or two associates such as Joe (later Lord) Kagan, who had business interests in Iron Curtain countries. Arthur Martin investigated these matters to the point of interviewing Tom Meyer, the boss of Montague L. Meyer Limited, the timber company that had engaged Wilson as a consultant. In his report Martin concluded that there were no grounds for questioning Harold Wilson's loyalty to Britain and that his 'links' to the Soviet Union were entirely innocuous. Nevertheless, Peter Wright and other officers, in what became known as 'the rogue element' within MI5, took a different view. They continued to harbour suspicions about Wilson and his associates, and started to circulate weird rumours to this effect around 1975–77. There is no doubt that some of this activity upset Wilson disproportionately. His mindset of paranoia was increased by two unexplained burglaries, apparently attempts to steal documents, at his London home in Lord North Street. Six weeks after he retired as Prime Minister, Wilson gave a series of interviews to a pair of young reporters from the *Observer*, Barry Penrose and Roger Courtiour, in which he accused a group of right-wing officers in MI5 of plotting against him. 'I am not certain that for the last eight months when I was Prime Minister I knew what was happening fully in Security,' he said. At least this part of the interviewing sessions made sense. Other parts made no sense at all, for example Wilson's baffling announcement to Penrose: 'I see myself as the big fat spider in the corner of the room. Sometimes I speak when I'm asleep. You should both listen. Occasionally when we meet I might tell you to go to Charing Cross Road and kick a blind man standing on a corner. That blind man may tell you something; lead you somewhere.'

The kindest interpretation of such ramblings is that Wilson was under great strain when he delivered them, believing that he was giving guidance to the reporters off the record, whereas in fact he was being covertly tape recorded on the record. When these tapes were published they were greeted first with incredulity and ridicule, then by a second wave of new conspiracy theories. The loudest of these was that Wilson had been forced to resign as Prime Minister in order to run away from some deep, dark secret which he was afraid would come out and do devastating damage to him and his office.

This 1970s' conspiracy theory was just as unfounded and ridiculous as the 1960s' canard that Wilson had been a Soviet agent. There had, however, been one genuine mystery which baffled some of the friendliest of Wilson-watchers. It was the question: Why on earth did the 59-year-old Prime Minister resign in April 1976?

The short, simple and by now totally convincing answer to this question is that Harold Wilson wanted to retire because he was tired, in poor health, and fed up with the exhausting power struggles within his government between the left and right wings of the Labour party. From the other side of the House of Commons, I was one of many Tory MPs who could easily see how debilitating these tensions were becoming as Tribunite MPs inflicted hostile speeches and votes against their own Government's economic policy. With the balance of payments crisis worsening, union militancy increasing, and the need for massive public expenditure cuts becoming imperative, it was obvious during the winter of 1975–76 that Britain was facing a looming economic and political crisis. Although some commentators predicted an apocalyptic end to these dramas, most observers predicted that the wily Harold would somehow wriggle out of the government's difficulties and yet again cobble together a Prime Ministerial left-right deal within the Cabinet and the Parliamentary Labour party which would avert the various spectres of widespread strikes, a no-confidence motion defeat in Parliament and a general election victory by the Conservatives.

A younger Harold Wilson, full of the energy he displayed in the 1960s, would probably have risen to these challenges. But he had lost his appetite for power, and to his inner circle it showed. He was drinking too much brandy by night and not attending to the detailed paperwork in his red boxes by day. His performances at Prime Minister's Questions lost their old wit and sparkle. He retreated into an introverted 'kitchen cabinet' at No. 10, although its key players were not a happy culinary team. His most loyal aide, Marcia Williams, was at daggers drawn with the Press Secretary, Joe Haines, and with several of the No. 10 team of civil servants. Various other cronies, staffers and ministers were full of mutual suspicions and antagonisms. The left-wing MPs in the Parliamentary Labour party became full of venom, particularly towards the Treasury's proposals for expenditure cuts. Instead of responding to these signs of turbulence with strong leadership, Wilson drifted into weakness and vacillation. He had become a semi-detached Prime Minister.

In December 1975 Harold Wilson confided to his wife Mary that he was going to resign at the time of his sixtieth birthday the following March. 'He was just terribly tired,' Mary recalled when I interviewed her for this chapter. 'Perhaps he knew that his concentration was not as good as it had been. Perhaps he had an inkling that the problems with his memory were just beginning. But he was very clear about what he wanted to do and of course I supported him.'

From that time onwards there was no mystery about the Prime Minister's coming retirement. Wilson spoke about his departure plans to various confidants including the Queen, Lord Goodman, Harold Lever, Barbara Castle and Marcia Williams. Some of them disbelieved him. Others, particularly Marcia, tried hard to persuade him to change his mind. None of this was affected one way or the other by what was going on, or not going on, within Peter Wright's group of rogue officers within MI5. Wilson made his decision to go for entirely explicable and honourable reasons.

For reasons that were perhaps slightly less honourable, Wilson tilted the succession firmly towards the Foreign Secretary, James Callaghan. The alternative candidate, Denis Healey, had made many enemies within the Parliamentary Labour party as Chancellor of the

Exchequer. It was an enmity sharpened by Healey's bombastic style, which had also deepened the tensions between Numbers 10 and 11 Downing Street. As a result of those tensions Callaghan was tipped off by Wilson about his imminent departure, whereas Healey received no such advance warning. So on the evening of Wednesday the 10 March 1976, when the Foreign Secretary was let into the secret that the Prime Minister would be announcing his resignation to the Cabinet the following Tuesday, the unbriefed Chancellor launched a kamikaze attack on a significant group of Labour backbench MPs who had embarrassed him by abstaining on a public expenditure vote in the House of Commons. Outside the division lobby after the vote an incandescent Healey bellowed at the abstainers: 'Go f*** yourselves!' It was not the canvassing technique he would have used had he known that an election for the job of Labour party Leader and Prime Minister was going to be held in a few days' time. Harold Wilson was greatly amused by Healey's over-reaction, telling Mary soon after-wards that he had done his best to help Callaghan, 'so I could make way for an older man'.

When he became a backbencher for the first time during his 31 years in the House of Commons, Wilson had a miserable ending to a great career. His own party turned on him in a mood of cruel rejection, bad-mouthing him continually and blaming him for just about every economic crisis, industrial dispute or political scandal that surfaced in British politics for the next three years. Only a tiny percentage of this blame-game hostility was remotely justified. The row over the 'lavender-coloured notepaper' resignation honours list of 1976; the Penrose–Courtiour interviews; and a complex 'who knows what?' dispute over Rhodesian sanctions-busting by oil companies were embarrassing episodes which would all have been more adroitly handled by a Harold Wilson in his prime. None of them were so bad that they merited the demonization of Wilson. Yet he quickly became a political pariah, booed when his name was mentioned at Labour conferences, snubbed by former colleagues, and consigned by the conventional wisdom of the party to the outer darkness of a discred-ited Siberian-style exile. It was revisionism at its most unfair and unattractive.

History will surely be kinder to Harold Wilson than his contemporaries were. For the reality of his record shows that he was a skilful and successful Prime Minister. In political terms he was the only Labour Leader, until Tony Blair, to win three general elections. As a foreign policy Premier he defused the Rhodesian crisis; managed the painful but essential withdrawal of Britain's huge military presence 'East of Suez'; kept what was then called the 'special relationship' with the USA in good shape; and against the wishes of most of his own party (even his wife Mary voted with the no's!) he achieved a yes vote in the national referendum of 1975 on Britain's entry into the Common Market.

On the domestic front it was Wilson's misfortune to be Prime Minister during an agonizing period of economic decline and industrial unrest. Yet he governed through the turbulence far more effectively than either his predecessor Heath or his successor Callaghan, for both their tenures of No. 10 collapsed in strikes, chaos and national anger. Britain was a happier country under Wilson who, paradoxically, remained popular with the ordinary voters, even when the Westminster politicians of both major parties were reviling him.

For the 31 years after he left No. 10 Downing Street until his death in 1995, Harold Wilson suffered in his physical health as well as in his political reputation. He had an operation for bowel cancer in 1981 which was successful in removing the malignant tumour, but the patient never fully recovered. Wilson told his wife Mary that he had heard someone saying in the hospital recovery room: 'We gave him too much anaesthetic,' and he blamed his subsequent loss of memory on this alleged medical mistake. Whatever the reason, Wilson went through a long and painful descent into increasing frailty of body and mind, although he managed to be a regular attendee in the House of Lords whose allowances were an important part of his slender income. He was the last Prime Minister to receive a non-indexed pension which was never adjusted for inflation in the three decades after he left office. Despite these financial difficulties, Harold Wilson was comfortable and contented in his twilight years thanks to the love of Mary. She cared for him and nursed him with devotion in their flat in Ashley Gardens, Westminster, right up to the end. He entered hospital two days before his death which took place, with Mary at his bedside, at ten minutes to midnight on the 23 May 1995.

Harold Wilson had become almost a non-person to his own party for the last 30 years of his life. No proper degree of recognition, let alone honour, was shown to him by his political supporters until after his death. Tony Blair then made amends by giving eloquent posthumous tributes at the time of the funeral in the Scillies and at the unveiling of a superb Wilson statue in his native Huddersfield. Yet the warmth of the historical mantle of praise spread over Labour's fifth party Leader by its eighth was also a chilly reminder of the intervening years of silence and hostility (or worse).

One of the few small gestures of respect to Harold Wilson during his retirement was, oddly enough, arranged by a Tory MP and minister. This was the occasion when I invited Wilson to visit the Ministry of Defence and to see his own portrait hanging on the walls of my office. The guests who gathered that morning around the Ruskin Spear painting were a small but interesting group. They included the Secretary of State for Defence, Malcolm Rifkind; the Chief of the Defence Staff, Field Marshal Sir Peter Inge; Marcia Falkender; my mother, Lady Aitken; various Generals, Admirals, Air Marshals and top MoD civil servants; and the guests of honour, Mary and Harold Wilson. We drank a toast to the portrait, and to its subject, in the Moet et Chandon champagne he enjoyed. Harold looked fragile but was evidently appreciating the occasion. He observed that this was the first time he had ever been inside the Ministry of Defence. 'Probably I should have come sooner to see how all that money was being spent,' he chuckled. But after one or two more such sallies and clinking of glasses the shutters of his mind slowly closed down. Indeed, towards the end of the formal proceedings Harold Wilson drew Malcolm Rifkind to one side and murmured to him, almost in the manner of confiding a secret: 'I used to be Prime Minister, y'know.'

It was a poignant touch but in its way a symbolic one. For these words were a sad reminder that the most successful political leader of his generation had been relegated to the shadows of oblivion. This was such a historical aberration that it could not possibly last. On the stock exchange of history, Wilson shares seem likely to rise. If this chapter of good memories about him encourages the process of re-evaluation and reassessment, may it contribute to a recovery in Harold Wilson's historical reputation that is long overdue.

CHAPTER 6

Jimmy and Aspers

'Can you join me and Jimmy for dinner tonight at Howletts? He has something important he needs to talk to you about urgently. He says it could make a big difference to the result in seats all over the country.'

The suppressed excitement in John Aspinall's voice as he delivered this message intrigued me. So did the timing of the message. For Britain was in the middle of the General Election campaign of May 1997 in which Sir James Goldsmith's Referendum party was making a considerable impact. He had financed candidates from his party to stand in over 100 constituencies. Although no more than one or two of them had the slightest chance of winning, their capacity to siphon vital votes away from sitting Conservative MPs in marginal con-stituencies was dangerous. I thought of the two seats where my dinner companions were standing: Putney where Goldsmith was challenging David Mellor and Folkestone where Aspinall was fighting against Michael Howard. According to the polls, both these senior Tories could be ousted if the Referendum party did well. Similar fears were being voiced all over the country, making the Goldsmith factor a wild card in the election. But why would the chief player of the wild card, not to mention his equally formidable partner at games of chance, want to talk to me so urgently in mid-campaign?

Although I was having a tough battle to defend my own seat in the election, I was not affected by the Goldsmith factor because the Ref-erendum party had decided not to put up a candidate against me.

This was partly on account of my longstanding support in Parliament for a referendum on Britain's membership of the European Union but more because I was counted as an ally by 'Jimmy and Aspers'. Having known both of them for over 25 years, I was well aware of their lifelong friendship and their extraordinary exploits. They had first bonded in the 1950s over poker games in undergraduate Oxford. Since then they had built financial and gaming empires; flouted conventions; changed laws; won court cases; made headlines; organized elopements, engagements, marriages and divorces; saved animal species; won, lost, and re-made fortunes; and been the ring masters of an exotic cast of risk-takers, deal-makers, life-enhancers, high achievers and beautiful women whose high-wire acts had often been orchestrated by these two extraordinary friends.

At the core of their friendship lay an unusual combination of virtues and vices. Their virtues were courage, loyalty, generosity, tenacity and vaulting ambition. Their faults included greed, grudges, ruthlessness, rages and occasional cruelties. Yet whatever one thought of their private lives, Goldsmith and Aspinall were public men. They achieved high profile results in their special areas of interest which at various times included gambling, global ecology, animal conservation, stock exchange coups, buying and selling businesses, championing the Zulus, and opposing the march of European Union federalism.

Paradoxically, however, their previous appearances in the passion play of politics had been not as stars but as spear carriers. I had occasionally wondered whether they would one day seize a particular moment and move to centre stage in a serious attempt to influence the causes they cared about. Suddenly in the General Election campaign of 1997 it looked as though their moment might be arriving. Naturally I wanted to know more about what they were getting up to. That was why I responded positively to John Aspinall's mid-election phone call.

As I lived only a few miles away from Aspinall's home and private collection of wild animals – his beautiful Palladian country house of Howletts, near Canterbury – it was easy for me to visit for dinner on the Saturday evening of Goldsmith's visit. However, there was a complication over my acceptance of his invitation which brought out a strange yet central feature of the Jimmy-and-Aspers approach to life – male chauvinism.

Aspinall and Goldsmith practised and preached a belief in the supremacy of dominant male primates. It derived from Aspinall's fascination with the animal kingdom. Long observation of elephants, lions, tigers and, above all, the gorillas in his gorillarium at Howletts had left him with the unshakeable conviction that the human species would be far better off if it reverted to the instincts of its animal forbears, did away with the conventional wisdom about equal rights for women and accepted that male supremacy was essential for the good order of the family, the nation state and the world. I once listened to Aspinall expounding a slightly modified version of this theory to Margaret Thatcher when she came to dinner at his home in Belgravia in the mid-1990s. The modification consisted of telling the former the Prime Minister that she was the genetic equivalent of a silverback dominant male primate gorilla, a transformation that had probably been due to 'a rogue gene' in her chromosomes. Thatcher appeared to be rather flattered by this theory.

There was, however, no help from a rogue gene theory over the feminine complication which for a while threatened to prevent me from coming to dinner with Aspers and Jimmy in May 1997. My problem was that I already had made a prior commitment to pick up my 16-year-old daughter Alexandra from her school in Canterbury and to give her dinner on our way home for a week-end exeat. I was not willing to break this commitment. Instead I asked if Alexandra might be included in the Howletts party. This produced much huffing and puffing from my host who had evidently been planning a male-primates-only evening. But when I insisted on keeping the commitment to my daughter even if it meant missing the meeting with Jimmy, Aspers gracefully gave way, although his animal logic for the invitation was unusual.

'Is Alexandra the one who didn't cry when Munga scratched her?' he asked. 'Yes,' I replied remembering the afternoon when 3-year-old Alexandra had entered Aspinall's gorillarium and had enjoyed an afternoon of mutual cuddles with a newly born baby gorilla named

Munga. All had been sweetness and light between the two young female mammals until Alexandra wanted to leave the cage to go home. Munga clung on to her human companion rather aggressively and could only be separated after inflicting a minor scratch or two on my daughter whose lack of tears had evidently impressed Munga's owner. 'Oh, Alexandra's all right then,' said Aspinall, 'she'll fit in.' Thanks to this judgement from the gorillarium, two Aitkens, Goldsmith and Aspinall sat down together for dinner on that Saturday evening.

Jimmy Goldsmith was in an apocalyptic mood. The Conservative party was finished for at least the next ten years, he declared – a prediction that looked doubtful at the time but has since come true. However, he went on to say that there was still time for party and nation to be saved if only the Tory leadership would reverse its policies on a European referendum and on gun control law. 'I'm with you on Europe,' I replied, 'but why gun control?' 'Typical short-sighted, blinkered politician's answer,' snorted Goldsmith. 'Go on Aspers! Tell him!' Aspinall explained that he had been doing some lobbying (i.e. canvassing) among what he called 'the hoi polloi' (i.e. the voters) of Folkestone. He claimed to have discovered the biggest reason why Michael Howard and the Conservatives were unpopular. This was the 'backlash' against the recently passed Firearms Act which had imposed tighter controls on the ownership of guns, rifles and revolvers in the aftermath of a recent massacre of schoolchildren by an insane marksman in Dunblane. 'The chairman of the Folkestone association of gun clubs has written to me saying that every single one of his members and their families will switch their votes to the Referendum party if we announce that we will repeal the Tory Firearms Act,' proclaimed Aspinall with the triumphant air of a conjuror who had pulled an extremely large rabbit out of his hat.

'This is true! It is true for gun clubs in constituencies up and down the country,' continued Jimmy Goldsmith, leaping up from his chair and pacing up and down the dining room as excitably as if he was one of Aspinall's tigers bounding towards his prey. 'So we are announcing tomorrow a new policy on firearms. It will bring us a landslide of votes.' He paused as though expecting me to be thunderstruck by his announcement. When I continued eating my smoked salmon without any visible reaction Goldsmith frowned and then moved to his real agenda for the evening which was to ask: 'What I'd like to know from you Jonathan, is how will John Major react to our initiative? Will he try to trump our ace? Will he try to discredit our policy? Or will he recognize the game is up and want to work out a deal with us?'

Knowing that John Major had already spurned various offers of deals from the Referendum party, I asked what its new policy on gun control would be. 'We will be announcing,' said Goldsmith in a voice of barely controlled triumph, 'that all controls on firearms will be lifted. What is more we will be saying that it will no longer be a criminal offence to shoot an intruder in defence of a citizen's home or property.'

For a moment I wanted to laugh but Goldsmith was in full, impassioned and totally serious flow as he continued: 'So in one fell swoop we will win the votes of all those who care about their constitutional rights, the votes of all gun club members . . .' 'And their families,' added Aspinall. 'And their families,' agreed Goldsmith, 'and the votes of all those who want to defend their property against criminals.' He paused for breath. I took a deep breath, wondering whether the Referendum party thought it was fighting an election in England or in Texas. As if to answer my unspoken question, Aspinall produced the letter he had received from the Chairman of the Folkestone Association of Gun Clubs and deposited it with a flourish on my side plate. It did indeed say that all members of the shooting fraternity in Folkestone would vote for candidate Aspinall if the Referendum party promised to repeal the new Firearms Act.

'Well?' demanded Aspers as I finished reading it, evidently under the impression he had just delivered a knockout blow. I responded with a counter-question: 'Aspers, how many people do you think belong to these gun clubs in Michael Howard's constituency?'

This simple enquiry set Jimmy Goldsmith off on another excitable stomp around the dining room table. 'Aspers, don't answer!' he commanded, 'it's a trick question. A politician's trick question.' 'We are not going to be deflected from making our announcement tomorrow, Jonathan,' he warned shaking an admonitory finger in my direction, 'that'll put a stop to you Tories and all those smart-ass people on television saying that we are a single issue party. From tomorrow we will be a party with two big issues – guns and referendums.'

It became obvious over the next few minutes that both Aspinall and Goldsmith were highly excited about the impact they believed their new policy would make on the outcome of the General Election. A draft press release of the announcement was passed round the table and Goldsmith talked with relish about the '50 plus' target seats (including Putney and Folkstone) which would now fall to the Referendum party as a result of its pledge to repeal the firearms legislation. Eventually I brought the conversation back to the question Aspinall had not been allowed to answer. How many members were there in the gun clubs of Folkestone? 'I don't know the exact figure,' said Aspers, 'but thousands.' 'Thousands upon thousands. Up and down the whole country,' declared Goldsmith. 'You're completely wrong,' I replied. 'I will bet you that there are less than 100 gun club members in the whole of Folkestone. The same goes for gun club membership in just about every other constituency.'

A bet was an irresistible proposition to these two legendary gamblers. So an excitable discussion started about the terms of the bet, the inside knowledge that I might or might not possess and the odds against my being right. Patiently I explained that in my own constituency I had been receiving letters and delegations from gun club enthusiasts for several months. As interest groups go they were small. In East Kent which had a population of around 500,000 and six Parliamentary seats there were only eight registered gun clubs. Two of them were in my constituency with memberships of approximately 60 and 40. On the national scale of recreational groups, rifle and pistol shooters ranked low, way down the list alongside players of tiddlywinks and cribbage. With these and other statistics that had been sent to election candidates as part of the daily briefings from Conservative Central Office, I demonstrated that the notion of gun club members being able to change the result in any constituency was political fantasy.

Jimmy Goldsmith listened to me in grim silence then slumped back into his chair looking devastated. 'Jonathan knows the score,' said Aspinall; 'don't bet against him.' The gloom that descended on the Howletts dinner party became oppressive as Goldsmith sorrowfully admitted that his exaggerated ideas about the political influence of the gun lobby had come from conversations with American friends. He had another little rampage round the table speaking at appropriately machine gun speed about the need for a written Constitution granting Englishmen the right to bear arms. However, it was clear that the stuffing had been knocked out of him by the facts about gun club members.

For in the middle of his enthusiasm for the right to bear arms as a vote-winning issue, his voice trailed away as if it was a tape recorder running out of power. Resuming his seat, Goldsmith buried his head in his hands, looking more disappointed, dejected and exhausted than I had ever seen him before. Aspers evidently had a similar reaction for he came over and put his arm round his old friend, saying 'C'mon Jimmy, there'll be other days and other bets.'

This was a far more poignant moment than either Aspinall or I realized. For Jimmy Goldsmith was harbouring a deep secret known only to his wife and mistress. A few days earlier he had been diagnosed with advanced cancer of the pancreas. Knowing that he only had a few more months to live, and realizing that he was now playing against death, the one gambling opponent who never loses, Goldsmith was making his final roll of the dice in the casino of politics. His Referendum party campaign, even it had partially succeeded in capturing just a handful of seats, would have changed the face of British democracy. It had the potential to be Goldsmith's last and greatest political coup. His naive ideas about gun clubs had encouraged him to believe that he was on the verge of pulling it off. I was the bearer of the bad tidings that the coup was bound to fail. No wonder that the dinner party at Howletts ended on such a melancholic note of gloom. The only ray of light came on the doorstep as my daughter and I were departing. Although hardly a word had been addressed to her all evening, Alexandra was suddenly showered with compliments for her beauty by Goldsmith, no mean connoisseur in such matters. As we drove away I asked Alexandra what she had thought of Jimmy and Aspers. She replied 'wonderful, but slightly mad'.

These words are a fair summary of the remarkable relationship between James Goldsmith and John Aspinall. They were both extraordinary characters, with many accomplishments to their respective names. However, they appear in this book not because of what they achieved separately but because of the way they bonded together in a unique Alpha male relationship which their contemporary, Taki Theodoracopulos, describes as 'the most profound friendship I have ever seen'. What united them in friendship was a special chemistry flowing through four principal interests they had in common: politics, risk-taking, breeding and outrageous behaviour.

The political threads that tied together the lives of Jimmy and Aspers have been underestimated. From a distant vantage point, an observer might conclude that neither of them were particularly serious about politics, and that it was the one game at which they were dilettantes and failures. This is far too simplistic a view, for in both seen and unseen ways they were political goal scorers. Yet their scores were lower than they should have been. For they were such right-wing romantics that whenever they became involved in affairs of state, the hard-headed realism they applied to all their other affairs of business or the heart deserted them.

John Aspinall's political romanticism stemmed from his belief that he was a great orator. Certainly he had a flair for the art of public speaking but more often than not he needed a good editor. Yet what he lost by prolixity he gained by originality. He was undoubtedly the most politically incorrect speaker with whom I have ever shared a platform. I have never forgotten his first-ever public speech which he delivered to a large open air crowd in Ramsgate High Street during the General Election campaign of 1974.

Passions were running high in that election, which ended with the fall of the Heath government. The miners were on strike and 2,000 of them from the East Kent coalfield lived in or around Ramsgate. Aspers, the grandee proprietor of nearby Howletts, had become Patron of the Thanet Conservative Association as a gesture of friendship to me. Typically, his friendship turned into practical action when the going got tough towards the end of the campaign.

'How can I help?' he asked. 'Can I make a speech for you?' 'Great idea!' I enthused, still too inexperienced a parliamentary candidate to realize that Aspers on the hustings might be something of an unguided missile. The crowd on that particular Saturday morning was large and boisterous. 'Aspinall the tiger man! Wot the 'ell does 'e know about politics?' shouted a heckler. Aspers, hunching over the microphone like one of his Silverback gorillas in possession of a bamboo tree, rose to the challenge. 'I may not know much about the squalid manoeuvres of politicians, but I know about England,' he began, 'and England is in trouble. Napoleon once said that England is a nation of shop-keepers. As I look round Ramsgate High Street this morning I see that England has become a nation of shoplifters.'

I wondered if my majority was about to evaporate in the face of such insults to the electorate, but Aspers was oblivious to the norms of political correctness. With his blue eyes blazing and his windswept locks of Heseltine-length blonde hair giving him the look of a Nordic invader, he told the crowd that they were a weak and supine lot because the fine old Anglo-Saxon blood in their veins had become diluted by a diet of socialism. Comparing them to some obscure wolf pack he had been studying on the steppes of Russia, he announced that the spirit of the English people was dying out from lack of genetic vitality. His voice dropped to the tone of a funeral dirge. But then he rallied to thunder: 'But at least you've had the sense to hire a strong, virile, red-blooded Canadian as your future MP!' The crowd was as surprised as I was to hear my North American ancestry extolled as a qualification for election to the British House of Commons.

As Aspers wove his iconoclastic way through history, natural history, *Jus animalism* (the rights of animals), animal behaviour comparisons (he described Barbara Castle as 'more of a vixen than a lioness') and tangential references to the election, his listeners had a great time. For he was not only a natural speaker, he was also a natural combatant with hecklers. One of his best jousts came when a small boy with a shrew of a mother started a rhythmic chant from a vantage point just beside the lorry trailer on which Aspers and I were standing. 'Tell us about the old age pension! Tell us about the old age pension!' they shouted in shrill unison. Aspers beckoned to the lad, an undersized shrimp of a schoolboy. 'Come here, sonny,' he said genially. Unwisely, the boy stepped forward only to have his right arm seized by Aspers, who lifted him up and dangled him like a baby monkey high above the crowd. 'How old are you, sonny?' demanded Aspers over his microphone. 'Eleven,' squeaked the boy. 'This is what's wrong with England!' boomed Aspers, 'He's 11 years old and he's worried about his old age pension.' 'Put him down,' shrieked the boy's mother, 'he was only asking about his granddad!' 'His granddad should come and ask me his own questions about his pension,' replied Aspers. 'And what could you do to help an old age pensioner?' shouted someone. 'I would invite him to dinner in my house, and show him how my tigers live out their old age with honour and dignity,' was the reply. So it went on for over an hour of rowdy give-and-take, with Aspers emerging the clear, if occasionally bloodied, victor.

'We've never heard anyone like Mr Aspinall,' said my lady Chairman at the end of the morning's excitement. How right she was. In public speaking – like everything else he turned his hand to – Aspers was a one-off original. But so was his closest friend Jimmy, who had his own way of travelling through the minefields of politics.

Jimmy Goldsmith was the son of the Member of Parliament for Newmarket, Major Frank Goldsmith, who represented the West Suffolk constituency from 1910 to 1919. I was also the son of a later MP for Newmarket, Sir William Aitken, who sat for the same constituency from 1951 to 1964. 'So we are both the offspring of Suffolk politicians!' exclaimed Jimmy with some surprise when I told him of this connection when we first met in 1973. 'Tell me, what did the people of Newmarket think of my father?'

'A lot – most of it very favourable,' I was able to reply. Having grown up in Suffolk, frequently accompanying my father to constituency functions in towns and villages like Newmarket and Cavenham (where the Goldsmiths lived) I often heard talk of previous incumbents of the seat of whom Major Goldsmith – usually referred to as 'The Major' – was the most colourful. On the surface Frank Goldsmith looked the part of an archetypal Conservative and

Unionist MP from the shires. He had a 'stake in the country' in the form of a 2,500-acre estate, Cavenham Hall; a history of public service, for he had been in local government as a councillor in London; a good degree from Oxford; and a sound military record, as he had been commissioned into the local army regiment closest to his family home, the Duke of York's Loyal Suffolk Hussars. 'We always thought the Major was a sure thing for the cabinet one day,' an elderly constituency activist once told me, 'he used to have lots of bigwigs like F. E. Smith and Winston Churchill staying the weekend at Cavenham. He was in with the right crowd, he was a good speaker, he dressed beautifully, and he cared about the poor in a patrician sort of way. The perfect English gentleman, you might say.'

The image of Major Frank Goldsmith was unjustly shattered just before the outbreak of war in 1914 when a telegram arrived from his German-Jewish brother in law, Ernest von Marx of Frankfurt. The telegram, taken down by the village postmistress of Cavenham, contained words to the effect of 'If war does break out, remember your loyalties are to Germany'. The village postmistress took it upon herself to announce the contents of the telegram throughout the local community. Within days the popular Major was being vilified as 'That Hun Goldschmidt'. One Saturday night a party of local yokels, inflamed by a combination of beer, and anti-German fever, set out from the village pub carrying buckets of pitch and fired torches towards Cavenham Hall. They made a serious effort to burn the house down. Its destruction was narrowly averted only after Goldsmith's staff and neighbours rallied round to fight off the arsonists.

Major Frank, who had changed his name from Goldschmidt before going up to Magdalen College Oxford, was bitterly hurt by this episode. Although he fought for King and Country throughout the war, the insult from a handful of his constituents rankled badly. In 1919 he resigned his seat in Parliament, despite strong urgings to the contrary from senior Conservatives in his constituency and from his friends in Parliament. The slur on his good name and patriotic loyalty had caused Major Frank such deep resentment that he resolved to live in France for the rest of his life, which he did, exchanging a career in British politics for a career as a French hotelier.

Goldsmith Senior's resentment was to some extent shared by Goldsmith Junior, as was the interest in British politics. For it was Jimmy Goldsmith who first told me about his father's Parliamentary life and about his father's unhappy experiences in the village of Cavenham in 1914. Jimmy was moved to hear the many good things his former constituents had said about 'The Major' while he was their MP. It was obvious that filial pride in his Suffolk heritage was a factor in Goldsmith's business life because he had called his principal holding company on the London Stock Exchange, Cavenham Foods. This nostalgia also had a political dimension to it. When we talked about Major Frank Goldsmith as an MP, Jimmy asked many questions about his father's old constituency such as: 'Is it still a Conservative seat?' 'Is it safe?' 'Who is the MP for it now?' This conversation began with Jimmy bristling with suspicion, but when he was convinced that his father's good name was still respected by the 'burghers of Newmarket', as he quaintly called them, he became enthusiastic. Towards the end of our talk, he made the revealing comment that he would like to know if the West Suffolk constituency 'ever came up for grabs'.

James Goldsmith was grabbing many things in the early 1970s as I saw from my vantage point as a young merchant banker at Slater Walker Securities, where I was employed as executive assistant to the chairman Jim Slater. In that job I saw a fair amount of Goldsmith. He was at various times the company's largest investor, its most active co-predator in takeover bids and eventually its chairman and saviour when the group's banking arm, Slater Walker Limited, got into trouble during the crash of 1974 and had to be bailed out by a Bank of England life boat arrangement.

By the time the Slater Walker crisis was at its height I was a newly elected Member of Parliament. When there was much unfavourable reporting on Slater Walker's troubles in the Press, I picked up a strong rumour in the corridors of Westminster that the Department of Trade was planning to set up a statutory inquiry into the group's banking transactions and share dealings. Such an inquiry would have had devastating consequences on Goldsmith's efforts to save Slater Walker from collapse. So I immediately warned him of the Department of

Trade's intentions. 'This is very serious indeed. It will wreck every-thing,' he said. 'I will have to go and see Harold.' 'Harold who?' I asked. 'Harold Wilson,' was Goldsmith's answer. I had no idea that the Prime Minister was on speaking terms with the new Chairman of Slater Walker. On the face of it they should have been antagonists because Wilson's left-wing socialism was the antithesis of Goldsmith right-wing 'extremism', as free market capitalism was often called in those days. Yet they had apparently become friendly after meeting at a dinner party given by David Frost. The start of their friendship was a shared dislike of *Private Eye*, which was distressing Mary Wilson with its Mrs Wilson's Diary column and infuriating Goldsmith by its attacks on his business and private life. Harold Wilson was delighted by Goldsmith's robust epithets about *Private Eye*'s writers, whom he denounced as 'maggots and scavengers'. Jimmy Goldsmith was fasci-nated by Wilson's wily manoeuvrings through national crises such as rows on public expenditure and runs on the pound sterling. In no time the two men had bonded. Goldsmith became a regular nocturnal visitor to Downing Street. Wilson had several meals at Pelham cottage, the Kensington home of Goldsmith's mistress (later his wife) Lady Annabel Birley. At one of these dinners the guests included both the Prime Minister and the Leader of the Opposition. It is hard to think of any host other than Goldsmith who could have attracted such eminent left and right adversaries as Heath and Wilson around the same private dining table.

Goldsmith's financial expertise was used to keep the Prime Minister well briefed on City of London matters, including the Bank of England's rescue operation to save Slater Walker whose demise would have shattered investors confidence in the banking system and the stock market. So, thanks to right words in the right ear, there was no Department of Trade inquiry into Slater Walker, which was saved at the cost of some £110 million of public money from the Bank of England's lifeboat. Wilson's helpfulness to Goldsmith was probably the right decision in the public interest because the collapse of Slater Walker would have almost certainly meant another run on sterling and a stock market crisis. Nevertheless it says much for Goldsmith's powers of charm and persuasion that he made the Prime Minister his ally in the City of London matters. For Harold Wilson was the same Labour politician who had once addressed his party's Brighton conference with the words 'There are no delegates here today from the Amalgamated Society of Share Pushers and Company Promoters, nor are there any representatives of property speculators, takeover bidders, dividend strippers or bond washers'. These were caps which could easily have fitted James Goldsmith.

One key Prime Ministerial aide who understood why her boss had been converted from this past hostility into a warm friendship with Goldsmith was Marcia Falkender. 'Harold found Jimmy quite extraordinary,' she recalled. 'He was fascinated by the big buccaneering tycoon who symbolized terrific success but was classless. They got on tremendously well.'

Marcia Falkender also got on tremendously well with Goldsmith. According to later reports he promised her a directorship of Cavenham Foods but this never materialized, possibly because of the row that exploded over Goldsmith's appearance in Harold Wilson's resignation honours list. During the honeymoon stage of their relationship, Wilson had talked of sending Goldsmith to the Lords as a Minister with responsibility for financial services. The prospect excited Jimmy but it was an appointment too far for a government in the final months of Wilson's premiership, just as a peerage for him was an enoblement too far in the eyes of the honours scrutiny committee. These grey Whitehall watchdogs looked askance at Goldsmith's bitter battles against *Private Eye* which went so over the top when he tried to get the magazine's editor Richard Ingrams jailed for criminal libel that the case did more harm to the wining plantiff than to the defeated defendant. Goldsmith's phyrric victory in the libel action cost him his peerage, but he was philosophical about having to settle for a lesser honour. 'For services to exports and ecology', said the citation attached to his knighthood. In fact Goldsmith's reward had been more personal than political for, as he said soon after receiving it: 'It was always absolutely clear in my conversations with Harold Wilson that I was an ideological conservative and I never in any way, wavered about that.'

Jimmy was not a waverer but he was mercurial. This is a polite word to describe his mood swings which could sometimes erupt into terrifying rages. The only person who understood how to handle Goldsmith during his volcanic explosions was Aspinall, who would calmly say 'It's the lion in him . . . let him roar . . . let him break the telephone . . . let him know throw his fax machine out of the window . . . he's a human with wild animal instincts.'

On one occasion when they were on holiday together with their families in Italy, Aspers took on the role of lion tamer. Goldsmith had gone berserk over the shortcomings of the Italian telecommunications system which kept disconnecting him in the middle of his calls. Suddenly he snapped and embarked on a rampage of phone smashing. Terrified by this tempest of fury, everyone else in the house party except Aspinall retreated to the garden as four telephones were torn from their sockets, stamped on and hurled out of the window. As Goldsmith seized the villa's fifth and last instrument of communication, hell bent on its destruction and defenestration, Aspinall physically restrained his friend, shouting: 'No Jimmy! I'll find you something else to throw out of the window. You'll need a phone for your next deal.'

'The next deal' was something permanently on the agenda of the two bondsmen. In the early years of their relationship Aspinall was the older, richer and more dominant character. They had met in March 1950 when Goldsmith was a teenage schoolboy and Aspinall was an undergraduate running poker games at Oxford. Temporarily flush with cash from an accumulator bet on three winners at Lewes racecourse, Goldsmith impressed Aspinall with the recklessness of his poker playing and the insouciant way he paid his losses with some eighty large white £5 notes casually pealed from his jacket pocket. After that evening the two young men struck up a friendship. The 16-year-old awkwardly adolescent Goldsmith, who had just walked out of Eton after a row with his housemaster, was seven years younger than Aspinall but the gap in years and sophistication between them was bridged by their overt passion for gambling and their covert understanding of each other's strengths and weaknesses. Aspers, outwardly bombastic and bohemian, was inwardly shy and snobbish, striving for acceptance by his aristocratic Oxford contemporaries. Goldsmith, whose exterior carapace was conventional and self-assured, was privately insecure and ill at ease, disinterested in social success but driven by material and political ambition. Both had absorbing hinterlands. Aspinall's was self-taught scholarship through deep reading of history, anthropology, ecological conservation and the cultures of India and Africa. Goldsmith's was excitable restlessness across a range of diverse passions from beautiful women and fine wines to homeopathic medicine and international geopolitics. In such areas of complementary interest they stimulated each other's curiosity and fuelled each other's ideas. Yet their greatest common interest was risk-taking and reward-making – for Aspinall through gambling, for Goldsmith through business.

Throughout the 1960s Aspinall was far more successful than Goldsmith; Jimmy lagged behind his older friend in the wealth stakes for many years. He was given little or no money from his father, the Major, who used to say of his volatile second son 'he'll either make a fortune or go to prison'. But after narrowly escaping jail during the drama of his elopement and marriage to the underage Bolivian heiress Isabel Patino, Goldsmith immersed himself in business after his young wife's tragic death in childbirth. For over ten years he toiled away at the hard grind of buying, revitalizing and selling manufacturing companies. At first his deals, often backed by Aspinall, who lent him £500,000 in 1968, were mainly based in France. But in 1971 came the takeover of the Bovril group of companies which was Goldsmith's breakthrough as a heavyweight financier in the London market. On the night that this £15 million takeover battle ended in victory, Aspers gave a dinner in honour of Jimmy at the Clermont club. Every course on the menu was a Bovril product. This meant a reduction in the clubs usual high gastronomic standards, but at all other levels the festivities were euphoric. Perhaps they symbolized that Goldsmith the business entrepreneur was catching up with Aspinall the gaming entrepreneur. Yet in the great game of wealth and power which they both played so enthusiastically, even after the Bovril acquisition it is probable that Aspinall was still ahead.

Aspinall accumulated a large cash fortune during the 1960s by concentrating all his energies on the business of gambling. At first it was an illegal business with movable chemmy parties operating from friends' houses. Aspinall ran the bank or 'shoe' and his mother, the formidable Lady Osborne (always known as Lady O), raked in the punters' losses with her charming catchphrase: 'Sorry it had to be you dear'. This family business whose clients were mainly family friends was making profits of around £30,000 a night until interrupted by a police raid. Aspinall and his mother were charged with 'keeping a common gaming house'. As the charge was read out to Lady O she replied to the police inspector: 'Young man, there was nothing common about this house until you entered it.' It was the first sign that the Aspinalls were ready to take on the authorities in a courtroom drama that put not only the defendants, but also Britain's ancient gambling laws on trial. The end result was that the jury, on the direction of the judge, returned not guilty verdicts. New gaming legislation had to be brought in by Parliament and licensed casinos became legal. Aspinall was awarded one of the first of these licences and used it to create the Clermont Club.

The Clermont was a palace of elegance and opulence. The combination of William Kent's eighteenth-century architecture and Aspinall's exquisite taste in furniture and paintings made this magnificent town house at 44 Berkley Square feel as comfortable as some great nobleman's country seat. I was an early visitor and small gambler at the Clermont. I described it in my 1960s book *The Young Meteors*:

> It is a club in the true sense of the word for everyone seems to know everyone, even well enough to 'come in' continually on each other's bets. There is a *fin de siècle*, Regency flavour to it with dukes and earls betting against each other across the table, liveried footmen bearing in free champagne on silver salvers, heiress debs perching on armchairs fiddling with their diamonds and a flow of banter to everyone from the proprietor, John Aspinall. With his Beau Brummel sideboards, his Charles James Fox wit, his Prinny-like obsession with health diets, and his prize fighter chest puffed out in a stance surely imitated from some member of his private collection of gorillas, Aspinall is a legend in his own lifetime though he is still under 40. He has a commanding personality that could easily have taken him to the top in politics or in business. Instead he has

used his charm and cunning to create to create the world's most celebrated gaming house.

The somewhat gushing tone of my 22-year-old reporter's account of the Clermont is an accurate reflection of the awed impression the club and its owner made on me. Later in the same chapter I recorded the extraordinary losses that flowed from the posh punters into Aspinall's pockets, although inevitably there were nights when the luck ran the other way.

Taki Theodoracopulos tells a good story of one legendary game of *chemin-de-fer* at the Clermont in the mid-1960s which had a twist in the tale. The big players around the shoe in the *salon privé* were the Earl of Derby, The Duke of Devonshire, Jimmy Goldsmith, Cubby Broccoli the producer of the Bond films, Taki, and Ernest Blow a Chicago billionaire. The remaining players were 'Blues', Aspinall's name for elegantly mannered house players like his friend Lord Lucan (at that table that night), whose only reward was 'blinner' – a free dinner in the club restaurant.

As this particular chemmy game progressed, the stakes rose higher and higher. The bank was losing badly. So was Lucan 'the Blue' whose losses were on the house. However, his fellow aristocrats were enjoying an amazing run of good luck. By 1 am Derby's winnings had reached £1million and Devonshire's were £400,000. It was the worst evening Aspinall had ever experienced in the history of the Clermont. He kept his cool but counting in other smaller winners, he saw that the club (i.e. himself) was down by over £1.5 million. The night was still young and his intuition told him there was little or no prospect of recouping his enormous losses. All he could hope for was that the game would end. There seemed little chance of this with the main punters doing so well until suddenly Ernest Blow vomited at the table and had to be helped to the cloakroom. After some mopping-up oper-ations, the next shoe was about to start when Aspinall came into the *salon privè* and announced in a sombre voice: 'I am sorry to have to tell you that Ernest Blow has just died. We will have to stop.' 'Oh, let's just have one more shoe,' said Lord Derby with the carefree insou-ciance of a winner whose luck was in. That spirit of 'on with the game' might well have prevailed in the atmosphere of success and alcohol. But Aspinall was insistent. He said the club could lose its licence if it ever got out that the chemmy had continued after a player had dropped dead. So the game ended. Taki and Jimmy Goldsmith went down to the basement of the Clermont's building in Berkeley Square to seek out female company in Annabels. A few minutes after arriving they were amazed to see Ernest Blow, healthy, hearty and far from dead. Indeed so miraculous was his resurrection that he was gyrating energetically on the nightclub dance floor. In astonishment mingled with outrage, Taki and Jimmy went upstairs to demand an explanation from Aspinall. 'Well I had to stop my losses,' said the unrepentant Aspers. 'When you're down £1.5 million you have to take desperate measures.'

The episode, which raised both Goldsmith's and Taki's opinion of Aspinall's outrageousness, was not typical of the financial record of the Clermont. In terms of today's money, the Clermont Club was making profits of £1 million to £2 million a month in the 1960s. With this success Aspers was becoming one of the richest self-made men in England. In these good times he acquired priceless works of art and furniture: two beautiful country houses; and expanded his private collection of wild animals to the point that it cost him £10,000 a week to feed them. Much of this expense was due to Aspinall's insistence that his tigers should eat the same quality fillet steak as his guests at the Clermont. He often mentioned this to departing gamblers if they complained about their losses. Gesturing towards a portrait of his most beautiful Bengal tiger which hung near the cashier's desk, Aspinall enjoyed saying: 'You wouldn't like to see that magnificent beast go hungry, would you?'

Jimmy Goldsmith was not in the same league as John Aspinall for flamboyance or financial success during the years when the Clermont Club was at its zenith. But with startling suddenness their roles were reversed as a result of a series of 'bad calls' by Aspers and one spectacularly good judgement by Jimmy.

Aspers by the early 1970s was in a state of *hubris*. He had made all the money he thought he could ever need. So telling his friends, that he was bored with humans in comparison to his animals, he sold the

Clermont Club. That was his first bad call. The second was the absurdly low price he took for it – a mere £500,000. The Clermont's purchaser, Victor Lowndes of the Playboy Organization, recouped the entire investment with the profits from the first three nights of gambling under the new ownership.

Aspinall's third bad call was to invest heavily in the US stock market using borrowed money. For a time he did well which added to his *hubris*. But in 1974 a global collapse in share prices followed by a run on sterling completely wiped him out. For months he teetered on the edge of bankruptcy. He asked his friend Jimmy to rescue him with a loan. Goldsmith could well afford to help. For with uncanny intuition he had foreseen the 1974 crash in equities and taken his profits at the top of the market. Yet the cash-rich Jimmy refused to bale out the over-extended Aspers and was aggressively critical of his beleaguered friend for the mistakes that brought him to the brink of economic disaster.

Aspinall was deeply hurt by Goldsmith's treatment of him. More serious than the emotional pain was the punishment of financial catastrophe. 'We were absolutely ruined,' recalled Lady Sarah Aspinall, John's newly married third wife, 'we hadn't a bean. Aspers had to go out gambling every night to keep the banks at bay with interest payments. He was shattered by Jimmy's refusal to help him.'

Sally Aspinall had a good understanding of her husband's relation-ship with Goldsmith. In 1971 when she was being courted by her future spouse he had taken her to Paris to meet his best friend Jimmy. A dinner for the three of them was arranged at the Ritz Hotel. However, as soon as the introductions had been made the two men abandoned Sally and began pacing up and down the long corridor of the Ritz on their own like a pair of racehorses training at the gallops. 'I don't think I've ever seen two people so totally engrossed in each other with so much intensity and animation,' she has recalled, 'eventually I had to shout at them to get their attention and ask "What on earth are you two doing?"'

It was Sally who eventually solved the Aspers–Jimmy crisis of 1974 by having her own one-to-one confrontation with Goldsmith. 'I said to him why are you being so cruel? Why are you hurting your best friend so badly?' she has recalled. It must have been a most effective wifely *cri de coeur* because Goldsmith relented and provided the funds that rescued Aspinall. However, the terms of the deal were harsh. Aspers had to hand over the *pièces de résistance* of his art and furniture collection, which to this day are in the Goldsmith family home, Ormeley Lodge near Richmond. Parting with these unique items caused Aspinall great distress. But he recovered, saying: 'I should have known the animal in Jimmy's human make-up. Once you know your animal you're never disappointed.' On that basis the friendship made a full recovery, yet from that time on the balance of power in the relationship changed – and none too subtly. To symbolize the shift in his status Jimmy insisted on sitting in Aspinall's chair at the long table in the Clermont whenever he came in to gamble there. Whatever his private feelings at this reversal, Aspers publicly turned the other cheek. With outward good humour, he paid obsequious homage to the new occupant of the pro- prietor's chair, addressing him as 'King Goldsmith'. But behind the humour there was no doubt that Jimmy Goldsmith was now the dominant male primate in the relationship.

Dominant male primates have strong libidos. This aspect of Jimmy's personal life fascinated Aspers who had a much more restrained libido himself. Indeed so amazed was Aspinall by his great friend's prodigious sexual energies that he could sometimes sound like Leporello singing the praises of Don Giovanni when he recounted Goldsmith's conquests. This was not because Aspinall ever played the role of procurer. However, in what became the most important rela- tionship of his friend's life, Aspinall emerged as the pivotal figure acting as introducer, encourager, romantic adviser, breeding consult- ant and closer of the deal. His role is affectionately acknowledged by the heroine of Aspinall's finest hour as Cupid, Lady Annabel Goldsmith, who says: 'I would never have become committed to Jimmy without Aspers' involvement. The seriousness of the relation- ship, especially the decision to have children with Jimmy, was 100 per cent down to Aspers.'

The Annabel–Jimmy romantic saga might never have happened at all had it not been for a row about a staircase. The row was between Mark Birley, the controlling shareholder of Annabel's, the nightclub he had named after his wife, and John Aspinall, the owner of the Clermont. Both establishments had the same address, 44 Berkeley Square. Annabel's occupied the basement and the Clermont filled the rest of the building. The two clubs were linked by an internal staircase. Mark Birley became tetchy with Aspinall about Arab gamblers descending down the stairs from the casino in states of dress and disorder which jarred with the tone of the nightclub. Aspinall thought Birley was being too fastidious. The two proprietors had a falling out which ended in Birley closing the staircase. It was not all that much of an inconvenience for the Clermont gamblers to have to use the front door of Annabel's via the street entrance but the estrangement became personal. Aspinall, who had a lifelong tendency to harbour grudges, may well have been looking for an opportunity to stir up trouble for Birley. The opportunity arose when Goldsmith arrived to gamble in the Clermont one evening, saying to Aspinall: 'I've just been dancing with the most amazing girl downstairs. I think you know her. Can you fix for her to have dinner with us tomorrow night?'

The amazing girl was Lady Annabel Birley. Unaccompanied that evening by her husband Mark, she was having dinner with a girlfriend when Goldsmith's roving eye fell on her. He took advantage of the club's custom in those days of members asking unattended ladies to dance. After a few minutes on the discotheque's dance floor Jimmy was smitten by Annabel, although not quite strongly enough to prevent him from returning to his higher passion – playing roulette upstairs at the Clermont. However, when he reached the casino he raved so excitably about his dancing partner that Aspinall made further inquiries and followed up with a phone call to Annabel the next day.

'Aspers kept saying that Jimmy had fallen for me in a big way and that I must join them for dinner that night,' recalled Annabel Birley. 'I was intrigued because I had found this tall handsome man very attractive. But I said no to the invitation from Aspers because I had small children and didn't want to leave them on their own for two late nights in succession.'

Aspinall was not deterred by the lady's unavailability. He kept on intervening, cajoling, encouraging and offering alternative dates for dinner with Jimmy. 'I think Aspers was delighted to have a chance of stirring things with Mark,' is Annabel's recollection of these approaches, 'he wanted to keep me on side and he wanted to please his best friend Jimmy. So he kept pushing me hard.'

Annabel did not need too much pushing. Her affair with Goldsmith started in his suite at the Ritz a few weeks later. Yet on her part there was no sense of serious involvement at first. 'I thought I would keep it to a light-hearted relationship,' she says, 'because although Jimmy was tremendously appealing with all his energy and confidence yet at the same time a certain vulnerability, he wasn't quite my sort. I sensed he was just too strong a force for me.'

Although the strong force soon turned the light-hearted arrangements into a serious passion that deepened and flourished, there was no talk of marriage or children from either party. Goldsmith, who is credited with the remark 'when a man marries his mistress he creates a vacancy', had already demonstrated the authenticity of his observation by marrying his former mistress in France, Ginette Lery, and then taking on Annabel as his English lover. As he remained close to both the women in his life, he was in the happy dominant male primate position of having his cake and eating it. He seemed unlikely to change this agreeable arrangement. The same went for Annabel. She was keeping her marriage to Mark Birley more or less on the rails, largely by downplaying to her husband the seriousness of her relationship with Jimmy. This unconventional sitcom might have run and run for years had it not been for Aspinall's no less unconventional second intervention into this *ménage à quatre* with a speech about breeding.

Aspinall was a considerable expert on the rearing of animals. At Howletts he had bred tigers, elephants, wolves, rhinoceroses, cheetahs, monkeys, baboons and gorillas. One afternoon in the spring of 1973 he took Annabel for a walk round their cages and offered his advice to her on the subject of breeding humans. 'You must mate with Jimmy, you really must,' declared Aspinall, 'it would be a great honour for you to bear his children.' Unaccustomed to being addressed as if she were a Siberian tigress, Annabel demurred: 'I can't do that, we're both married' was her response. It was not the first time she had turned down this proposition. Jimmy had unexpectedly raised the idea of their having children together a few months earlier but Annabel had refused to take it seriously. She thought her life was already complicated enough and so was Jimmy's. Both of them had families of their own. On Annabel's side she had a circle of conventional relations some of whom, especially her adored cousin Lord Plunket, were bound to disapprove strongly. She explained this to Aspinall. 'You're making a great mistake,' he replied. 'Jimmy wants to have a child with you so badly . . . he would rather have a child by you than play roulette.' This was hardly the most persuasive of arguments but Aspinall persisted. As the walk round the animals continued, he expounded the case for the honour of being the mother of Goldsmith's children, adding the ominous observation: 'If you don't do this soon, one of these days the affair will be over and you will be left with nothing.'

Aspinall's advocacy using the carrot of honour and the stick of the affair ending was sufficiently effective to set Annabel pondering deeply on the question of to breed or not to breed. Eventually she concluded that Jimmy's desire to make her the mother of his children was a wonderful commitment on his part. So she said yes to the proposal of motherhood. 'I would never have thought of doing it without Aspers pushing me into it,' Annabel recalls, 'it was only when I saw the wisdom of what he was saying that I was won over.'

Annabel's 'breeding' began soon after her decisive conversation with Aspinall. She produced Jemima in 1974, Zac in 1975 and Ben in 1980. Aspers took an almost proprietorial interest in each of their births, spending noticeably more time in attendance at the maternity hospitals than their father did. Aspinall's crucial role as the persuader of Annabel into motherhood was frequently praised by Jimmy. It was also delightfully acknowledged by the couple's first born child Jemima, who was Aspinall's god-daughter. In a book of memorial tributes published after her godfather's death in 2000, Jemima wrote: 'I have a lot to thank Aspers for: in fact I even have to thank him for my own conception, since he was the one who persuaded and coerced my reluctant mother into "breeding" with my father in the first place.'

Success in the role of 'breeding adviser' restored Aspinall to the pinnacle of friendship with Goldsmith. Those tense times between them over debts, loans and pieces of furniture were replaced by Eldorado times of money-making in each other's businesses and ever closer personal intimacy. They remained in daily telephone contact, usually with the identical opening line 'What's new old boy?' several times a day, even when thousands of miles apart. 'You could soon understand how much they stimulated each other,' recalled Sally Aspinall, 'their minds led to one long sharing of ever-developing ideas on politics, history, personalities and business.'

Business for Aspinall meant returning to gambling club ownership which, with Goldsmith's backing, was a role he played better than anyone else in the world. Between them they owned and managed casinos in Belgravia, Mayfair, Darwin (the most profitable of all because of visiting Chinese gamblers) and Sydney. Eventually they sold their stakes in the holding company, Aspinalls, for a profit of around £40 million each. This was big money for Aspers who promptly poured it back into a trust to look after his beloved animals at Howletts and Port Lympne. However, it was only a small part of Goldsmith's fortune, for he had become enormously wealthy from merger and acquisition deals in the USA.

Jimmy Goldsmith began moving the focus of his business interests to America in the mid-1970s, partly because the rewards for his style of corporate raiding were so much bigger on Wall Street; partly because of his loathing for certain British newspapers which continued to plague him in the aftermath of his *Private Eye* libel case; and partly because of a major political misjudgement of Margaret Thatcher.

Goldsmith met Thatcher for the first time in 1975 soon after she had been elected Leader of the Opposition. In advance of their appointment, Goldsmith sent her a copy of a political speech he had delivered to a conference of editors from United Press International. It contained many policy ideas which Goldmith thought were likely to appeal to a radical new right-of-centre leader, such as reforms of the electoral system, the House of Lords, the trade unions and education. Instead of finding something to agree with in Goldsmith's speech, Thatcher subjected it to a detailed critique with arguments of such length that she hardly drew breath throughout their 55-minute meeting in the House of Commons. Goldsmith came out of the Leader of the Opposition's office in a ferment of indignation. 'That bloody woman – she talked to me as if she was my nanny,' he steamed to Annabel. More seriously he decided that nanny would be no good at governing Britain or running its economy. This negative view of Margaret Thatcher was the crucial factor in Goldsmiths decision to sell his Cavenham group of companies in Britain and to move his interests to the USA. The reasons for the decision were wrong but the results from it were gloriously right. Goldsmith's takeovers of giant US corporations such as Grand Union and Diamond International soon made him a 'Master of the Universe' on Wall Street and a billionaire.

Aspinall, for all his outward displays of male chauvinism, was shrewder in his early assessment of Margaret Thatcher than Goldsmith had been. This may have been something to do with his experience at Howletts of wrestling with lionesses, tigresses and lady gorillas possessed of 'the rogue gene' he believed was the source of Thatcher's strength. Eventually he converted Goldsmith, who came to regard Britain's first woman Prime Minister as one of his greatest idols.

Both Goldsmith and Aspinall had in them a need to hero worship. Quite a lot of this activity was devoted to themselves, for they were a mutual admiration society dedicated to *egoism à deux* – Stendahl's definition of love. But when they moved on from self-love, they created a pantheon of heroes whose highest pinnacles were reserved for an unlikely quartet of right-wing politicians – Margaret Thatcher, Ronald Reagan, Richard Nixon and Chief Mangosuthu Buthelezi. Thatcher and Reagan were predictable choices. Nixon was revered for his foreign policy triumphs and for his blunt realism as an international elder statesman in his later years. Both Goldsmith and Aspinall saw a fair amount of Nixon in the 1980s. They were not backward in suggesting new causes for the former President to endorse. I recall their extraordinary propositions to him at a dinner I gave for Nixon in 1989 when I was writing his biography. Aspinall wanted some ex-Presidential support for his campaign to save certain endangered breeds of tigers and gorillas from extinction. He invited Nixon to join him on a jungle tour of the Congo. 'The best way to stop journalists from calling you "disgraced"' advised Aspers, 'is for you to become a world hero as the saviour of the animal kingdom.' Nixon pretended to be interested in the idea at least to the point of calling other guests over to his table and solemnly asking them what they thought of this proposal from 'Professor Aspinall'.

Assuming Aspers to be a professor was a more understandable case of mistaken identity than regarding Jimmy as a politician. For Goldsmith was apt to spout eccentric opinions with the force of a volcanic geyser. One of them was his view that a nuclear war between Russia and China would be 'no great disaster if it reduced the threat of the urban biomass by bringing down the world's population by two or three billion'.

Nixon ignored such lunacies and enjoyed the company of Goldsmith for his electrifying energy. He was intrigued by the Jimmy and Aspers friendship, once describing them to me as 'competitors in coming on strong'. This was a perceptive comment for the two friends were constantly upping each other's ante in the outrageous stakes. Sometimes they were like a couple of naughty schoolboys egging one another on to juvenile japes. More often they fed off the excitable chemistry which their strange blend of supportiveness and competitiveness produced. Towards the end of their lives, they plotted together like a pair of political Svengalis to exercise manipulative power over politicians and political events. But why did they turn to politics at all?

Both Goldsmith and Aspinall fancied themselves as *hommes sérieux* in the arena of history. They were well read, well informed, well connected and well heeled. Success at making money had been extraordinary for Jimmy and good for Aspers, but by the beginning of the 1990s they were searching for new fields to conquer. 'I think Jimmy had done everything else except politics and he felt unbelievably strongly about Europe,' says Annabel Goldsmith. 'Aspers always had this deep romantic thing about Africa,' says Sally Aspinall.

Europe and Africa. Romance and politics. Money and power. These were heady combinations for the two restless 'competitors in coming on strong'. It was Aspinall who led the first charge into the politics of Southern Africa. Inspired by his youthful reading of Rider Haggard's adventure novels, Aspers had long worshipped fictional African

Uncle Max, Lord Beaverbrook

(Photo: Yousuf Karsh, Camera Press, London)

Winston Churchill

(Photo: © Empics)

Randolph Churchill

(Photo: Yousuf Karsh, Camera Press, London)

Lord Longford

(Photo: © Empics)

Harold and Mary Wilson with Marcia Falkender and Jonathan Aitken alongside a portrait of Harold Wilson in his office

Jimmy and Aspers

Margaret Thatcher and her family

(Photo: © Corbis)

Sir Frank Williams

(Photo: © Empics)

Michael Portillo

(Photo: © Corbis)

Nicky Gumbel speaking at an Alpha Course at Holy Trinity Brompton

heroes like Umslopogas, the fighting warrior in *Alan Quatermain*, and Sharka King of the Zulus in *Nada the Lily*. As a result of buying a beautiful home in South Africa when both the rand and property prices were at rock bottom, Aspinall became fascinated by the politics of that country just as the era of apartheid was ending. Ignoring all the realistic political advice about the near-certainty of Nelson Mandela and his ANC party coming to power, Aspers set off on a romantic crusade to install a Zulu King as ruler of South Africa. He formed a passionate political friendship with the Zulu leader of the Inkatha party, Chief Butheleizi, and backed him financially. In an astonishing speech at an Inkatha rally, Aspinall announced to cheers and throbbing drums: 'I am a white Zulu.' He also urged his audience to 'sharpen your spears' for the coming battle with their enemies in the ANC. These words were not just the colourful imagery of a speech to African tribesmen. Aspers put his money where his mouth was and persuaded Jimmy to follow his lead. Between them the two gamblers-turned-warriors made donations of well over £1million to the coffers of Inkatha. Most of that money was used by the Zulus to finance their battles against the ANC, often using expensive weapons that were far more lethal than sharpened spears. Despite their high risk gamble in support of the Inkatha movement, the Aspinall–Goldsmith foray into the power struggles of Southern Africa made no difference to the outcome. The ANC, which Goldsmith denounced as 'an evil communist organization', won the election easily and installed Nelson Mandela as President. The rest is history.

Jimmy Goldsmith had better luck in his efforts to change the history of Europe. His motivation for attempting to do this was inspired by a dream. One night while asleep at Montjeu, his home in France, he had a vision of himself standing on a mountain top from which he could see a railway line far below him. On the track was a train whose passengers included his family. This train was speeding towards a landslide which Jimmy could see but which was obscured from the driver by a bend in the line. From his mountain top Jimmy could do nothing except wait for the inevitable crash with growing horror. When he woke up from this nightmare he believed he had received a mystical warning about the disastrous consequences of

Britain continuing on its collision course of joining the euro and plunging into a federal European state. So after confiding with various friends, particularly Aspinall who doubled up as both an interpreter of dreams and a political adviser, Goldsmith launched the Referendum party in 1995.

Unlike most political party leaders, Jimmy Goldsmith never wanted to win power. Instead he hoped to change the course of British and European history by enshrining in legislation the voters right to a referendum on Britain's European Union membership before further moves towards European integration, such as the euro and the constitution, were imposed. At first the Referendum party was a gigantic game of bluff. Goldsmith believed that his demands were so reasonable that they would quickly be met by the Conservative party promising a referendum in the Tory election manifesto. I will never forget Jimmy Goldsmith's exuberance at Margaret Thatcher's seventieth birthday party in October 1995 after he had a conversation on this subject with John Major. 'We're getting there. We're winning,' Jimmy told me with feverish excitement after the Prime Minister had agreed to meet him for a private dinner to discuss the referendum issue.

Thanks to intermediaries such as Alan Clark and Charles Hambro, Goldsmith and Major had several secret conversations in the run up to the 1997 Election. The sticking point was that Goldsmith wanted a referendum that would give the electorate a chance to say 'no' to all recent developments in the European Union including the Maastricht Treaty. Major could not possibly agree to this as any political observer less naive than Goldsmith would have realized. So it was only a matter of time before the stalemate in these discussions became a standoff. Eventually Goldsmith declared 'I vomit on the government' and spent over £2.5 million in launching the Referendum party which put up 100 candidates in constituencies across the country.

Although Goldsmith's political heart was in the right place on Europe, he was easily outflanked as a political tactician by both Major and Blair. Before the end of the campaign the Labour and Conservative parties had also offered specific pledges to hold a referendum on the issue of joining the euro. This eclipsed Goldsmith's party which was proposing a much more general referendum on Europe with a longwinded question for the voters. The result was that the issue became blurred. Goldsmith had at one stage in 1996 been winning support for his party at the level of 15 per cent, according to the opinion polls. By the time of the General Election in May 1997, that support was below 5 per cent. No wonder Goldsmith was clutching at the straws of votes from gun club members during the Howletts dinner described at the beginning of this chapter. He had fought a good fight but the electorate was not sufficiently convinced by his cause and the big parties had outmanoeuvred him.

Of all the Referendum party's candidates, only two made any impact – Aspinall and Goldsmith. Although they were both defeated, they went down in style. Aspers polled a respectable 7,000 votes in Folkestone, the highest total in the country for any Referendum party candidate. He subsequently argued, with some justification, that if he had stood in his home seat of Canterbury he would have done at least twice as well. The reason Aspinall did not put up in the constituency where he was a well known and popular local figure was that Goldsmith insisted he should take on Michael Howard in Folkestone. 'Jimmy had a personal aversion to Howard which I never quite understood,' said Aspinall, 'he kept saying that Howard was "the wrong kind of Jew" – an Ashkenazai Jew.' With such eccentric criteria governing the decisions on who should fight which constituency, perhaps it was not so surprising that the Referendum party was an electoral failure.

Although Jimmy Goldsmith failed, he failed with amazing personal courage. For in the middle of the campaign he received the diagnosis that he had terminal cancer of the pancreas. He was soon in acute pain, debilitated by the disease and by the chemotherapy he was being given by his doctors in Paris every weekend. In the Putney constituency where he was running against the Conservative ex-Cabinet Minister David Mellor, Goldsmith campaigned with amazing vigour although some of his supporters were surprised by his mysterious absence from the hustings at the weekends. 'Why isn't Sir James out on the streets this Saturday?' a Putney voter asked Lady Annabel Goldsmith. She was the only person in Britain to know that her husband only had a few more weeks to live. Annabel was not able to give the real reason, which was that the candidate was undergoing chemotherapy in a Paris hospital in order to keep him alive.

No-one would have suspected Goldsmith was dying of cancer as they watched the television coverage of the count in Putney on election night. Although he polled only 7 per cent of the votes Goldsmith was by far the most charismatic and dominant figure among the candidates. The sitting Tory MP who went down in defeat, David Mellor, blamed his billionaire opponent for the loss of the seat for he said bitterly: 'As for Sir James Goldsmith and his Hacienda La Referenda Party you can all go back to Mexico with all your zoological society friends.' This pejorative reference to Aspinall excited the wrath of Taki Theodoracopulos who was attending the count. He began shouting scatological insults at Mellor which included the rather more pejorative epithet 'toe sucker'. Perhaps a little over sensitive at this reference to a well-publicized incident in their departing Member of Parliament's private life, David Mellor's supporters shouted back worse insults about Goldsmith. Within seconds scuffling, booing and slow handclapping threw the Town Hall into chaos. Goldsmith, who could not quite hear what the fuss was about from his position on the platform, started up his own version of a slow, slow, quick, quick, slow handclap which made it look as though he was beating time to some mysterious dance rhythm. What had begun as a serious political campaign ended in a farce.

It would be easy to conclude from this scene and from other disappointing results for Referendum party candidates around the country that Jimmy Goldsmith the politician had achieved nothing. Yet a deeper analysis would suggest that only because of the pressure from the Referendum party did the Conservative and Labour parties include in their election pledges a promise to hold a referendum on joining the euro. It is this Goldsmith-induced promise which has for the last ten years preserved the pound sterling and avoided the euro. For no government dares to hold a referendum asking for a yes vote on a cause that is so unpopular with the electorate. That is a historical legacy which brings honour to the political career of Sir James Goldsmith.

Goldsmith did not live long enough to take the credit for his legacy. Within days of the general election he was paralysed with pain. Despairing of chemotherapy treatment, he turned, on the recommendation of a business friend, to an Indian doctor who offered an alternative medicine cure for cancer based on a strict vegetarian diet mixed with ground-up metals. It did not work. Retreating to his beloved Montjeu, Jimmy faded away swiftly but with characteristic courage. Although agonizingly thin and fragile in his last weeks, he loved having visits from his family and closest friends. The visitor who amused him most was Sean Connery. The former James Bond star said he had an important piece of advice to impart. With complete seriousness he told Goldsmith, 'Whatever you do Jimmy don't make any deathbed confessions – you might survive and then regret them.' Goldsmith loved retelling this story, complete with his impressions of Connery's whispered counsel and amused speculations on the question of whether the actor had ever made a much regretted 'deathbed confession' himself.

Apart from when he was relating the advice he received from Sean Connery, Goldsmith never allowed words like death or dying to be used in his final weeks. Aspinall, who towards the end spent long hours lying on Jimmy's bed holding his hand in silent, mystical communion, was amazed by his friend's refusal to face reality. 'That was totally out of character,' Aspinall said to me soon after Jimmy's funeral. 'Throughout his normal life Jimmy was such a great hypochondriac that he had frequent panics that he was about to die – of colds, flu, or indigestion. Only when he was really dying did he become absolutely confident that he was going to recover to full health. Typical Jimmy. Always betting against the odds.'

Soon after Goldsmith had departed for the great casino in the sky, Aspinall was also diagnosed with terminal cancer. He faced the prospect of his demise with the *sang-froid* of a true gambler. Two days before I was sentenced to prison I went to see him to say what I thought would be my last goodbyes. Aspers immediately turned this valedictory conversation into a bet. Which would be longer – my time in jail or his time on earth? He bet on a short window for his own survival, giving himself six months. However, if he lost and was still around when I emerged from incarceration then he would pay up by giving me 'a great lunch'.

The bet was honoured. A week after I came out of prison in January 2000 Aspers hosted a marvellous 'welcome back' lunch party for me. I was shocked by his appearance. The melanoma had spread so badly over his face that it was scarred with weeping sores that had to be dressed twice daily. He was obviously in terrible pain but you would never had thought so from the warmth and gaiety of his conversation. When we were alone together I said I was sorry that he was having such a tough time, 'Oh well, one has to play with the cards one's been dealt,' he replied, 'I'm down to my last cards. Love and sympathy cards you might call them. Mostly twos of clubs and threes of diamonds, but Sally's an ace and I have friends like you who come to see me who are my court cards. So on my good days I can still play a few more hands before I go.'

Playing life's cards in their own inimitable style, always challenging the odds and the conventions, these were the vital elements in the bonding between Jimmy and Aspers. They neither thought nor behaved like other people. Both were *sui generis* characters. They enhanced many lives with their charm, courage and capricious spirits. Yet it also has to be recorded that they damaged a few lives in their circle by insensitivity, ill temper and occasional excursions into cruelty. There was a dark side to the Aspers and Jimmy friendship. The suicide of Dominic Elwes; the lifelong ostracism of Aspinall's half-brother Sir Peter Osborne; the obstruction of the police inquiries into Lord Lucan's disappearance; and a long list of ruined personal fortunes are among the negative areas that can be traced back to one or other of the two protagonists, both of whom could be ruthless towards those they believed had crossed them.

Yet seen in the round, James Goldsmith and John Aspinall were heroes, not villains. I admired them warts and all, because they were big men motivated by high ambition and exciting vision. Occasionally they failed or behaved badly. Yet the real pattern of their lives was to be continuously striving for high endeavours, combining a grandiose eccentricity of style with a serious excitement of purpose. The world would have been a much duller place without them. Their footprints in the sands of time were not as deep as either of them would have wanted but their trails were colourful and original. Like two comets lighting up the sky as they traverse the galaxies, Jimmy and Aspers blazed a path across the hearts of their friends with a dazzling illumination that will not be forgotten until our time is come.

CHAPTER 7

Margaret Thatcher and Her Family

'That young man needs his wings clipped,' said Margaret Thatcher in a piercing *sotto voce*. I was the young man, 29 years old, recently selected as the Prospective Parliamentary candidate for Thanet East. She was Secretary of State for Education in Ted Heath's Cabinet. We had both been addressing a conference of Young Conservatives at the Nayland Rock Hotel, Margate in 1972. Unfortunately for me, the audience applauded the speech of the candidate far more enthusiastically than the speech of the Secretary of State. As I waved back to the crowd with reciprocal enthusiasm, Thatcher's put-down from the back of the platform may or may not have been intended to reach my ears. But it was an unpromising start to our relationship which over the next three decades was sometimes disturbingly cold and hostile; sometimes, surprisingly warm and intimate, but never for one moment, dull.

I could never have imagined at the time of Margaret's first sardonic comment about needing my wings clipped that I would soon get to know the entire Thatcher family rather well. They have sometimes been called a 'dysfunctional family', which is not an unfair label since the interaction between the four members of it – Margaret and Dennis, Mark and Carol – has so often been fraught with tensions and misunderstandings. That said, I found the Thatchers a fascinating quartet, not only in terms of Prime Ministerial history but also as private individuals in their own right, since each one of them could be so sharply different from their public perceptions. They have never before been written about as a family so I will attempt such a portrayal in this chapter. Inevitably it must begin with my earliest glimpses – some good, some bad, all interesting – of Margaret Thatcher.

Within a few months of being elected to Parliament in 1974 I was asked what at the time seemed an extraordinary question by my fellow MP Peter Morrison.[1] 'Would you support Margaret Thatcher in a leadership election?' he enquired as we were towelling down after one of our regular games of squash. 'But she's not even on the radar screen of possible runners,' I replied. 'Not yet,' said Morrison 'but I talked to her last night and she's ready to go for it if enough of us are willing to back her.'

I was not willing, partly for reasons of self-preservation. Ted Heath, the Tory leader *in situ*, had been born and brought up in Broadstairs in my constituency. His elderly father, who lived in the town, was a prominent figure in the Thanet East Conservative Association. He and other Heath loyalists dismissed Thatcher as too shrill and divisive to be taken seriously as a leadership challenger. They also derided her ignorance of defence and foreign policy issues. I shared this opinion and was unwise enough to express it in what I thought were the safe surroundings of a Beirut dinner party. Towards the end of that dinner one or two of the guests, including a former President of Lebanon, kept pressing me on what the potential contenders for the Tory leadership thought of the latest developments in the Middle East peace process. In particular they wanted to know Mrs Thatcher's position on the various options for Israeli troop withdrawals from the Sinai area.

Taking a deep breath and a sip of post-prandial Dom Perignon champagne, I replied: 'Frankly, Margaret Thatcher knows so little about the Middle East she probably thinks that Sinai is the plural for sinuses.' By the time this *bon mot* found its way in to the columns of *Private Eye*, Margaret Thatcher had been elected leader of the Opposition. She was not amused. Her new chief of Staff, Airey Neave MP, summoned me to his office to tell me of his boss's displeasure. 'You must apologize to her,' he said. Although surprised by the seriousness the new regime attached to snippets of political gossip in *Private Eye*,

I agreed to eat humble pie. 'Good, the Leader will see you in the Division Lobby at the ten o'clock vote,' said Neave. 'She'll be wearing a green dress,' he added. Even without this sartorial sign-posting I had no difficulty in finding the leader of my party. In contrast to Neave's heavy-handed approach, Margaret Thatcher (who was indeed wearing a green evening dress) was graciousness personified as I stumbled out my words of apology for what had been said in Beirut.

'Oh please don't worry about it,' she said. 'I sometimes say the most dreadful things in private about my colleagues. You were just unlucky that someone let it leak out.' As she added some kind words about a speech I had recently made in the House, I came away feeling that the blot on my copybook had been a minor one. However, less than a month later, I was back in Airey Neave's office, apparently on the carpet again. 'Are you running some sort of subversive right-wing operation against the Leader?' he asked. 'What's this I hear about you starting up a new political group to keep on supporting Hugh Fraser?'

Airey Neave, who had known a lot about subversive operations, from his days as a wartime intelligence officer, was on the wrong track in suspecting me of being a dark blue under the bed. However, I could understand where he was coming from because the Rt Hon. Hugh Fraser MP, something of an unguided missile politically, had been a maverick candidate in the recent leadership election with me as his campaign manager. Although he had scored the lowest total of votes,[2] Fraser had written some of the highest quality articles about future policy ideas for the Conservative party. Alone of the leadership candidates he had advocated a liberalization of exchange controls, a halt to state investment in failing nationalized industries and a reversal of Ted Heath's drive towards greater British involvement in Jean Monnet's grand designs for a federal Europe. Three youthful enthusiasts who had played an amanuensis role in helping Hugh Fraser to set out his stall were Roger Scruton (then a lecturer in philosophy at Birkbeck college), Dr John Casey (a Cambridge don), and myself. When drinking sorrowfully together in the aftermath of Fraser's defeat we had talked hopefully about keeping his ideas alive. To do this we formed a supper club which we called the Conservative Philosophy Group. Our rather vague purposes were more intellectual than political and the whole enterprise would probably have fizzled out into academic oblivion had it not been for Airey Neave's sudden concerns about our potential to become a hotbed of anti-Thatcher subversion.

In my response to Neave I more or less managed to convince him that the fledgling Conservative Philosophy Group had been formed to generate new ideas for the party, not to settle old scores. Neave came up with a surprising request. 'So, could The Leader be invited to join your group?' he asked. 'Of course,' I replied, promising to send her an invitation to our next supper, which she promptly accepted.

Once Margaret Thatcher started coming to the Conservative Philosophy Group, everyone else wanted to come too. We had no difficulty in attracting academic speakers of the calibre of Professors H. W. R. Wade, Michael Oakeshott, Friedrich Hayek, Hugh Trevor-Roper and Anthony Quinton. Distinguished Americans such as Milton Friedman and Richard Nixon addressed us, respectively, on economic and foreign policy. But most of the talks were given by our own regulars such as Robert Blake, Paul Johnson, John Lucas, Roger Scruton, John Casey, Edward Norman and Hugh Thomas. Margaret Thatcher came as often as she could and thoroughly enjoyed these evenings. Although not an intellectual herself in the sense of being a thinker who lives *for* ideas, she came across as a Leader of formidable intelligence who was hungry to live *off* ideas. At a time when she was still being caricatured in the media as a shrill and superficial housewife, in the privacy of the Conservative Philosophy Group (untroubled by journalistic leaks for the first two years of its existence) she was seen as a deeply serious changer of the national agenda. She would seize on ideas and phrases that came up in the discussions, sometimes domineeringly but more often creatively. I have never forgotten how she pounced on a throw-away line from Professor Michael Oakeshott who said: 'Stop talking about de-nationalization. Call it some thing more attractive like privatization.' Eventually that idea which originated in the Conservative Philosophy Group became one of the most enduring legacies of Thatcherism.

Perhaps because we were getting on well as fellow participants in the Conservative Party Philosophy Group, Margaret Thatcher seemed pleased rather than displeased when I started going out with her 21-year-old daughter Carol in 1977. We met at a summer barbecue given by John Moore MP at his home on Wimbledon Common. Carol and I were just about the only young singletons at this party which was full of senior Conservative functionaries and shadow ministers keen to hover around the Leader of the Opposition. By contrast Carol and I retreated with a large jug of Pimms to some stone steps at the far end of Moore's garden. We talked so long and enthusiastically that we were almost the last to leave. On that first evening I was captivated by several of the same qualities in Carol which 31 years later were to make her 'Queen of the Jungle' in the ITV programme *I'm a Celebrity, Get Me Out of Here*. I found her funny, feisty, full of energy, slightly wacky but highly attractive. At that time she was a trainee solicitor, doing her articles with Norton Rose, a leading City law firm. She looked the part of a future legal eagle in her horn-rimmed spectacles and a charcoal grey suit, but I soon discovered that beneath her conventional exterior lay an unconventional spirit of adventure. For Carol was determined to abandon her promising career as a solicitor as quickly as possible, talking excitably about travelling around the world and becoming a writer. 'Oh I'm not going to continue with bo-wing old law,' she said with the lisp that in those days gave her difficulty in pronouncing her r's. 'I don't want to be a clone of Mum. As soon as I've qualified I'm going to start a life of excitement and wo-mance.'

As Carol and I started our own romance, it became clear that she was determined to be staunchly independent from anyone else in her family. I had the impression that Carol admired Margaret from a distance but did not enjoy being close to her. Their's was a tense relationship, with more chill than warmth in it. The same could be said of Carol's attitude to Mark, but without the admiration. Even in those early days, brother and sister were like chalk and cheese. Long before the controversies and conflict of interest allegations surrounding Mark, which Carol later blamed for their bad relationship, their sibling antipathy in the 1970s was put down to 'being a couple of Leos'. But there was more to it than astrology. Mark was outwardly kind and solicitous towards Carol. 'Take good care of my sis, won't you?' he said to me in a friendly way once or twice. Carol never had a good word to say about Mark. She felt a rivalry, perhaps a resentment that her brother seemed to be in so much closer communication with both their parents than she was, even though it was Carol's choice to keep her distance from them.

I was involved in an episode two years after Margaret became Leader of the Opposition which revealed flaws in Thatcher family communications. An assiduous *Daily Mail* reporter discovered that Denis had been through a divorce before marrying Margaret. The *Mail's* Diary column planned to run the item as a lead story about the first Mrs Thatcher. I learned about this drama when Denis rang me at home asking if I knew where Carol was. He sounded so fraught that I wondered what could be bothering him. A few minutes later I discovered that Margaret's private secretaries were making frantic efforts to track down Mark who was away on an accountancy course in Edinburgh. The reason for these panic searchings was that the Thatcher parents had never told their children about Denis's first marriage. Even though it was a case of shutting the newsroom door after the *Daily Mail* had bolted with the story, Denis and Margaret were desperate to avoid Mark and Carol being shocked by reading the revelation in print. That concern was understandable. It was harder to understand why all knowledge of Denis's short-lived wartime marriage had been suppressed as if it were too dark a secret to tell the children. When an emotionally overwrought Margaret eventually reached her offspring to break the news that she was the second Mrs Denis Thatcher, her overwhelming concern was to soothe what she imagined would be their bruised feelings. In fact both twins were calm and supportive. However, the maladroit 'in denial' attitude to the first marriage surprised Mark and elicited the comment from Carol: 'My family can be quite dysfunctional at times.'

I was beginning to understand that Margaret could sometimes have guilt feelings about her children. Her worry was that she had worked so hard at her political life that her career was damaging her maternal life. Because of this angst she had a tendency to over-react negatively or over-compensate positively about whatever was happening to Carol and Mark. In many published stories about Margaret it has been reported that her overprotective concern was concentrated exclusively on Mark, thus making him a 'Mummy's boy'. Not so. The Margaret I saw at close quarters in the 1970s was even-handed in her efforts to help Carol just as much as Mark. The story of our Verbier skiing weekend is an illustration of this.

In the winter of 1978 Carol was given a 15-day holiday in the Swiss resort of Verbier by her parents. I planned to come and join her there for a long week-end in the middle of it. Because of problems with airline seat availability at the height of the skiing season, my travel plans only worked if I flew back to London on a Monday evening flight from Geneva. Unfortunately, after the tickets had been bought, this particular Monday turned out to be a date unexpectedly chosen by the Opposition for some contentious parliamentary voting which required all Conservative MPs to be present in the House on a running three-line whip from 3.30 pm onwards. As I could not be on the ski slopes and in the division lobbies at the same time and as no alternative flights were available, my week-end with Carol in Verbier had to be cancelled, to our great disappointment.

Although I accepted the disappointment, Carol in Verbier did not. Unknown to me, she telephoned her mother with a wail of protest about the unfairness of the Opposition's three-line whip and its wrecking effects on our romantic week-end in Verbier. Margaret's heart evidently melted. A cheerful Carol came on the line with the announcement: 'Mum says she can change the voting for Monday.' 'That's impossible,' I replied. I was wrong. For at the last minute the Opposition day's business was switched and the three-line whip was miraculously dropped. Carol and I had a wonderful weekend together in the joys of the Alps. The day after my return I was back in the division lobbies of the House of Commons when I saw the Leader of the Opposition a few feet away from me. So I went over and started to say thank you for her amazing favour in re-arranging the parliamentary business.

'Sshh!' she said putting a finger to her lips and giving me a theatrical wink. 'Did you two have fun?' 'Great fun,' I replied. 'Come to my office and tell me about it then.' Five minutes later I was sitting in an armchair drinking Scotch with Margaret Thatcher in the Leader of the Opposition's office. Kicking off her shoes, she brushed aside my repeated thanks by saying that her Chief Whip, Humphrey Atkins, had wanted to change the Opposition's voting plans anyway. Then she wanted to know everything about Verbier, asking me about snow conditions, ski-runs, restaurants, the local fondue, and whether Carol had any other friends or skiing companions. 'I get so worried about Carol being out there all on her own,' she explained in a worried voice. Even more poignantly, as I was leaving her office Margaret said, 'You won't tell Carol that I was worrying about her, will you? She will think I am being overbearing.'

I liked what I saw of both Margaret as a mother and Denis as a father. Some of my best glimpses of them were in Lamberhurst where the Thatchers rented a flat in a National Trust property, Scotney Castle. It had beautiful grounds. Looking out of the window one morning I saw Margaret and Denis strolling around the garden holding hands. It struck me that this was the first time I had seen any two members of the family in warm human contact. They were not a tactile foursome. Hugs, cuddles and kisses never seemed to be on their agenda. Years later I asked Mark if my impression was correct. 'Yes,' he said, 'even Mum was not in the slightest bit tactile. But she communicated her love by the way she looked at you.'

In the privacy of her home Margaret Thatcher could deliver looks that were far from being loving. I got one of them during a visit to Scotney when I noticed hanging in the dining room an exotic picture of Islamic art which Margaret said had been given her by the Syrian Ambassador. In the centre of the painting was some elaborate Arabian calligraphy. 'Do you know what it says?' she asked me. 'It says "There is only one God and his name is Allah."' I replied, foolishly adding, 'I hope you don't invite too many of your constituents from Finchley to come and have lunch here.' This was supposed to be a light-hearted reference to the high percentage of Jewish voters in her Finchley electorate. Margaret was not amused. Fixing me with a gimlet stare, she replied, 'I will invite anyone I like to lunch here.' I resolved to cut out humorous remarks when receiving Thatcher hospitality in future.

The Thatchers were good at being hospitable. Margaret insisted on doing all the cooking and washing up herself, her speciality being coronation chicken. Denis, a man of his time, expected no less of his wife and could get pernickety if his breakfast bacon was not grilled by her to perfection. In the evenings he enjoyed his glasses of gin, wine and Scotch. They did not make him drunk but he could become a little repetitive. I felt I had heard the details of his great coup in selling his business to Castrol Oil many times over, but it was his feet-on-the-ground common sense deriving from his business life that had made him such a rock. In those pre-No. 10 days he called Margaret 'my woman', and Carol, 'my girl', and they both often deferred to him.

Carol sometimes became prickly in the presence of her parents. She could be provocative, aggressive and witty at their expense, none of which went down well even, or especially, when she was in the right. There was an incident when I was driving Margaret and Carol somewhere around Lamberhurst. Carol, in a puckish mood that afternoon, embarked on a shopping quiz saying: 'Come on now, let's see if you two Tory politicians know what inflation is doing to the food prices. How much is a pint of milk? How much is a half pound of margarine?' and so on. I was a miserable failure at answering these questions but wriggled out with the explanation that my cleaning lady usually did my shopping. 'Mum' also failed several of the questions which was a far greater surprise as her political opponents had at various times labelled her 'a food hoarder', 'a milk snatcher' and other epithets which suggested that frugality and domesticity were central to her character. Far from enjoying Carol's teasings, Margaret Thatcher became furious. It was one of my first glimpses of the iron in the Iron Lady, but she may have drawn long-term political advantage from her temporary discomfort. For a few weeks later, 'Thatcher's shopping basket' became an effective weapon of election propaganda as the leadership of the Opposition unveiled her groceries on television with emphasis on their price rises under Labour's inflation.

The job of winning the next election was, quite rightly, the supreme priority of Margaret Thatcher's life throughout her three-year period as Leader of the Opposition. She had little or no spare time for family, friends or recreation. Yet despite her pressures she made considerable efforts to show warmth towards me and my family once she realized that the Carol–Jonathan relationship was a serious one. Those efforts included occasional *en famille* excursions to restaurants and theatres. One night Carol organized an evening at the National Theatre which was performing Noel Coward's *Blithe Spirit*. My sister Maria was playing the female lead in the part of Elvira, a spirit who comes back from the dead. We all went backstage afterwards for champagne in the star's dressing room where Margaret Thatcher made a good fist of being a luvvie, offering extravagant compliments to members of the cast. Denis was less effusive.

'Your sister's a damn good actress but I can't stand Noel Coward,' he said brusquely. Expanding on his aversion, he continued: 'Chap got his timing completely wrong with that play didn't he? It came out in the middle of the war. Struck a wrong note making all those jokes about people being brought back from the dead. Didn't please the chaps doing their bit in uniform when people around us were dying left right and centre. Upset us a lot I can tell you.' Then he pulled out a silk handkerchief and blew his nose on it. In that fleeting moment, I caught a glimpse of some deep emotions that lay buried inside Denis Thatcher.

No member of the Thatcher family liked to 'let it all hang out', in terms of communicating their emotions. Yet all of them could be emotional people. I misjudged that, especially in Carol. I even misjudged the friendly, perhaps emotionally friendly, signals that Margaret may have been sending me. For as I look back, with the added insight of now being a father with three daughters of my own, I think that Margaret did her best to show many kindnesses to her daughter's boyfriend. At her invitation, we had several nightcaps together in her Flood Street home when she would kick her shoes off, relax and gossip. When I was ill in hospital with typhoid fever she sent me two charming handwritten letters. At a politically fevered moment in the House of Commons, she sent an emissary with a personal message urging me to mend my fences with her Deputy, William Whitelaw. When the General Election of 1979 was under way and Carol was staying at my constituency home in Thanet for part of the campaign, Margaret found time in her hectic schedule to telephone surprisingly often.

In retrospect I think I was rather bad at reciprocating those green shoots of incipient affection. I was paradoxically both an arrogant and at times insecure young man. I found it difficult to imagine having a relaxed and happy relationship with a woman of such formidable strength and character as my future mother-in-law. This leap of the imagination became more difficult after Margaret Thatcher won the election and was the new Prime Minister.

For reasons too private to write about, my love affair with Carol ended in the summer of 1979. She was in Sydney. I was in London. I handled the break-up badly. The fundamental cause of our parting was that I had fallen in love with Lolicia, a Swiss lady whom I married later that year. Carol was hurt. Margaret Thatcher was upset.

No mother can be expected to take an even-handed approach towards the complex reasons for the ending of a relationship that might well have ended in her daughter's marriage. The Prime Minister was no exception. Some of her closest courtiers at No. 10, particularly her new Parliamentary Private Secretary Ian Gow, brought me news of 'the distress of the lady', as he called it. Years later, in a somewhat emotional scene, I apologized to Margaret Thatcher for this distress (see page 147) but at the time I kept my distance. It was a long distance and a chilly one too so far as the Prime Minister was concerned. However, Denis kept his lines of communication open, at least to the extent of making a point of chatting to me very pleasantly on many social occasions.

It took a long time before my relations with the Thatchers warmed up again, but eventually the ice melted thanks to three episodes in which I was a passionate supporter of the Prime Minister. One was a war, the second was a bombing, the third was a political coup.

The war was the Falklands war. It is often forgotten how badly it began on the political front. On Saturday the 3 April 1982, the morning after the Argentine invasion of the islands, the House of Commons held an emergency debate. Immediately before that debate there was a meeting of the 1922 Committee of Conservative backbench MPs. Their mood was a mixture of despair, panic and recrimination. I happened to make one of the few positive contributions, saying that although things looked bleak right now, if we kept our nerve and got the military operation right, yesterday's mistakes could be turned into tomorrow's glory. Later in the day the Chief Whip, Michael Jopling, told me that he had written down my comments and passed them on to No. 10 where they had pleased the Prime Minister.

Margaret Thatcher was initially a lonely figure in the Falklands war. Her iron determination to retake the islands was not well supported in her own Cabinet, even though her policy had much better backing in the country. That her will prevailed and that she maintained such strength of resolve through the darkest moments of the war owed much to the two members of her family who were resident with her at the time in the Prime Minister's flat above No. 10 Downing Street.

Denis Thatcher's support was indomitable but predictable. He had to look up the Falklands in an atlas to discover where they were on the day of invasion, but his ex-soldier's conviction that 'Getting the Argies off' was the right policy never wavered. He stood where he always stood – totally behind Margaret.

The part played by Mark Thatcher in sustaining his mother throughout the crisis has never been written about. It does him great credit and may perhaps help to explain why the bonds between the two of them have stayed so strong through so many of Mark's personal difficulties. The record of his small but precious contribution is preserved in the private archive of personal notes he wrote to Margaret at various moments in the drama – when the task force sailed; when South Georgia was recaptured; when the bombing of Port Stanley airport began; when Goose Green was taken; when HMS *Sheffield* was hit by an Exocet and when the Argentine forces surrendered. Usually these notes were just one liners with the simplest of messages such as 'I love you' or 'I am so proud of you'. Sometimes they ran to two or three lines of devoted filial support. Occasionally Mark would scribble down a verse of poetry for his mother to read on her pillow at night such as these words of Kipling which he gave her as the British troops made their beachhead on the island:

> Dear bought and dear a thousand years
> Our father's title runs
> Make we, likewise their sacrifice
> Defrauding not our sons.

More important than such written offerings was Mark's physical presence throughout the Falklands war. At the time he was occupying a spare bedroom in the flat above No. 10. He had a son's intuitive understanding of the emotional burdens his mother was carrying at this most testing moment of her Premiership. As a war leader she could not show her vulnerability to the emotions she felt over lost lives in the Falklands to anyone other than Mark and Denis. Although wonderfully supportive in a multitude of ways, Denis's military experience could make him seem a little too matter-of-fact about casualties. 'What are you making all this fuss for? When there's a war on you've got to expect things not to go right all the time,' was his first reaction to the losses on HMS *Sheffield*. Mark, who at 22 was much the same age as the servicemen in the Falklands, had gentler and more sensitive reactions. The morning after the attack on the *Sheffield* Mark heard the telephone ring at 5 am in his mother's bedroom. Guessing it might be more bad news, he bought her a cup of tea and sat with her in a time of silent emotion. Few words were spoken. 'I could see she was suffering. I think it helped her to have a member of the family beside her sharing in her feelings. It wasn't necessary to say anything.'

After ten agonizing weeks of conflict, the Falklands war ended in glory. On the night the Argentine forces surrendered, Denis was with Margaret in the House of Commons. After she made a Prime Ministerial statement, they travelled back to No. 10 together. As Denis liked to describe of their entrance: 'We went inside and as we walked past the famous bulldog pose portrait of Winston hanging in the anteroom to the Cabinet I swear the great man bowed and said, "Well done girl."'

Both Denis Thatcher and Mark Thatcher had extensive business interests during Margaret's years as Prime Minister. Denis's directorships and consultancies never caused a ripple of trouble. Mark's more entrepreneurial activities, particularly in Oman and Saudi Arabia, became flashpoints for journalistic investigation and censure. Much of the investigation was done by the *Observer*, whose proprietor Tiny Rowland held a fierce grudge against Margaret Thatcher and her government for permitting the takeover of Harrods by Mohammed Al Fayed. I read these investigative newspaper stories with special interest. Although I never had any business interests connected with

Mark Thatcher, as chairman of the Aitken Hume Banking group I knew many of the countries and the people with whom he was said to be involved including Qais Zawawi, Tim Landon and Sultan Qaboos in Oman; and Wafic Said, Prince Bandar bin Sultan and others in Saudi Arabia. In the last analysis, the principal allegations against Mark Thatcher boiled down to two claims. First he was alleged to have been paid substantial commissions on a Cementation construction contract in Oman and on one part of the Al Yammamah contract in Saudi Arabia. Secondly he was alleged to have earned these commissions through having access to his mother, the Prime Minister, which in turn allegedly created, 'a conflict of interest situation'.

It has never been credibly suggested that Margaret Thatcher herself acted improperly in any situation or contract linked to her son. It is the job of the British Prime Minister 'to bat for Britain', as Margaret herself so often said. If her batting was better because of Mark's influence who was harmed or damaged? In the turbulent arena of fighting for or batting for international export contracts there is a world of difference between actual impropriety and allegations of impropriety by rivals, enemies or critics. Mark Thatcher was undoubtedly tarnished by the latter but both he and his mother have always been adamant that Mark had nothing to apologize for. Is this wilful blindness on the part of Thatcher *mère et fils* or could they be right and the *Observer*'s journalists wrong? Attempting detailed answers to these 1980s questions nearly a quarter of a century after the events is a pointless exercise. My personal view is that Mark Thatcher was vilified for who he was than for what he did. Because in the presence of curious strangers his insecurities can give him a curt and abrasive manner, he can appear dislikeable and therefore all the more attackable. Nevertheless there is a case for Mark Thatcher, and a different side to his character, which have largely gone unreported. In his commercial activities while his mother was Prime Minister, he was no saint, but he was far less of a sinner than his journalistic detractors would like to believe. I think he made his money honestly but paid a price of media scrutiny that portrayed him as venal. That judgement has been harsher on him than on any other comparable risk-taker among British businessmen operating in the Middle East in the 1980s.

Perhaps because I occasionally made public and private comments that were supportive of Mark Thatcher when he was under attack in the 1980s I returned to the No. 10 invitation list for dinners and receptions. At these events Margaret Thatcher began talking to me again with increasing friendliness which blossomed into a rekindling of our former warmth during one particularly testing episode of her Premiership.

In April 1985, President Reagan ordered the bombing of Colonel Gadaffi's military headquarters and security services buildings in Libya. The US Air Force F111 aircraft executing this operation, which was in response to Libyan terrorist attacks, needed to fly from USAF bases in Britain. The British government's consent for this was essential particularly as France, Spain and Germany refused the American request for overflying nights. Margaret Thatcher was herself initially cautious about granting the necessary consent, not least because British co-operation with the bombing of Libya was opposed by her own Foreign Secretary Sir Geoffrey Howe. Apparently the Foreign Office was concerned about the effect of British co-operation on world opinion, particularly on Arab opinion in the key capitals of the Middle East. In the middle of these still secret to-ings and fro-ings, the Prime Minister called me in to her room in the House of Commons to ask what I thought would be the effect of the use by the USAF of British bases upon the important decision-makers in Saudi Arabia, particularly on King Fahd whom I knew well.

My reply was that I thought the Saudis would criticize Britain publicly but would be far from unhappy privately to see Colonel Gadaffi punished for his terrorist adventures. There would be no change in British–Saudi trade or diplomatic relations, I predicted. As for King Fahd, who I knew had greatly resented some of Gadaffi's personal jibes at the Saudi monarchy, I offered the thought that the King's attitude to the Libyan leader's discomfiture might well be one of 'that young man needs his wings clipped'. In a more serious vein, I told the Prime Minister that if she did decide to authorize the use of UK bases for the F111 raids then I would support her publicly.

As it happened, my support came in handier and sooner than expected.

Immediately after the F111s bombed their targets in Tripoli, public opinion in Britain, let alone in the Middle East, was overwhelmingly hostile to Thatcher's decision. Even a number of normally sound Conservative MPs and newspaper editors were loud in their criticism of the F111 deployment from British bases. In the middle of this furore, I drew question No. 1 in the first Prime Minister's Questions after the Libyan air strike. Keeping my promise, I praised Margaret Thatcher for her 'difficult, courageous and right decision'. She sent me a generous note of thanks later that day, saying that she thought I had 'steadied the party at a difficult time'.

The steady support of Parliamentary and Cabinet colleagues should never be taken for granted by any Prime Minister. Like Lloyd George in the early 1920s Margaret Thatcher made this same mistake with increasing high-handedness in the late 1980s. At that time I was enjoying myself on the backbenches, rebelliously opposing many items of European legislation which the Thatcher government was forced to bring before the House at the behest of an increasingly bureaucratic and interventionist European Union. Perhaps the greatest misjudgement that Margaret Thatcher ever made was to allow herself to be pushed, against her instincts, into the Single European Act and membership of the Exchange Rate Mechanism as a result of heavy pressure from her Foreign Secretary Sir Geoffrey Howe and her Chancellor Nigel Lawson. Eventually there were signs that she was beginning to recognize her mistakes on the European issue. One such sign was her demotion of Howe from the Foreign Secretaryship to the high-sounding but largely powerless positions of Deputy Prime Minister and Leader of the House.

Thatcher underestimated the bitter resentment felt by Geoffrey Howe, and even more by his wife Elspeth, over his removal from the Foreign Office. His demotion meant the loss of the cherished job perks which go with the Foreign Secretaryship, particularly the week-end use of Chevening House in Kent, which the Howes adored. Thatcher nurtured a feline resentment of what she called 'Geoffrey and Elspeth holding court at Chevening'. The removal of this particular perk rankled. Howe became increasingly sympathetic to Michael Heseltine's tireless scavenging for support in the *salons de refusés* of disaffected Tory backbenchers. This unholy alliance of Howe's bitterness and Hesletine's plotting was to prove Thatcher's undoing.

I did not understand the lethal negativity of the Howe–Heseltine axis until the afternoon of Tuesday the 13 November 1990. I was in my usual place on the fourth row of the government backbenches below the gangway when suddenly Geoffrey Howe took a seat immediately in front of me. He had come there to make a statement explaining the reasons for his resignation from the Cabinet a few days earlier. As he rose to speak, it was clear that his real mission was to inflict maximum personal and political damage on the Prime Minister. It was the most poisonous speech I had ever heard during my 23 years in the House of Commons. My reactions to it were recorded for posterity because of what was known as 'doughnutting'. This was the practice, unintentional in my case, of squeezing into the same television frame as the speaker, in order to be filmed by the cameras.

As a result of this proximity to Howe my grimaces of horror mirrored his most offensive words of character assassination of the Prime Minister. As those frequently replayed television images show, I was close to being physically sick down the back of the ex-Foreign Secretary's neck as he moved to his peroration with the words 'the time has come for others to consider their own response to the tragic conflict of loyalties with which I have myself wrestled for perhaps too long'.

As Howe and Heseltine had so obviously planned, this attack on Thatcher set off an immediate conflict of disloyalties. Hezza threw his hat into the ring and all hell or rather all canvassing broke loose. To this day I do not fully understand the collective mood of madness that gripped the Tory party at Westminster in those extraordinary weeks of Lemming-like self-destruction in the autumn of 1990. As I said on BBC *Newsnight* on the evening when the Howe–Heseltine coup started, I could not believe that the greatest peace time Prime Minister of the twentieth century was going to be overthrown in a mood of backbench panic over the unpopularity of the poll tax. But I also could not believe two unforeseen developments in the unfolding drama – the treachery of Thatcher's Cabinet and the inefficiency of her campaign managers.

The first of these two fatal ingredients was exhaustively reported on at the time. The second was less well understood, partly because there was no point in playing the blame game among Thatcher's inner circle after her fall. Such finger pointing as did take place was largely directed against Peter Morrison MP. In his role of Parliamentary Private Secretary to the Prime Minister, he was responsible for the over-optimistic forecasts of 'definite' votes before the first ballot which created such misguided complacency in the Thatcher camp. Under the arcane rules of that electoral contest (in which 16 MPs abstained), Thatcher needed to win at least 206 votes from her colleagues to avoid a second ballot. In the event she scored 204 votes to Michael Heseltine's 152. For the want of two votes, a Prime Minister was destroyed.

The destruction was not immediately obvious. Immediately after the ballot Margaret Thatcher declared: 'I fight on – I fight on to win.' There were several MPs willing to reconsider their votes cast in the first ballot against Thatcher. The enormity of removing a sitting Prime Minister by the plottings of backbenchers rather than by the votes of the electorate was beginning to cause growing unease even among some of the plotters. If the Cabinet had stayed loyal there might have been a very different result in the second ballot. But the Cabinet was not loyal. Several senior ministers were longing to get rid of their boss. Where those ministers led, additional backbenchers prepared to follow. It was apparent that her support was haemorrhaging and that Thatcher was doomed.

Denis was one of the earliest to realize that Margaret's fate was sealed. 'Don't go on, love,' were his first words of advice to her after the ballot. As the realities of the reports from the front line confirmed his pessimism, Denis was effective in suppressing the fighting spirit of his wife and also in preparing their children for the end of her Premiership. One time when the Thatchers do function well as a family is when under attack. In a rare moment of tactility with Carol, Denis hugged her on a walk across Horse Guards Parade. 'He pushed up his glasses and I could see the tears in his eyes,' recalls Carol. 'It was the only time I have ever seen him cry.'

There were many tears shed among Thatcherites, including mine, during the next few days. Margaret Thatcher's departure from No. 10 was one of the saddest days of my political life, yet paradoxically it resulted in a big improvement in my personal relations with her. For she was well aware that during the leadership contest I was one of her most ardent supporters. She appreciated that Teddy Taylor MP and I had worked hard to firm up a large block of eurosceptic votes (we had over 40 reliable colleagues in the Conservative European Reform Group of MPs) which were delivered into the Thatcher camp, but, alas, in vain. When I met her a few days after her resignation I thought she was the unhappiest person I had seen in my entire life. Torn from the job she loved she was totally and utterly miserable. The concept of magnanimity in defeat was clearly alien to her, at least in private conversation. She ranted and railed against 'my betrayers' with a bitterness that was as sad as it was embarrassing. For her, the withdrawal symptoms from power were excruciatingly painful. She was going through the political equivalent of cold turkey and my heart went out to her.

The cold-turkey period was made more bearable by the devoted love and the financial support of her son Mark. One of his unsung virtues is kindness to people in trouble. For many years Mark had been an anonymous donor to individuals down on their luck, his surprised beneficiaries ranging from pensioners, hospital patients and deprived children to sportsmen who had problems that became known to him. Suddenly the individual in his life most out of luck and in trouble was his own mother. Recognizing the enormity of the gap in her life, Mark was generous with his time and care. This was important because life with Margaret Thatcher after she lost power was difficult. Denis and Carol saw the difficulties too, but they were much more down to earth about the emotional problems of an ex-Prime Minister. Mark, understanding that a time of healing was essential, gave his mother his filial empathy and sympathy with great love.

Mark was also practical in his help. 'Lots of people were around being extremely kind to Mum, but when it came to signing the necessary cheques and getting the things done that she most needed to get done I was the one who stepped up,' he says with justified pride. Mark's good deeds including paying for a lease on an office in Chesham Place, setting up the Thatcher Foundation and organizing the first major overseas speaking engagement for his mother. This was a mega one-off event in Dallas in March 1991. Mark's Texan contacts clubbed together to provide a speaking fee of $250,000 for the ex-Prime Minister. 'It gave my mother an enormous boost of confidence at a time when she was feeling very uncertain about her future,' said Mark, who continued to play a useful behind the scenes role in securing high fees for his mother in her new career on the international lecture circuit.

While all this was happening, John Major won the 1992 General Election and appointed me as his Minister of State for Defence. The strategic implications of my job were particularly challenging because almost every important decision on future equipment programmes centred on the question of the future military threat, or lack of it, from Russia. I asked Margaret Thatcher if I could come and talk to her about this strategic issue, not least because she was in touch with Gorbachev and some of his former advisers. It was a fascinating and illuminating discussion. Thatcher was still at the top of her game in assessing the various political and geopolitical factors that might cause a Russian resurgence as an aggressive power. 'The Bear may get hungry and angry towards its neighbours but not for a generation or two' was her conclusion. It made my future plans for defence equipment orders much easier.

At the end of our talk I said I would like to mention something rather personal. Taking a deep breath I began: 'We were last on our own together nearly 13 years ago, and I have often thought since that if we ever found ourselves in a one-on-one situation again then I would like to apologize to you. You see, I think I handled the break-up with Carol terribly badly. I am on good terms with her again but I know I made such a mess of things that I upset you too as her mother. So I just wanted you to know that I am very sorry for that.'

Margaret Thatcher looked totally stunned and was then visibly moved. Neither of us wanted to discuss what had just been said. So I took my leave quickly, anxiously wondering as I got into my ministerial car whether I had made a mistake in reopening, a painful memory. However, a week or two later Denis Thatcher came over to me at a large cocktail party and said as we shook hands: 'Thank you for what you said to Margaret the other day. She appreciated it a lot and so did I.' Between two somewhat inhibited Englishmen it was a moment of deep communication, confirmed by Denis's strong handshake.

Communications with Margaret Thatcher got better. For a period I was a regular guest at her drinks and dinner parties. Attending her seventieth birthday dinner (at which Jack Profumo sat between the Queen and Margaret Thatcher – a beautiful touch of kindness by the two great ladies), I had an amusing conversation with her on the unlikely subject of Psalm 90 verse 10 which says: 'The days of our age are three score years and ten and though some be so strong that they come to four score years, then is their strength only labour and sorrow . . .'

Bill Deedes had quoted this verse in his birthday toast but without attribution. Apparently thinking that these sentiments were from Bill rather than from the Bible, when Thatcher came to respond she gave Deedes a good handbagging in her speech along the lines of 'What's all this stuff and nonsense about labour and sorrow after three score years and ten?' Later in the evening when she was mingling with her guests I asked if she realized that the stuff and nonsense was a quotation. 'Who wrote it?' she demanded. 'King David – in the Psalms' was my answer. Margaret Thatcher, on the crest of her seventieth-birthday wave, could have been back at the despatch box at Prime Minister's Questions: 'Well, he got a lot of things wrong,' she retorted 'as Kings in the Middle East still do!'

Although she was good at off-the-cuff repartee, a sense of humour did not come high on the list of Margaret Thatcher's finest qualities. Jokes had to be explained to her, even by her speech writers before she delivered their best lines – often with incomprehension but usually with faultless timing. Despite, or perhaps because of, her blindness to humour, she could be the unconscious creator of richly comic scenes and situations. One that I cherish involved a furore Thatcher created over a major defence export order.

In 1993 when my responsibilities as Minister of State for Defence covered Britain's arms exports, a crisis arose over a Kuwaiti order for £1 billion worth of Warrior armoured cars made by GKN. The order had been announced and confirmed by the government of Kuwait, but just before the contract was due to be signed an American defence manufacturer put in a highly opportunistic counter-bid. Under the usual ground rules a new bid in such circumstances would never have been considered. But this particular American counter-bid was accompanied by extraordinary political lobbying which climaxed with a telephone call to the Kuwaiti Crown Prince from the US Vice President Al Gore and a personal letter to the Emir from President Clinton.

On learning that the British order was likely to be lost as a result of these pressures from the USA, I tried to organize some high-level British counter-lobbying in the hours before the Kuwaiti Cabinet met to review its decision. Unfortunately Prime Minister John Major was embroiled in a Maastricht treaty vote crisis and could not be persuaded to break away from it to make the telephone calls to Middle East potentates. So who else would carry weight with the Kuwaiti rulers? I decided to enlist the help of Margaret Thatcher. This was an unorthodox, indeed risky manoeuvre. Because of her increasingly critical views on the Maastricht treaty, the former Prime Minister was going through a period of chilly relations with her successor. Ignoring these tensions I went to see the Iron Lady at her house in Chester Square some 13 hours before the vital Kuwaiti Cabinet meeting was due to take place.

The action of the next 40 minutes was a marvellous demonstration of Thatcher power at its fiercest, funniest and most effective. As I recounted the sequence of events in the contract battle so far, my narrative was punctuated by a succession of explosive epithets from Margaret Thatcher: 'Outrageous!' 'Appalling!' 'Disgraceful!' and finally, 'I will not allow this!' Having aroused Queen Boadicea to wrath, my next move was to persuade her to charge at the right target. No such persuasion was required. The lady was for phoning. 'Do you have the Crown Prince of Kuwait's home telephone number?' she demanded. Fortunately I had and dialled it. Amazingly, Sheikh Jabr Al

Sabah answered the line himself. 'Your Highness, I am in Margaret Thatcher's house. She is right beside me and would like to speak to you about an urgent matter,' I began. 'Jonathan, you must be joking,' chuckled the bemused heir apparent. Before I could explain that jokes were not on the evening's agenda, Margaret Thatcher seized the receiver. In tones of rising passion she reminded the Crown Prince of the part Britain had played in the liberation of Kuwait and of his pledge that Britain would get its fair share of the armed forces re-equipment programme. She also reminded him that debts of honour were debts of honour, and that only a month or so ago he had personally assured her that Britain had won the armoured vehicle competition.

'Now what I want to know is: do Kuwaitis keep their promises?' The answer was apparently less than satisfactory. 'Your Highness, I do not like what I am hearing. Let me ask you again. Do Kuwaitis keep their promises? Are you going to keep your word or break your word?'

'I'm beginning to feel a bit sorry for this chappie,' observed Sir Denis *sotto voce* as he sipped his gin and tonic . . . His sympathy was evidently not shared by his spouse. Her decibels rose as she enlarged on her strong feelings to the Crown Prince. 'So what exactly are you going to do at your Cabinet meeting tomorrow?' she crescendoed. 'You are not going to run away from your responsibilities, are you?'

I was beginning to wonder whether my bright idea would provoke a major diplomatic incident in Anglo-Kuwaiti relations when sweetness and light broke out. 'Thank you so much, Your Highness. I knew you would be a man of your word,' I heard Margaret Thatcher coo in dulcet tones.

'He was wobbly, but he'll be all right,' she declared as she put down the receiver. 'Now I must sort out the Americans. Let's get Al Gore on the line.' I confessed that my skills as an impromptu switch-board operator did not include carrying around the telephone number of the Vice President of the USA. 'Well then, get Robin Renwick. He'll know it.' The number of the British Ambassador in Washington was not at my fingertips either.

Margaret Thatcher was in no mood to be thwarted by these petti-fogging obstructions. 'Then I must speak to Ray Seitz at once. He must be made to order the Clinton Administration to stop their dirty tricks immediately.' With some difficulty I tracked down the Ambassador of the USA to the Court of St James, only to be told by the butler at the US Embassy Residence in Regent's Park that His Excellency was unavailable to come to the telephone because 'he was having a shower'. For the second time Margaret Thatcher seized the receiver from me. 'This is Margaret Thatcher. Please tell Ambassador Seitz that I will hold on until he comes out of the shower.'

The butler did not argue with these orders and apparently delivered them to the Ambassador's bathroom, for a couple of minutes later a presumably wet and dripping Raymond Seitz came to the telephone to receive a broadside, from which he escaped only by promising to pass on a 'back off' message to Washington immediately

Justifiably pleased though she was by her evening's work, Margaret Thatcher had not quite finished. 'Now, our last task tonight is to tell the Prime Minister exactly what's been happening. I'd like him to know that I can still bat for Britain.' I said I would tell John Major about all the boundaries his predecessor had scored in the morning. That was not good enough. 'A Prime Minister likes to know these things at once. Do it now!' was the command. With some trepidation, I rang No. 10 and was relieved to be told that the Prime Minister could not be disturbed. 'And perhaps it might be wiser not to disturb him at all on this one,' murmured the well-trained private secretary. 'Let's take stock in the morning.' I agreed with alacrity to this proposition.

By the time we got round to taking stock the following morning in Whitehall, the Cabinet in Kuwait had approved the final details of the armoured vehicle contract and authorized the Defence Minister to sign it in the British Embassy. So GKN got its £1 billion order and the Warrior subsequently performed superbly both in the snows of Bosnia and in the sands of Kuwait. Britain had achieved a great export success – but we would never have done it without Margaret Thatcher.

Unfortunately Margaret Thatcher was not often invited to bat for Britain during the years after she left No. 10 Downing Street. Nor was she much asked to play for the Conservative party at home. Her growing opposition to British Policy towards the European Union and her criticism of the government's policy in Bosnia made her an uncertain ally of the Prime Minister she had backed to follow her. There were times when Thatcher's mood of sourness towards her successor became almost as acidic as Ted Heath's attitude to his replacement. However, there was one important difference between these two ex-Prime Ministers. Heath's sulkiness was motivated by personal pique: Thatcher's unhelpfulness was driven by political passion. Moreover, while Heath let the whole world know about his dislike of Thatcher, Thatcher spoke only privately of her reservations about the policies of John Major. The distinction was not as obvious as it should have been because the reservations were too often leaked by mischief-makers. But on the whole, Thatcher tried to play the role of ex-Prime Minister with dignity and fairness. She let her true feelings show only in the privacy of country houses and dinner parties from which her fulminations should not have been conveyed to newspapers.

Two country houses where I saw a good deal of Margaret Thatcher in her retirement years were Rannoch Barracks in Perthshire, owned by the Eurosceptic crusader Lord Pearson, and Rest Harrow in Sandwich Bay, the home of Julian Seymour who was head of Thatcher's private office from 1993 to 2000. Although neither the sporting life of the Scottish highlands nor the beach life of the English channel were naturally congenial diversions for the former Prime Minister, I have good memories of her in both establishments as an enthusiastic and participatory guest. At the Barracks, where Malcolm Pearson arranged a panoply of events and expeditions, from lakeside picnics to mountain climbs by Argo,[3] Thatcher showed a good appetite not only for the local venison, grouse and malt whisky but also for in depth briefings from the local lairds, stalkers and ghillies on the finer points of deer conservation, cattle feeding, trout stocking, Munro bagging and Highland estate management. After one day on the hills spent grilling all those sources of local knowledge, she settled down by a roaring fire and allowed herself to be quizzed for nearly two hours by four teenage boys, including my 16-year-old son William, who were staying in the house. A mutual admiration society had been formed by the end of the evening, with Thatcher declaring that her interlocutors were much brighter than backbenchers at Prime

Minister's Questions and a member of her schoolboy fan club announcing that she was the greatest Englishwoman since Queen Elizabeth the First.

Margaret Thatcher may have enjoyed this youthful interrogation because she so much missed the cut and thrust of political debate. Her visits to country houses were sometimes an escape route from the frustration she felt at being out of office. Occasionally that frustration boiled over. When staying one weekend with Julian and Diana Seymour, she and Denis came over to lunch at my home at Sandwich Bay which was a few hundred yards along the beach. What should have been an amicable Sunday lunch turned into a verbal punch-up. I was in the Cabinet at the time and Margaret Thatcher was in a mood to attack the Major government's policy towards former Yugoslavia. 'Handbagging' was much too gentle a word to describe her onslaught. She tilted her lance and charged. I did my best to deflect her blows by defending the government's position but this annoyed her so much that she worked herself up into a rage, firing salvoes like 'are you ministers so weak that you are going to twiddle your thumbs while the Serbs inflict genocide?' The going got so rough that Denis eventually broke the silence into which all the other guests had fallen with the quiet command: 'Cut it out, girl!' Amazingly she did, making an abrupt and barely polite exit a few minutes later. After her departure our housekeeper Jean Wildin said to me: 'Lady Thatcher is really scary! I was shaking like a leaf as I handed round the vegetables and it wasn't me she was attacking!'

Thatcher's aggressive style was not meant, nor in my case was it taken, to be a form of personal attack. She was not a bully. She gave no quarter in the ferocity of her argument but she only took on those she thought were strong enough to stand up for themselves. In government, weak or ill-prepared ministers often felt the rough edge of her tongue, as did underperforming civil servants. But they were legitimate targets for a Prime Minister's wrath. She respected those who had the courage of their convictions, however unfairly she bombarded them with arguments from her own fortified position as a conviction politician. In that row with me over Bosnia she went completely over the top with some of her more aggressive statements, so much so that an inexperienced Thatcher watcher (several of whom were present) could easily have concluded that the two of us would never speak to each other again. But without a word of apology, which was never her style anyway, she was back in touch within a couple of weeks' time as though nothing had happened. It was just part of her nature to be ferocious one moment and friendly the next. She was not an easy character but she was a remarkable one – personally as well as politically.

Margaret Thatcher was also capable of remarkable kindnesses. I was the beneficiary of this little-known side of her character at the time when my career fell into deep trouble and again when I came out of prison.

Following my resignation from the Cabinet in 1995 I knew that I would face a tough fight to get re-elected. Quite apart from my personal difficulties, I took a far more pessimistic view of the general Conservative prospects in the 1997 election that most of my colleagues did. Over a drink with Margaret Thatcher several weeks before the campaign I predicted (alas, all too accurately) that Labour would gain about 200 seats and that mine would be one of them. Thatcher said I was being far too pessimistic but then added 'But you know your patch very well. Is there anything I can do to help?'

As a result of this generous offer a Thatcher walkabout in my constituency took place on the Saturday before polling day followed by a Thatcher public meeting at the biggest hall in Ramsgate. It was a huge success. Large crowds greeted her in the streets and in the hall she was cheered to the rafters for a rip-roaring speech, one part of which became so passionately eurosceptic that it stopped only just short of advocating a complete renegotiation of Britains' membership of the European Union! One way and another Margaret Thatcher could not have done more to improve my chances of re-election, but in the polling night landslide where 15 per cent swings to Labour became the norm across South East England I did not survive.

Losing my Thanet seat was the first of a series of personal catastrophes which became a downward spiral into defeat, disgrace, divorce, bankruptcy and jail. Nevertheless, within days of my release from prison Margaret Thatcher was making solicitous enquiries about me in a telephone call to her former Parliamentary Private Secretary Michael Alison. As a result of that call, a dinner party was arranged in Michael and Sylvia Mary Alison's home in Chelsea. The only guests were Sir Denis and Lady Thatcher, General Sir Michael Rose (an Alison cousin) and myself. Both Thatchers enveloped me with a warmth of friendship that was unprecedented in the 25 years I had known them. Margaret said at one point, 'You have paid a very high price for one foolish mistake. Now we must all rally round and help you rebuild your life.'

I do not know whether Margaret Thatcher co-ordinated a series of family initiatives as a follow-through to that remark or whether the events of the next few weeks were just coincidences involving Denis, Mark and Carol. The first member of the family to get in touch was Mark. I was surprised when he called up to say: 'I've been thinking a lot about you. Can I help? Would you like to have lunch?'

Over that lunch in a Knightsbridge restaurant, Mark poured out the milk of human kindness. Was there anything he could do? Did I need money? Would I like to have a get-away-from-it-all holiday in his guest house in Constantia outside Cape Town? He would send me the air tickets and guarantee my privacy.

For family reasons I did not want to travel abroad at this time so I could not go to South Africa but I mentioned that my efforts to earn a living as an author were being disturbed by the chaos of having to move out of my home. Mark immediately offered me the loan of office space, a secretary and a computer. I did borrow the computer which was a great help.

These kindnesses were not confined to one lunch. Mark twice wrote to me repeating his invitation of an all expenses paid holiday in Cape Town. He called several times to find out how I was bearing up. We met again, at his suggestion, for no reason other than for him to offer more help. His offers were not taken up but they were greatly appreciated. I was touched by his genuine compassion, which had no hidden agenda. There was only one explanation for it. Mark Thatcher, for all his outward brusqueness and occasional surliness can be a very kind man.

Like father, like son. Some time after these contacts with Mark an unexpected voice called my telephone number. 'Denis Thatcher here,' it said. 'Would you do me the honour of joining me for lunch at my club?'

A few days later we were sitting in 'DT's corner' of the bar of London's exclusive East India club. A couple of two large sniffers before lunch and a bottle of claret on the table during it reduced the barriers of shyness between host and guest. To prepare myself for the encounter, I had glanced through an inscribed copy of *Below the Parapet*, Carol's biography of her father. I mentioned this. 'Never read it,' said Denis. 'Why Not? It's very good,' I replied. 'Oh well . . . it's just I don't like reading about myself. Not my style.' I told him he would enjoy Carol's filial portrait which was fond and favourable. 'By George, you do surprise me,' he said with a fervour which suggested that Thatcher dysfunctionalism must be flourishing. As if to change the subject, he asked how I was getting on in my post prison life. 'I suppose going through all this has made you realize who your friends are,' he observed. 'Yes,' I answered, 'and one unexpected friend who's been astonishingly kind to me is Mark.' 'The boy Mark?' said Denis sounding rather startled. 'Tell me more.'

So I told him. Suddenly the atmosphere at our corner table over-looking St James' Square became emotional. My host took out a blue silk handkerchief, blew his nose loudly on it two or three times, and took off his glasses to wipe his eyes. 'Mark's made his mistakes and he can be a complete b.f. at times but the boy's got a heart of gold, God bless him,' declared Denis, raising his glass. 'You've seen a part of him that few people have spotted. It comes out best in the way he looks after his mother.'

Looking after mother has not been Carol's forte. Towards other people, she too can have a heart of gold as I found when she poured warmth and kindness over me after I came out of prison. Yet greatly as I enjoyed the generosity of spirit that flowed in my direction from Carol during my post-release summer of 2000, I was simultaneously worried by how little of that same spirit was flowing towards members of her family. Resentments and rows were the main charac-teristics on her side of those relationships. The resentments were mostly to do with money. In Carol's eyes, Mark was her parents' favourite, seen as the palm-outstretched recipient of an overly large slice of the inheritance cake. Mark himself strenuously denies this: 'In everything they have given away to us my parents have been even handed, in fact they have favoured Carol,' he told me. Carol does not accept this and has made her feelings known loud and clear. After one recent clash with Margaret, Carol stormed out of the house in Chester Square shouting: 'Lady Thatcher you were a great Prime Minister but you are an awful mother!' Scenes like this confirm the trend of the mixed feelings between the exasperated matriarch and the belligerent daughter. If anything their emotional sores seem to be festering rather than healing. In 2004 Carol became openly contemptuous over her mother's decision to bail Mark out from house arrest in South Africa over his alleged involvement in the foiled coup attempt in Equatorial Guinea. The episode deepened their estrangement. In December 2005 it was widely reported that Margaret Thatcher had a fainting fit while at her hairdresser. In fact, as insiders knew, her collapse was caused not by fainting but by a stroke. Mark rushed to his mother's hospital bedside. Carol, although in London at the time, stayed away. She was also away from Chester Square over the Christmas that followed the stroke. One way and another Carol's alienation from her mother is now almost as bad as her alienation from her brother. This seems sad, particularly to someone who knows as well as I do that all three surviving Thatchers are full of likeable qualities that include great generosity and compassion – except it would sometimes appear towards each other as a family unit.

Denis died in 2003. His last words: 'How kind – but then you always were,' came as a farewell murmur to Mark who had made characteristically caring efforts to ensure that his father's last days were comfortable. The obituaries and other tributes lauded Denis as if he was a national treasure and hero. It was a status he deserved.

Carol, for all her problems with her nearest and dearest, deserves her new status as a TV icon, 'Queen of the Jungle'. Until this victory she had been undervalued as a personality, as a public speaker and as a powerful force in her own right. As soon as I heard she had entered ITV's bizarre world of *I'm a Celebrity Get Me Out of Here* I was sure she would carry off the victor's laurels. Accordingly I bet on her when her odds were 33–1. My confidence in her prospects came from knowing her character. The Carol I have long admired may be more vulnerable and volatile in her private emotions than the world knows. But in any kind of public arena she is tough and tenacious. The grit in the oyster that made her a winner is her gutsy, earthy stubbornness. Perhaps it might be said that she has inherited something of the Thatcher courage. Mark has acquired his share of it, too, as his stoicism in the face of unfair media vilification shows. And in their different ways Margaret and Denis personified this greatest of virtues.

So for all the ups, downs and dysfunctionalties in their family life the celebrated iron in the Iron Lady was shared by all four Thatchers. So were some of her failings. Perhaps these same qualities made it so difficult for them to get along together. None of the Thatchers are easy people. Yet all of them have strengths and weaknesses, convictions and compassion that have made them one of No. 10 Downing Street's most intriguing families of the twentieth century.

Notes

1   Peter Morrison, MP for Chester 1974–92, was the first backbench Tory MP to approach Margaret Thatcher with the suggestion that she should challenge Ted Heath in 1975 for the leadership of the Conservative party. He was later appointed Parliamentary Private Secretary to the Prime Minister.

2   The result of the first ballot among MPs in the Tory leadership election of the 4 February 1975 was Margaret Thatcher 130 votes, Ted Heath 119, Hugh Fraser 16.

3   An Argo is a rubber-wheeled motor vehicle, much used in the Highlands of Scotland, suitable for climbing in rocky or boggy mountain terrain.

CHAPTER 8

Sir Frank Williams

'Your Royal Highness, Frank Williams is the most determined man I have ever met.' 'Why do you say that?' 'Because of the way he waits to see you.'

This symbolic dialogue I had with the Saudi Arabian Prince whose backing transformed the fortunes of the Williams Formula One racing team took place long before Frank Williams won his first Grand Prix. The iron determination I had spotted in the intensity of his waiting outside Arab offices and palaces (sometimes for days at a time) in the mid-1970s was but a small sample of the same extraordinary qualities that drove Williams to become a legendary winner and record breaker on the fastest track in the world – F1 racing. Determination also enabled him to beat death after a car accident that would have killed almost anyone else; to fight back from his shattering injuries; and to achieve greater Formula 1 triumphs and personal honours in his past 20 years of life as a paralysed quadriplegic than he achieved in his first 44 years as a super-fit entrepreneur and motor racing legend.

Inside the jealous world of F1 competitors there are Williams watchers who say that his dedication to being a race winner has made him an emotional loser. He has been pejoratively described as 'robotically inhuman', 'the coldest of cold fish', 'utterly impersonal' and 'incapable of having a human relationship'. Frank Williams would probably regard such negative sound bites as positive marks of success in keeping his personal feelings well behind a wall of privacy. Yet I have been on the other side of this wall enough to know that journalistic portrayals of Williams as a cold and unemotional stoic are not the whole story. To me, he is a quintessentially English hero. Steeped in old-fashioned virtues such as loyalty, generosity and patriotism, he thinks that doing the impossible is normal and being reticent about it is essential. The complexity of his mind is hidden by the intensity of his discipline. His need for privacy masks the magnitude of his legacy. His pain is no less real for being concealed behind a mask of endurance. Naturally he did not like the idea of a chapter about him appearing in any book, let alone one with this title, but because we go back a long time together, he gave me his co-operation. The result, I hope, is a fascinating portrait of the deeper Frank Williams.

The upbringing of the young Frank would probably intrigue child psychiatrists. But the boy turned the negatives of an unloved childhood into life-enhancing positives. His early emotional deprivation developed into later career dedication. Parental neglect was the spur to self-motivating success. Tough schoolmasters produced a much tougher school leaver, and a lonely childhood was transformed into a gregarious young adulthood. From his earliest years Frank Williams was full of surprises.

The first unpleasant surprise came when Frank's father, Owen Williams, an RAF squadron leader piloting Wellington bombers, left his wife just as their only son was born in April 1942. Unable to connect with his father, the boy was also strangely disconnected from his mother. She was a respected teacher of mentally handicapped children whose dedication to her pupils does not seem to have included giving comparable love and attention to her son. For at the age of 4, Frank was sent to his first boarding school, a convent in Liverpool. From then on he was shipped around the homes of grandparents, uncles and aunts, making only occasional visits to his mother who had become deputy head teacher at Dumpton Park school in Broadstairs. She was an austere woman whose priority for Frank was education, so she made considerable financial sacrifices to send him away to a Catholic boarding school in Scotland. This was St Josephs College, Dumfries.

The monastic regime of St Joseph's imposed on its pupils a spartan zeal which inculcated into Frank the spirit of 'never give up' drive which dominated his early years in motor racing. The ethos of the school emphasized religious faith, ascetic lifestyle and classroom discipline. The faith was the least important to Frank although today he says: 'I still believe it all even though I don't practise it.' The asceticism was responsible for his obsession with physical fitness, his lifelong teetotalism and his seven-days-a-week work ethic. The discipline was harshly enforced by the Marist brothers who ran St Josephs. Frank remembers them as 'frequent wielders of a three-pronged leather strap who took no prisoners'. However, their mixture of corporal punishment, cold baths (the school was without hot running water until the mid 1950s) and muscular Christianity somehow resulted in a good international education. For the Marists were from several different nationalities, and they taught their subjects thoroughly, particularly languages. Frank emerged from St Josephs speaking French and Italian fluently, and German competently, and was near the top of his class in Latin. These linguistic skills served him well when he began moving around the motor racing circuits of Europe.

During his schooldays Frank became obsessively interested in cars. Part of his obsession was fuelled by avid reading of two weekly magazines, *Autocar* and *The Motor*, whose contents he often knew by heart. Another part resulted from hitch-hiking rides in various different makes of cars on his long journeys from school in Scotland to his mother's home on the Kent coast. Saving his money from the train fare was secondary to the pleasure he derived from travelling in a variety of vehicles on the 400-mile journey. His most thrilling experience was a ride in the outstanding sports car of the 1950s, a Jaguar XK150S owned by a prosperous bookmaker. The drive, he said, left him 'speechless with excitement'. From then on he was 'absolutely nuts about fast cars', getting a grounding in how their engines worked from a motor mechanic in Ramsgate, a mile or so down the road from his mother's school.

Frank's own schooldays ended ingloriously but interestingly. He failed all his A levels yet won three Higher Entry level certificates which qualified him for a place at a Scottish university. These confusing results perhaps indicated that when he wanted to work at a subject he did well at it. However, he was not interested in higher education so he said no to university. In the greatest disappointment of his youth the army said no to him when he applied for a place at Sandhurst. After that rejection he was out on his own in the big wide world with the valedictory words of his favourite schoolmaster Brother Cazimir (who taught him his excellent Italian) ringing in his ears: 'Williams, you may think you're a clever dodger, but we've seen through you.'

Clever dodging was a fair description of Frank's life for the next few years. His first job was to be a management trainee for Cripps Brothers, a Rootes Main Dealer in Nottingham. After six months in the body shop and another six months in the truck shop he was certainly learning about life at the axle grease end of the motor trade but he was fired for playing truant from the classes his traineeship required him to attend at Nottingham Technical College. Another trainee job that kept body and soul together by paying him £10 a week was as a travelling sales representative for Campbells Soup. The Ford Anglia car the company gave him was useful but the lifestyle was uncongenial. Visiting food stores wearing the required formal attire of suit and bowler hat was not the occupation Frank had in mind. He wanted to be where his heart was, driving on the motor racing circuit, which he had fallen in love with after going as a 16-year-old to the 1958 British Grand Prix at Silverstone.

By the time he was 19, Frank had scraped together the money to buy his first car for club racing. It was a battered Austin A35 whose engine had been race-tuned by Speedwell Conversions. This was a motorsport company owned by Graham Hill, a rising star among Grand Prix drivers. His infant son Damon, who would one day win the world championship in a Williams F1 car, had just been born.

Frank entered his car for a 1500cc touring car race at Mallory Park near Leicester in July 1961. He crashed it at Gerards, a long right-hand bend on the circuit a few seconds after another young amateur driver with the same surname had rolled his car over the same bank. He was Jonathan Williams who later in the afternoon introduced his namesake to a third young competitor. This was a 20-year-old Old Etonian, Piers Courage, who was to become Frank's closest friend and first Grand Prix driver. The rapport between Jonathan Williams, Frank Williams and Piers Courage took off with instant combustion. Jonathan initially thought Frank was 'a right lunatic' but that was on the basis of his driving, for when he got into conversation, 'I could tell right away that Frank was just like the rest of us. A perfect fit. We were all mad on motor racing. We would rather not have eaten if it meant going somewhere and racing something. We hadn't got much money – and Frank had even less.'

A few months later Frank Williams abandoned his never-very-promising career with the bowler hat at Campbell Soups and became a fully participating member of the Jonathan Williams–Piers Courage set. These two shared a flat in Chelsea as well as a passion for motor racing. Although he was a few steps below the two flat mates on life's financial and social ladders, Frank was their equal if not their superior in the passion of his commitment to speed. So they bonded as a triumvirate. One of the first practical manifestations of that bond was when the two Williams namesakes set off on a gypsy-like tour of Europe's motor racing circuits in 1963. Jonathan, financed by his father, owned a Lotus 22 race car which he strapped on the top of a Volkswagen camper van. Frank was the 'mechanic' of this two-man team, although only in the loosest sense of the word, since according to Jonathan: 'He was hopeless. He didn't know a piston from a piece of tin. He would pick up a spanner and if you were lucky he would go to the correct end of the car.'

Despite his inadequacy as a mechanic, Frank had a dream summer as Jonathan's companion. The two excited young men spent five months on the road travelling each week to different European race tracks from Trieste to Trondheim. Start money of around £100 per race kept them afloat. Sleeping rough underneath the Volkswagen camper, they were often uncomfortable but always happy. Frank's language skills were a bonus and so were the new skills he was developing as an entrepreneur. For as he mixed with continental motor racing enthusiasts, many of them rich young men with money to burn on their sport, Frank found he could offer them a service of getting quick delivery of spare parts for their Lotus, Lola, Cooper and other British made cars in the Formula Junior class. In this way he began building a network of contacts which later enabled him to create his first serious business in motor sport spare parts.

Eventually in that summer of 1963 the money ran out and the broke but exhilarated duo of Williamses had to come home. But the experience had kindled the sparks of Frank's enthusiasm for motor racing into a blazing fire that would never be quenched. On one of the last stops of the tour, in Sicily, he found himself gazing out at the circuit at the end of the day's racing saying to himself: 'One day I'll be back, with a team of my own.'

Returning to London, Frank Williams joined a different sort of team. It was a motor-racing obsessed group of young men who at various times shared a ground floor flat at 283 Pinner Road, Harrow. Frank slept on the sofa paying the smallest share of the rent. He was much poorer than his posh new flatmates like Piers 'Porridge' Courage, Charlie Crichton-Stuart, Jonathan Williams and Anthony 'Bubbles' Horsley. Yet despite his poverty and his Geordie accent, Frank was totally accepted as one of the gang on account of his infectious enthusiasm and passionate commitment to the sport they all loved. Even so, Frank felt an outsider. There were times when he fell so far behind in paying the rent for the sofa, that in embarrassment he moved out for weeks at a time. 'I had so little money that I had to live as a bit of a vagabond,' he says. This meant going hungry, sleeping in the back of a borrowed Morris 12cwt diesel van and dodging his creditors. On one occasion when he was totally skint, Frank became so desperate that he broke into a friend's house who was away and 'burgled' some food. Eventually the Williams determination saw him through these tough times as he gradually built up his business of supplying British spare parts and later British racing cars to European motor sport enthusiasts. By 1966 Frank Williams (Racing Cars) Limited was becoming a serious business with its own workshop premises on the Bath Road outside Slough.

Although he was delighted to be making ends meet behind the counter in business, Frank Williams still yearned for success behind the wheel in motor racing. He actually won an F3 race at Knutsdorp in Sweden, but despite this one-off victory he was slowly getting the message that he did not have what it takes to be a championship driver. In one big race, the Coppo D'Oro Pasquale Amato at Caserta he was given this message loud and clear. Driving what *Autosport* described as 'an unstable looking Cooper', Frank came last. In the final stages he had to endure the humiliation of being lapped by the race winner, Piers Courage, who when overtaking his flatmate weaved his

Brabham from one side of the track to the other in the style of a jubilant Spitfire pilot making a victory roll.

This dashing, if dangerous, manoeuvre in the middle of an F3 race was typical of 23-year-old Piers Courage. Debonair, charming and brave, he was both a talented driver and a magnetic personality. As it happens, I knew Piers or 'Porridge' Courage rather well in his teens since he was my classmate at school. Full of fun, flamboyance and *joie de vivre* in the private company of his friends, he was paradoxically unhappy as a public schoolboy, perhaps because he was too much of an individualist to fit in with the herd instinct of 1950s Eton. More surprisingly he was unhappy in the family business, Courage Brewery, chaired by his father. To considerable paternal disappointment, Piers decided to quit his accountancy training and the golden road to the Courage boardroom. Instead his individualism took him into the impecunious, hazardous, but more exciting life of full-time motor racing. It was his dedication to that life which brought him close to the equally dedicated Frank Williams.

At first it was not a social closeness. Although the two 24-year-olds got on well together, often sharing five-shilling dinners at a Turkish café in Shepherds Bush, Frank was awed by Piers' background and social standing. The distance between them was accentuated, so Frank thought, when Piers married one of the most beautiful models of the 1960s, Lady Sarah Curzon, daughter of Earl Howe. Their marriage, colourfully reported in the gossip columns, took place at Holy Trinity, Brompton, Knightsbridge, on the 29 March 1966, with a glittering attendance of society guests, wedding photographs by Patrick Lichfield and a champagne reception afterwards at Searcy's in 30 Pavilion Road. Although Frank knew both Piers and Sally well, the outsider complex in him produced an attack of social nerves. 'I was there but I didn't come into the church,' he recalled. 'I hung about outside. I was just too shy to come in.'

The shyness evaporated when the bridgegroom and the nervous wedding guest were reunited just three days after the marriage ceremony at Oulton Park for the first F3 race of the season. The weather was appalling and the race had to be cancelled but not before Piers had qualified for second place on the starting grid. 'A good

165

driver is always best in wet conditions,' recalled Frank. 'I saw from his quick reactions and his car control that he was developing into a formidable talent.'

That talent was beginning to be recognized by others, as Piers had offers from several teams which resulted in him having entrances, exits and crashes in both F1 and F2 races in 1966–67. But there were many more disappointments than successes and by the summer of 1967, the Courage career was in danger of stalling. It was put back on the map by Frank Williams. He was doing well in business. Frank Williams (Racing Cars) Limited was now turning over £200,000 a year from its Slough premises, selling cars as well as spare parts. Having become an unofficial agent for Brabham, Frank had acquired its 1968 F3 prototype and he needed a driver to showcase it at the high-profile last race of the season, the Motor Show 2000 at Brands Hatch. He persuaded Piers to drive for him, which was not easy as it meant a come-down from F1 racing. 'Piers' F1 future was looking very bleak so I offered him a plan to re-establish his confidence and his career by winning the Motor Show race,' recalls Williams.

The plan worked. Although Piers Courage did not actually win the race in the new BT21B owing to water getting into the car's electrics, he performed brilliantly, winning the qualifying round and beating the F3 lap record for Brands Hatch. It was a good debut for Frank Williams as a racing manager and for the new combination of Courage and Williams. Fired up with enthusiasm they agreed to do a programme of F2 races together.

During the 1968 season Piers did not win a race for Frank in F2 but his performances were fast and consistent. The team was building up a reputation for thorough preparation and elegant presentation. The thoroughness came from the meticulous attention to detail applied to the car and its engine by Frank and by his outstanding New Zealand mechanic Johnny Muller. The elegance came from the charisma of Piers, the beauty of his much-photographed wife Sally and Frank's stylish touches to the team's dark blue Brabham, such as equipping it with gold plated fuel injection trumpets.

Impressed by the rising profile of the Williams team, the organizers of the 1969 Tasman race series offered Frank £6,000 if he and Piers would make the trip to Australia and New Zealand. They jumped at it. With the help of a Belfast businessman Derek Mackie, Frank got together the money to by a Brabham BT26 car for £3,500 and two Cosworth V8 engines for £7,500 each. The Cosworths were 3-litre capacity engines for Formula 1 racing but they could be adapted to the 2.5-litre capacity required by the Tasman rules. There was no technical reason why they could not be adapted back again to full 3-litre F1 power.

As the Tasman car was being assembled in the Slough workshop of Frank Williams (Racing Cars) Limited, it dawned on one junior employee that the team had in place all the ingredients for Grand Prix Racing. This employee was Frank's secretary, Norma Robb. While she was making toast and coffee for her boss in his flat above the workshop one November morning, she suddenly said, 'I don't know why you don't do F1?' 'Norma, I think you're right,' replied Frank Williams. It was the moment of birth for Williams F1.

It did not require much effort from Frank to persuade Piers Courage to become his Formula 1 driver. Paying for a new Grand Prix Racing Team was harder work. But the entrepreneurial Frank was something of a lateral thinker. Back in the 1960s, motor racing was dominated by self-funding works teams like Lotus, Brabham and Ferrari. Commercial sponsorship was in its infancy, as were cash injections from trade suppliers. Frank broke new ground by getting a tyre deal with Dunlop worth £10,000 and an oil deal from Castrol for £2,000. The biggest sponsor of all was a machine tool manufacturing company T. W. Ward. Its owner Ted Williams was sold the idea of associating his firm's products with Formula 1 and bringing his customers to Grand Prix races. This was pioneering work by Frank Williams whose money-raising successes alerted the rest of the Grand Prix world to the huge potential of sponsorship from businesses with no direct interest in motor racing.

Among all his frenetic business deals and racing car preparations at the premises of Frank Williams (Racing Cars) Limited there was a personal development in his life. At the time when it began in December 1967, it could easily have been dismissed as 'another of Frank's flings'. This was the relationship he embarked on with Ginny Sawyer-Hoare, the lady who seven years later became Mrs Frank

Williams. Ginny, a young married woman when the romance began, had fallen in love with Frank at first sight. Frank, who played the field with many girlfriends throughout the swinging sixties, treated her rather casually at first. He was too wrapped up in his business to consider any sort of serious romantic involvement. Although Ginny soon realized that women came a long way behind cars in Frank's life, she was besotted with him, enchanted by his infectious energy, his charm, his lean physique, his self-discipline and perhaps above all by his dedicated perfectionism. This last quality was single-mindedly applied to every aspect of his team manager–driver partnership with Piers Courage as they prepared for their debut in Grand Prix racing.

The Williams team made its first appearance in a World Championship race at the Spanish Grand Prix on the 5 May 1969. There was considerable press interest in the two 27-year-old British buccaneers who were bursting on to the stage of international motor racing. An article in the *Daily Telegraph*, published on the eve of the race, caught the chemistry between them: 'Piers Courage strides by in a light suede cowboy jacket looking young and unruffled,' reported the paper. 'Frank Williams in a blue blazer looks worried and is beginning to lose his hair. He smiles now and again.'

The same article quoted Frank as saying: 'My ambition is to win. I have terrific faith in Piers and we have a fabulous relationship. The racing has strangled my business because I've put all my money into it. But I want to do it better than anyone else. I'm not sure what I'll be doing in two years' time but whatever it is I'll be trying to make money. I need money to succeed.'

He was right to be emphasizing the need for money, for Frank describes his financial position at the start of the season as 'wickedly precarious'. It was not improved by a bad result in the Spanish Grand Prix. Piers Courage had to abandon the race, pulling into the pits after 19 laps because of engine trouble with his BT26 Brabham. But the perfectionist Frank, now aided by three mechanics, went to work to iron out the snags in good time for the next Grand Prix at Monaco, where the team had an unexpected breakthrough.

The Monaco race, with its punishing course through the streets of the Principality round devilish hairpins, chicanes and adverse cambers, is the toughest of tests for both cars and drivers. Piers Courage, presciently equipped by Frank with unbreakable driveshafts and reinforced fuel tanks, had a car which could take the punishment and he drove it brilliantly. The most exciting feature of the race was Courage's 40-lap duel with the Belgian Jackie Ickx for second place. It was a thrilling contest nose to nose with first one car and then the other inching ahead as the crowd roared their appreciation. In the pits Frank Williams could barely contain his excitement as a third place result would have been spectacular for the new team. He began to worry that the duel was getting too exciting so he held up a sign to Piers 'P3-OK' meaning in effect, ease off, third place is good enough. 'I didn't want him to mix it and crash,' recalled Frank; 'we wanted to get good solid results and points.'

Before Piers had time to obey these instructions Jackie veered off the track just ahead of the tunnel when his rear chassis snapped. So the unknown young Williams team found themselves in a safe second place, too far behind the race leader Graham Hill to catch up but well ahead of the rest of the pack. All Piers had to do was to keep his nerve and his speed for the next 31 laps, which he did through gritted teeth as he was in acute pain from foot cramp. Even though he had to hobble up to the royal box for a handshake with Prince Ranier, he was ecstatic at coming second. It was a result which brought new prominence to both driver and team manager. As *Autosport* commented in its editorial on Monaco: 'Piers Courage drove the race of his life on Sunday, thoroughly justifying the faith Frank Williams has in him.'

Piers and Frank were bonding into a profound personal and professional relationship. It needed faith on both sides. They were running a car in Formula 2 as well as in Formula 1 which meant they were racing virtually every weekend in the summer of 1969. The pressure was enormous on both partners but they delivered. Frank brought in the money and Piers continued to drive with a maturity that had eluded him in previous seasons. He came second in the US Grand Prix at Watkins Glen, picking up valuable prize money of $20,000 for the team and was in the points for fifth place results at Brands Hatch and Silverstone. By the end of the season the Williams team was a new force to be reckoned with in F1. It had given the greatest names in motor racing a run for their (much bigger) money.

That big money came after Piers Courage. Ferrari offered him a package of £30,000 which was ten times the £3,000 driver's salary he was getting from Frank Williams. The financial temptation was huge. Piers went to see Enzo Ferrari, *Il Commendatore* of motor racing, accompanied by Frank whose fluent Italian came in useful at the meeting. The combination of Frank's toughness and Piers' loyalty resulted in a rejection of *Il Commandatore's* proposition. 'We went to see Mr Ferrari,' recalls Frank Williams, 'and he was a little bit disdainful of my being here. But I was there as Piers' manager. He was just another bloke as far as I was concerned, always was . . .'

Sally Courage was in favour of her husband signing up with Ferrari. 'Frank was seriously under-funded and I just wanted, I suppose, for Piers to have a bit of security,' she recalls, 'you do need something to pay the bills with!'

Piers, who had very little money of his own, was not unmindful of the importance of paying bills. But when Frank was able to come up with some £15,000 of new personal sponsorship for him, all thoughts of moving to Ferrari, Lotus or other teams that were interested in him faded from Piers' mind. 'He wouldn't leave Frank,' recalls Sally. 'He said Frank knows me. Frank understands me. I have faith in Frank, Frank has faith in me.'

Frank Williams reciprocated those strong emotions 'I pretty much adored Porridge,' he says. It was evident that these two young men, still only 28 years old as the 1970 Grand Prix racing season began, had united in a long-term friendship that transcended short-term money considerations. They were so excited by what they had achieved together in their first year of F1 that they wanted to live out their dream of showing what their small partnership could do against the giant companies of the motor racing industry.

Sadly the dream ended in a tragic nightmare. Frank had done a deal with an Argentine motor manufacturer, De Tomaso, to supply the team with a new F1 car. No-one knew how good or bad the De Tomaso would be because it had never raced before. First outings were not encouraging. The car was heavily overweight by some 120lb and there were other problems with the brakes and the electrics. After re-engineering by Frank and his team, the extensive mechanical problems were gradually sorted out, but after the first four Grand Prix races of the 1970 season Piers Courage in the De Tomaso had not won a single championship point.

By the time the Williams team reached the fifth round of the world championships for the Dutch Grand Prix at Zandwoort they were confident that the De Tomaso had put its troubles behind it. Both driver and car performed well in the practice, with Piers securing ninth place on the grid. On the day of the race Piers got a farewell thumbs up in the pits from Frank who said 'Cheerio, see you later'. At the start Piers took the De Tomaso off to a fast getaway. By lap 12 he was in seventh place after pulling away from several competitors in a superb mid-field dice. Ten laps later he was driving superbly and looking in good shape to move higher and collect championship points. Then on lap 23 disaster struck. No-one knows exactly what happened. According to Jackie Stewart, the most likely explanation was that the De Tomaso hit a bump in the road which upset the car's balance and sent it out of control. The consequence was that Piers Courage, travelling at 140mph, veered off the track, hit a fence post and overturned. With over 20 gallons of fuel on board the car burst into flames with the driver trapped inside. The only mercy was that Piers was likely to have been killed instantly rather than burned alive slowly because the car's explosive impact with the post ripped the wheels off the front of the car: they catapulted backwards into the cockpit, hitting the driver's head with such force that it ripped off his crash helmet and ended his life.

Although Piers Courage was dead, many minutes went by in complete confusion at the pits with his wife Sally and his manager Frank believing he had survived. There were two causes of the confusion. The first was that two drivers had dropped out of the race on lap 23, one in the accident (which was soon sending plumes of sinister black smoke over the crowd) and one with engine failure. The second was a trackside report that Piers was out of the car, reported as walking about and then taken away in an ambulance to hospital. This 'good' news was broadcast over the public address system by the race commentator. Frank Williams became desperately worried when he saw the Citroën ambulance return to the pits with no occupant. He rushed to get confirmation of Piers' condition from the Clerk of the Course, John Corsmit, who told him that Piers had not got out of the car and had been burned to death. 'You must tell me three times that Piers is dead before I can go and tell his wife,' said the distraught Frank. 'Yes, Piers Courage is dead,' said the Clerk of the Course. In shocked disbelief, Frank asked: 'Can you repeat clearly, Piers Courage of England is dead?' The official repeated it twice.

Sally Courage, who was sitting in a car behind the pits, saw Frank coming back: 'He did this sort of dance,' she has recalled. 'He didn't come straight towards me; he went round all the different cars so I knew something was wrong. When he reached me he had to say 'I'm sorry, he's dead.'

Sally poured out her grief. Frank bottled his up. She flew back to England on a private plane, under heavy sedation, to her two infant sons, Jason, 3, and Amos, six months. Frank stayed in Holland, had a morose dinner with Jackie Stewart and the following morning performed the grim duty of identification. 'I had to go to the police station to identify the remains of the car,' he recalls, 'all that was left was in something like a little porter's barrow from a station, a wire caged thing . . . it had taken them a long time to put the fire out because the bulkheads were magnesium. Piers I never saw. But his helmet turned up. It had a big black smudge on the top and a little bit of hair and scalp on the inside.' The impossible task of identifying Piers' remains was officially done by another friend of the family. Frank was asked by the police what he wanted done with what was left of the car. 'Get rid of it . . . I don't ever want to see it again . . . get it away,' he said in an emotional outburst. It was melted down in an incinerator.

Four days after the tragedy Piers was buried in the country church-yard of St Mary the Virgin in Sheffield, a short distance from the Courage family home. Most of the great names of motor racing were present, many wearing dark glasses to hide their tears. 'It was my first exposure to death of any kind,' recalls Frank Williams, 'the most emotional impact ever in my life.'

*　　　*　　　*

In the aftermath of Piers Courage's death, something may have died within Frank Williams. He suppressed his grief so strongly that he seemed to cut himself off from the expression of his emotions. Inwardly he was the same, a positive and enthusiastic man. But outwardly he seemed colder and even more driven. He coped with the loss of Piers in the only way he knew how to – by pushing himself harder and faster. 'I never thought of giving up,' he has recalled, 'I knew I had to press on in F1.' This was tough, for the next seven years of his life were to be his wilderness years of famine and frustration.

Although Frank Williams made a brave attempt to keep going on the Grand Prix circuit for the remainder of the 1970 season in the aftermath of Piers Courage's death, the unsatisfactory De Tomaso car with inexperienced new drivers at the wheel achieved no points and no finishes. The team was hopelessly underfunded and its debts were alarmingly high. Any other manager might have become dispirited but Frank remained as determined as ever. For the next four years he lurched from financial crisis to financial crisis. Sometimes he was only one step ahead of collapse, using any new money he charmed and cajoled out of sponsors to pay last year's creditors. Often he was ridiculed and insulted. Behind his back he was called 'Wanker Williams'. Yet miraculously he stayed in F1. His cars raced even if they often failed to qualify and rarely finished. But there were two turning points in Frank Williams's life in 1973–74. He became a constructor and he became a husband.

Being a constructor meant that the team's cars now bore the name Williams because Frank was manufacturing his own chassis. Seen from the outside, his new status looked good but a constructor who tries to go Grand Prix racing without an engine for his factory's cars is like a parachutist who tries to jump without a parachute. Frank jumped just the same. At the last minute, he persuaded his oldest sponsor Ted Williams of H. W. Ward Machine Tools Ltd to come in with £25,000, his newest sponsor Marlboro came in with £15,000 and in the nick of time the team managed to purchase a couple of Ford-Cosworth V8s with which to go racing. Such brinkmanship on the eve of the new season was par for the course for Frank Williams. More and more people became astonished at his tenacity. How he survived against all the odds on the horrendously expensive battlefield of F1 in the early 1970s was the stuff of which legends are made. In addition to his permanent guerrilla warfare to pay suppliers and conjure sponsors out of thin air, all sorts of unlikely people chipped in with cash or kind to keep Frank afloat. One of them was his girlfriend Virginia (Ginny) Sawyer-Hoare. Madly in love, she sold her flat in Chelsea and lent him over £8,000 at a time when Frank's finances were at their most perilous. Their relationship had gradually become less casual. Five years after their romance had started, Ginny was brought out of the closet and invited to her first Grand Prix in 1973. That was one of several signs of a growing closeness which at times seemed to make Frank nervous. But when Ginny finally became pregnant he overcame his nervousness. After walking round a field saying to himself, 'perhaps I'd better make an honest woman of her', he proposed on the eve of the Austrian Grand Prix in August 1974. Hardly believing her luck that the man she thought was not the marrying type wanted to marry her, Ginny fixed up the earliest possible date at the nearest registry office. The arrangements were that the knot would be tied at 2 pm on Tuesday the 20 August 1974, with lunch for bride, bridegroom and the witnesses at 12 noon before the ceremony. At 1 pm there was no sign of Frank. Had he got cold feet? Suddenly the phone rang. The groom was on the line. 'Ginny? What time are we meeting at the registry office?' 'Two o'clock, Frank. Aren't you coming for lunch?' 'No. I'm sorry. I'll have to leave it. I'm running late at the factory. I'll see you there.'

To everyone's relief he did get to the Reading Registry Office in time, said his vows in a strong, clear voice, and put the 18-carat gold wedding ring on his bride's finger. Ginny had bought it for £30 out of the rent money. One of the witnesses loaned the couple £8 to pay the fee for the marriage licence. Frank on his wedding day was broke, outwardly unemotional and in a high-pressure hurry. As Mr and Mrs Williams took their leave of the registrar, the bridegroom gave his bride a brief kiss, looked at his watch and said, 'OK. I'm off back to the office. I'll see you later.'

The guests were appalled by the husband who skipped both the wedding lunch and the wedding reception. Frank was delighted that he had only needed to be away from his factory for 35 minutes. Ginny found the situation hilarious. One of the reasons why she was so madly in love with Frank was his dedication to his work. It was a quality on full display in the engagement and marriage of Frank Williams.

Although the family expanded with the couple's first child, Jonathan Piers Williams, arriving in February 1975, Grand Prix life remained cripplingly expensive. By the end of the 1975 season, Frank Williams (Racing Cars) Limited had debts of over £140,000. This time survival was impossible and the wolf (literally) was at the door.

In November 1975 Frank sold his company to an Austro-Canadian oil equipment millionaire Walter Wolf. The Wolf–Williams team was created in its place. This was not a marriage made in heaven. Although Frank, for the first time in his life was paid a salary (of £6,000) he was soon downgraded from the role he loved – managing a racing team. In what was effectively a sacking, Frank was moved sideways, assigned to looking after sponsors for the team and to other general duties. Frank's pride was hurt. Instead of running the show, he was on the periphery of it, treated at times as little more than a glorified gofer by the new proprietor. He found himself doing chores such as picking up Walter Wolf's personal Mercedes from Stuttgart or driving his Lamborghini to Paris. On one occasion Frank was asked to find a married couple to be live-in domestics for the Wolf family. The last straw came when the Wolf–Williams team set off to Argentina for the first Grand Prix of the season, leaving Frank behind in London. This was a deep wound and salt was rubbed into it by the team's new driver, Jody Scheckter, winning the race. Press reports of the Wolf–Williams victory implied that it was all down to the new management. This was more than Frank could bear. He parted from Walter Wolf and returned to running his own motor racing business, this time under the name of Williams Grand Prix Engineering.

A key figure in this new enterprise was Patrick Head. He also parted from Walter Wolf at this time out of personal loyalty to Frank. Head had originally been recruited to the pre-Wolf Williams team back in 1974 when it urgently needed a designer. Patrick Head was actually in the business of boat designing but he had done a smattering of work on Lola's F2 cars. 'To be honest I was pretty desperate' recalled Frank. 'I didn't know one designer from another. But I instinctively liked Patrick the moment I saw him. He talked good sense. He was tough, down to earth, and intensely practical. I liked him for his English military background. His father was a Colonel and his great-great-grandfather had fought at Waterloo. I liked him because his hero was the great English designer Isambard Kingdom Brunel. So I took Patrick on. It was the best move I ever made in my life. I soon saw he was the Vicar's Knickers so far as car designing and team leadership are concerned. He became my rock and my partner. Over the last 30 years he's been every bit as responsible for the success of Williams as I have.'

Success at Williams Grand Prix Engineering started to gather momentum from 1977 onwards. Patrick Head began to produce some revolutionary new aerodynamic designs using ground effect technology. The money that turned these designs into F1 cars was found from no less revolutionary sources. The first was a totally unexpected overdraft facility of £20,000. This came from an innovative Barclays Bank manager making a cold call at the company's new premises in Didcot. His arrival was greeted by Frank diving under his desk and instructing his secretary to say he was out. This was because all previous visits from bank managers had been debt recovery missions. Once Frank had regained his equilibrium and in wonderment accepted the loan he set off in search of further miracles. One of them came via his old friend from flat-sharing days in the 1960s, Charlie Crichton-Stuart, who arranged an appointment with Saudi Arabian Airlines. In return for having the slogan 'Fly Saudia' on the back of the car the airline put up £30,000. This was a useful but not huge sum of money, yet it was pivotal because it started Frank on the trail of the much bigger Saudi sponsorship that was to transform his company.

Saudi Arabia in the mid-1970s was entering its greatest oil boom period, yet it was an impenetrable country to all but the most determined of Western businessmen. Visa delays were interminable, the telephone system was unworkable, hotels were primitive and most Saudi offices were chaotic in everything from making appointments to clearing cheques. However, there were a handful of younger generation Saudis who were starting to open offices in London. One of the youngest of these new business leaders was HRH Prince Mohammed bin Fahd bin Abdulaziz the son of King Fahd, whose company Al

Bilad had just won a massive $5 billion contract in co-operation with Phillips of Holland, Ericsson of Sweden and Bell Canada to build a new telephone network for Saudi Arabia. To facilitate this and other major contracts Al Bilad set up an office in the heart of Mayfair on Park Lane. It was this office that started my relationship with Frank Williams. For thanks to a friendship with Prince Mohammed which had begun three years earlier, I had been appointed managing director of Al Bilad (UK) Limited in 1976 and was in charge of the Prince's London office.

On one of Prince Mohammed's visits to Britain, he and some of his cousins who were also princes began asking me: 'Do you know Mr Frank Williams?' Although I had never met him I knew about him because I had closely followed the tragic death of my Eton classmate Piers Courage. So I reported favourably on Frank to my Saudi friends, putting some emphasis on how well he had cared for Sally Courage in her bereavement and how much he had adored Piers. The Saudis were fascinated by the story.

It then emerged that Frank Williams had been visiting Saudi Arabia in search of sponsorship and had met with Prince Sultan bin Salman, a first cousin of Prince Mohammed. Both young princes were enthusiasts for fast cars. Prince Mohammed was a serious collector of them. One evening he took me to a large building in the grounds of his home in Riyadh. He called it his garage but it was more like an Aladdin's cave filled with over 60 gleaming Ferraris, Maseratis, BMWs, Aston Martins, Jaguars, Lamborghinis and other renowned marques. All were in pristine condition, many of them custom-made or specially adapted. As the Prince walked me round the jewels of his collection, enthusing over their finer points of style and speed, I began to understand his passion for unique cars. Extending this passion into an involvement with the fastest and most expensive cars in the world – Formula 1 racers – was an idea that caught his imagination. As the idea developed after he had watched film clips of a Williams F1 emblazoned with 'Fly Saudia' doing practice circuits at Brands Hatch, Prince Mohammed asked me to check out Frank Williams when I returned to London.

Despite my complete ignorance of Grand Prix motor racing, it did not take me long to recognize that Frank Williams was a remarkable man. I liked him from the moment we met in Prince Mohammed's office on Park Lane in December 1977.

My first impression of him was as a fitness fanatic, for Frank arrived at our meeting clutching a bag full of running kit in which he had completed two 3 mile circuits of Hyde Park before breakfast in the impressive time of thirty five minutes. I quickly began to enjoy his laconic sense of humour and his laid-back charm, two qualities which balanced the intensity of his dedication to motor racing. He knew as little about the Saudi royal family as I knew about Ford V8 Cosworth engines so the learning curves in both directions were steep but enjoyable. However, one less than enjoyable surprise for Frank was learning about the whimsical attitude to time prevalent among prominent Middle Easterners. His appointment to see Prince Mohammed took weeks to arrange. Finally when Frank thought he had a meeting 'firmly in the diary' (a concept unknown to Saudis of that era) it had to be cancelled and rescheduled on three consecutive nights. During this frustrating period Frank practically slept in my office, bombarding me with questions in between his prowls up and down Park Lane on tenterhooks of high anxiety. Finally as I fixed an appointment on the fourth day at the vague hour described by one of the prince's henchmen as 'sometime after evening prayer but before dinner' (i.e. roughly between 7 pm and 11 pm), Frank asked me 'do you have one last recommendation for anything more I can do to make this meeting go well?' I replied, 'Well if I were you I would bring your car along. Once Prince Mohammed sees it I think you will really get his interest.'

Frank gulped as I offered my suggestion which would not have tripped so easily off my tongue if I had realized that moving a Formula 1 racing car into the heart of Mayfair involved a mammoth logistics operation. However, my advice worked wonders. At his meeting in the office with Frank, Prince Mohammed listened politely but cautiously to the presentation of the good prospects for Williams Grand Prix engineering. But his eyes lit up when Frank said, 'Come and see the car we'll be racing – it's parked just around the corner!'

By the time Prince Mohammed and Frank Williams strolled together towards FW06, the prototype racing car which had been manoeuvred out of its vast pantechnicon on to the roadside half an hour earlier, an admiring crowd had gathered around it. Upper Grosvenor Street is normally a quiet location at 9 pm, but the crowd of bystanders, the team of Williams mechanics in their race overalls, the entourage of Prince Mohammed, the arc lights, the pantechnicon and the arrival of a couple of fascinated but friendly police officers transformed the atmosphere of the Mayfair side street into an excited buzz worthy of the pits at a Grand Prix. Prince Mohammed could not suppress his excitement, particularly when Frank Williams suggested that he might like to sit in the car. Clambering into the cockpit, the Prince was strapped into the driver's seat. Frank explained the various dials and gauges, then instructed his royal driver on how to execute 'heel n' toe', a fancy piece of footwork on the pedals for making high speed gear changes when racing at 170mph. Prince Mohammed was as thrilled as a schoolboy turning the steering wheel, practising heel n' toes on the car's brake and accelerator, and making Brrrm–Brrrm noises through his lips. Away in his own dream world for several minutes, he eventually came back to reality and pulled himself out of the car when his eye caught Frank's cheekiest gambit of the evening. The blue and white logo of the Prince's company Al Bilad, whose Arabic script Frank had lifted from a sheet of notepaper he found in my office, was already boldly painted on the bonnet of FW06. Prince Mohammed was amused. 'I see we are going to sponsor the Williams team,' he chuckled. When they returned to the office, Prince Mohammed became a serious sponsor, handing Frank Williams a cheque for £50,000. It was the beginning of the flow of big time Saudi money which ended Frank's hard-scrabble years of dodging creditors, pleading with suppliers and fighting for survival. At last he had access to the resources to fight and win world championship races.

In fact the money did not flow quickly or easily. After handing out four more cheques for £50,000 in the next three months, even Prince Mohammed began to realize that personal sponsorship of an F1 team is an immensely expensive business. Having the Al Bilad logo on the front of the car brought no commercial gains to his company, although in the London office I did receive ingenious proposals for launching contraceptives and cigarettes under our own brand name! However, Prince Mohammed kept up his support for the team not as a personal ego trip but because he had the vision to see that a Saudi-backed competitor in Formula 1 could be good for his country's international image.

Prince Mohammed's greatest contribution to the success of Frank Williams was to persuade several other Saudi princes, companies and individual businessmen that it was their patriotic duty to join him as co-sponsors of the Williams team. The only problem was that what was promised patriotically to Prince Mohammed in Riyadh, Saudi Arabia did not always arrive commercially in the form of cheques delivered to the Williams factory in Didcot, Oxfordshire.

Closing the gap between the promises and the cheques was one of Frank Williams's finest achievements. He spent many agonizing weeks hanging around in Riyadh and Jeddah clinging with limpet-like intensity to hopes of appointments with elusive Saudis who were forever on the move elsewhere, summoned away to see their uncles or simply showing whimsical disregard for the priority that Grand Prix team managers have to give to the pressure of time and money. Yet gradually and painstakingly, Frank overcame all these delay factors that are inherent in the Saudi way of life and tied his sponsors down. Interestingly one young prince who was such a keen motor racing fan that he became Frank Williams's most helpful companion in this sponsor-catching process was Mohammed bin Nawaf. Perhaps his role as Frank's principal encourager and escorter around Riyadh gave him some early training in diplomatic perseverance, for in 2006 Prince Mohammed bin Nawaf was appointed as the new Saudi Ambassador to Britain.

For all the encouragement he received from his Saudi friends Frank Williams succeeded because he brought to his task a special brand of patience and perseverance that bordered on the heroic. This was why, after watching him endure one of his most testing periods of Riyadh waiting, I described Frank to my boss, Prince Mohammed bin Fahd, as 'the most determined man I have ever met'. Yet in his own regal way, so was Prince Mohammed. Intuitively sensing the dedication to winning that Frank Williams personified, the Prince began scrutinizing the team's budgets, immersing himself in details such as wind tunnel test results of the team's cars, the evolving aerodynamic designs by Patrick Head and the choices of Alan Jones and Clay Regazzoni as the team's drivers. Prince Mohammed also made his own plans to come and watch the team race in the British Grand Prix of 1979.

Early on in the 1979 season it was apparent that the team's new car FW07 was performing exceptionally well in terms of speed and power. But reliability was a problem. The car was fast yet it did not win any of its races in May and June because of a series of electrical and mechanical failures. The promise showed again in the qualifying times before the British Grand Prix at Silverstone. Alan Jones took pole position with a record-breaking lap at the stunning average speed of 145mph. This pre-race success generated huge media speculation. Could Frank be about to win his first Grand Prix in front of the home crowd with his British-made car?

Sunday 14 July 1979 was a day of drama, agony and ecstasy for the Williams team at Silverstone. There were pre-race dramas such as a fuel pump breaking in Alan Jones's car just before the start (it was repaired in the nick of time) and Prince Mohammed nearly missing the last possible helicopter ride to the track from Battersea Heliport (he caught it with seconds to spare). I was with him in that helicopter and as it circled over Silverstone I recall my own and Prince Mohammed's astonishment as we absorbed the atmosphere of the 110,000-strong crowd; the feverish activity in the pits; the flags, posters and emblems around the circuit; and above all the sound of some 40 F1 racing cars roaring like a pride of hungry lions when their drivers moved towards the start, revving their engines at full throttle as they took their places on the grid. Because of the noise, colour and pent-up passion, the build-up to the start of a Grand Prix surpasses the opening of any other sporting contest for explosive anticipation.

The early stages of the race could not have gone better for the Williams team. Alan Jones and Clay Reggazzoni both made brilliant starts. For the first 17 laps the Williams cars were in positions 1 and 3 split by a Renault until its tyres burned, forcing a return to the pits. Then for the next 22 laps Jones and Reggazzoni were way out in front on their own. Would they hold out and bury the team's demons of unreliability once and for all? Frank Williams sat on the edge of the pit wall, his eyes drilling like lasers into the lap charts in front of him, his face totally immobile as if encased in an iron mask of concentration.

On lap 38 he suddenly announced in the unemotional tones of an I-speak-your-weight-machine 'Something's gone. I give him two more laps.' Frank's eagle eye had spotted a thin wisp of white smoke seeping out of the back of Alan Jones's car. This harbinger of failure was enough to put an end to the dream of victory (or so we camp followers thought at the time) because by the next lap Alan Jones was back in the pits, his car disabled from finishing the race by a leak of engine coolant liquid.

The gloom in the Williams camp over Jones's withdrawal was soon dissipated by the realization that a Williams car was still leading the race. Clay Reggazzoni, a popular figure with the crowd, was having the drive of his life. Coming into his own after the departure of Jones he promptly clocked the fasted lap time of the race, extending his lead over the rest of the field by 15 seconds. For the next 28 laps both car and driver continued to demonstrate their combined superiority. No other competitor came close. It was clear that in design, engine power, speed and (at last) reliability, the Williams team had produced a world-beating F1 racing car. As the chequered flag came down at the end of lap 68 to set the seal on the Williams triumph, the crowd went wild. The frenzied cheering was not only the public celebration of a great British victory. It was also a personal tribute to Frank Williams. In his epic trials and tribulations during the past ten years as a team manager he had been mocked, pitied, condescended to and ridiculed as the poor little underdog of Formula 1. Suddenly he was its master. Winning his first Grand Prix in front of his home crowd at Silverstone was the proudest and most glorious moment of his life.

Although emotions were surging through him, Frank was charac-teristically careful not to put them on display. Instead he concentrated on symbolic touches directed towards his chief sponsor. The first was having the Saudi flag as well as the Union Jack hauled up on 36ft high poles at opposite sides of the finishing line just as FW07 crossed it. The second was instructing Clay Reggazzoni not to indulge in the usual Grand Prix ritual of spraying champagne from the winner's podium. Instead as a mark of deference to Islam's prohibition of alcohol, Reggazzoni circumspectly sipped a glass of orange juice. Frank had planned both details 'just in case' well ahead of the race. Prince Mohammed was moved by them and by the general rejoicings.

He remained at Silverstone for another two and a half hours, talking at length with Reggazzoni (who was handed a generous princely cheque), conferring with Frank Williams and getting cheered by the fans. 'What a day! What a great day!' said Prince Mohammed as he got back into his helicopter. The Saudi–Williams partnership had made Grand Prix history. Drivers' Championships and Constructors' Championships were soon to follow, but as Frank sat with his arm around his wife Ginny savouring Silverstone by moonlight until 1 o'clock in the morning, he felt that he had reached the summit of happiness and high achievement.

The glorious day of the 1979 British Grand Prix at Silverstone was the start of a golden era for Frank Williams and his team. Four more Grand Prix victories came that year and many more followed afterward. With them came championships, titles, new sponsors, the Queen's Award for industry, invitations to Buckingham Palace and Chequers, worldwide recognition and a great leap forward in the company's revenues. Frank enjoyed being richer and more success-ful but he did not let his triumphs go to his head. If anything, he became tougher on himself and on others. His relationships with his drivers were rarely easy. Alan Jones, who won the world champi-onship in 1980, left by mutual consent in 1981. The breach came because Frank Williams thought Jones had 'let himself down'. This meant that in the opinion of his boss Alan Jones had thrown away his chances of winning the title for the second year running by losing his concentration in key races. Later fallouts with championship winning drivers such as Nigel Mansell, Nelson Piquet and Damon Hill were always about money. 'Patrick Head and I never lost sight of the fact that it is the car, its engine, aerodynamics, horsepower and tyres that achieve success in Formula 1, so we put every spare penny into technology and development and not into overpaying drivers,' says Frank bluntly. Another factor in his uneasy relationship with the men who drove Williams F1 cars was a remoteness which may have dated back to the death of Piers Courage. There had been no remoteness in the Courage–Williams friendship, but after their intimacy was ended by tragedy, Frank seems to have been deter-mined never again to get close to a driver as a personal friend. Keke

Rosberg, who drove brilliantly for Williams as Nigel Mansell's team mate in the 1980s illuminates this aspect of his boss's character:

> I don't think Frank is the sort of man who builds great friendships. He doesn't let you come close. It's not because he's the boss. He's a caring sort of a person but not as much as he liked to think he was. We used to tell a joke about how Frank would go into the workshop and pat one of the lads on the back. 'How's it going Pete?' he would ask. Pete would say, 'Not so good Frank. My wife died this morning.' And Frank would say 'Okay, never mind. D'you think that front suspension will be ready for the test next week?' Frank thought in his own mind that he was very caring and yet he seemed to forget to do it. It was a strange thing. He wasn't very distant – and yet he was very remote.

There may be a touch of caricature in Keke Rosberg's portrayal of Frank Williams, but his aura of aloofness was real. He could 'do gregarious', as they say in show business, but in his true character he was the ultimate loner. Away from the factory and the motor racing circuit he had no hinterland of wider interests or friendships. His only other passion was running but his way of training for this sport reinforced his remoteness, for Frank personified the loneliness of the long-distance runner. By the mid-1980s he was running 65 to 70 miles a week at speeds of around 5 minutes 45 seconds per mile. He was competing only against himself and his stop watch, but occasionally he entered a race to test his times in the atmosphere of a 10k or half-marathon. In March 1986 he entered the Portsmouth half marathon. He was determined, after a winter of hard training, to beat his own PB (personal best) of 1 hour 18 minutes for the 13-mile course. This was the race entry that was to change his life.

On Saturday the 8 March 1986, the evening before the Portsmouth half marathon, Frank was at the Paul Ricard circuit in the South of France where he had been testing FW16 the new Williams Formula 1 car for the coming season. He finished later than he had intended, cutting it fine for his next deadline which was catching the last flight out of Nice to London at 8 pm. 'I was in a real hurry because I didn't want to miss running in Portsmouth and trying to beat my best half marathon time,' Frank recalls. So I was overdoing it even by my usual standards of hooligan driving. I wasn't paying enough attention. No excuses. No one else involved. No one but myself to blame. It just happened.'

What happened was that Frank Williams had a terrible accident. He lost control of the rented Ford Sierra he was driving and it left the road at about 75mph – a high speed for the winding B class roads that lie between the Paul Ricard circuit and the main autoroute to Nice. The rented car soared into the air, nose-dived into a gully and somer-saulted downwards until coming to a mangled stop with its wheels in the air. In the course of the helter-skelter descent into the gully the roof of the car caved in, inflicting devastating injuries to Frank's neck and other parts of his upper body.

The passenger in the car, Peter Windsor, was almost unhurt. He managed to drag Frank's bleeding and unconscious body clear of the wreckage. An ambulance rushed him to the Timone hospital in Marseille where neurological surgeons carried out a six-hour operation on his multiple injuries. At the end of this surgery the prognosis was grim. The X-rays showed that Frank Williams had broken his neck with irretrievable damage to the spinal cord. He would be paralysed for the rest of his life. To make matters worse, his life was unlikely to last much longer. So acute were his breathing dif-ficulties and so bad was his general condition that he was not expected to live for more than four or five days. When Ginny Williams arrived at her husband's bedside 24 hours after the accident she soon discov-ered the depths of the hospitals pessimism about Frank's survival prospects. 'Are you telling me you believe my husband is going to die?' she asked the doctor in charge of the intensive care unit. 'Oui, bien sûr,' he replied with a shrug.

The only person who seemed to be 'bien sûr' that he was not going to die was the patient. Despite being in intense pain, drifting in and out of consciousness, with no feeling in his limbs and overcome by the intense cold that accompanies paralysis, Frank was determined to fight for his life. Lung congestion and breathing difficulties were his worst problems. Fluid was pooling in his lungs but the Marseilles hospital's intensive care team could not provide him with round the clock nursing, his lungs were not being suctioned with the frequency necessary to keep him alive. After a night which he only survived because of the peak lung fitness built up by his running, Frank managed to croak to his wife: 'Get me out of here Ginny . . . last night I wanted a nurse to help me . . . there wasn't one . . . I'm cold . . . I can't breathe . . . do something.'

Ginny did wonders. Bernie Ecclestone, the F1 Boss, sent a plane and a top British doctor. Margaret Thatcher issued orders from No. 10 to the British consulate in Marseille, requesting maximum co-operation from the French authorities. The net result was that the patient the Marseille hosptial was expecting to die there, instead left it alive with a police escort to the airport and was flown by air ambulance to Biggin Hill in Kent. Thanks to more orders from No. 10, the patient was then rushed with another police escort to the London Hospital in Whitechapel Road. In that renowned intensive therapy unit the battle to save the life of Frank Williams began in earnest.

In its early stages the battle had many more defeats than victories. Frank's condition deteriorated steadily. He came close to drowning in the secretions of his own lungs. As a last desperate measure after the near-brutal chest clappings of a team of physios had failed to move the secretions, an emergency tracheotomy was performed. The surgeon who carried out the operation was so despondent about the chances of its success that in an overwrought moment he shouted at Ginny: 'Just how much more effort do you want us to make to keep your husband alive?'

'I want every effort made,' she shouted back. She knew her man. For Frank was making every effort too, and soon he was winning. Seven days after being flown in from Marseilles he was out of intensive care. Ten weeks later he was out of hospital. The journey in-between was interspersed with terrifying crises such as a bad bout of pneumonia and an obstruction caused by a boiled sweet that should never have been given to Frank. However, Frank's will-power was the prevailing force in his survival. Against all the medical odds, his granite determination pulled him through.

But pulled him through to what? Additional tests and X-rays showed that what had happened as a result of the accident was a severance of the spinal cord between the cervical vertebrae known as C6 and C7. As a result of this total break of the spine all the nerves controlled by the cord below C6 had been permanently lost. This meant that Frank no longer had the use of his legs, lower arms and had lost all the muscles and feelings in his body below the lower level of his upper chest. For the rest of his life he would never again be able to touch, cough, sneeze or laugh. No wonder he had a few despairing moments when the full realities of quadriplegia hit him. In one of those dark periods he said to Ginny: 'God is punishing me. He's punishing me for having led such a selfish life.'

Frank Williams now looks back at this cry of anguish as 'an old-fashioned Catholic guilt trip'. It was a fleeting plunge into pessimism from a patient whose tenacity in adversity has kept him astonishingly optimistic. Even when his physical prospects could not have been worse, Frank developed a positive mental attitude which enabled him to see visions of a future life far beyond the horizons of other spinal injury victims. The first of these visions was Frank's determination not to follow the usual medical advice to patients in his condition. When he was stabilized and growing stronger in the London Hospital, his consultant Professor Watkins said to him: 'I think the time is coming when we ought to think about transferring you to a spinal hospital.' 'Not for me thanks, Prof,' Frank replied. 'I would rather go home.'

This was mission impossible. Every consultant, doctor, physiotherapist, nurse and medical adviser in the intensive care unit of the London Hospital urged that Frank should be transferred to Stoke Mandeville or some other equivalent specialized spinal unit. It was the recommended route of rehabilitation for quadriplegics. A stay at Stoke Mandeville usually lasts about 12 months before the full potential of the patient's still functioning muscles could be realized by intensive physiotherapy. Only then could someone with Frank Williams's degree of injuries think of returning home.

Frank, however, thought differently. He was not only planning to return home, he was talking about going back to work, about running his F1 team, and about returning to Grand Prix races. Some of his nurses thought he was delirious. It was not the dreams of delirium but the reality of his resolve that gave Frank the power to achieve these objectives within a timescale that defied all medical advice and experience.

After much arguing with his doctors, the patient was allowed to get his way. Eleven weeks after the accident Frank was carried on a stretcher into Boxford House, the Williams' family home near Newbury. It had been equipped with all the latest medical technology, including an £11,000 bed, and was staffed by two resident nurses supported by a back-up team of local doctors and physiotherapists. Ginny Williams had worked wonders to ensure that her husband was well cared for and comfortable.

There is no such thing as 'a comfortable quadriplegic'. Yet if any patient could possibly be described by such an oxymoron it was Frank Williams. His personal resources (he was worth at least £10 million at the time of his accident) made it possible for him to create his own spinal injury rehabilitation unit at home. However, it was not money but motivation that powered his recovery back to motor racing.

After coming home, Frank 'took a few days off', as he put it. His doctor called on him a week later to see how his patient had been getting on since leaving hospital: 'So how does it feel to be at home?' the doctor asked with a smile. 'Great,' replied Frank, 'but it'll feel better still to be back at the factory . . . I'm going to work this afternoon, Dr Britz.' The doctor stopped smiling once he realized that Frank was serious and tried to put his foot down. 'Just understand that I want nothing to do with this,' said Dr Britz, 'I think that its utterly foolhardy and I won't be held in any way responsible if you insist on going. It is absolutely against my advice. I can't say that strongly enough.'

Frank took no notice of this medical prohibition. He was determined to make a surprise visit to his team. So off he went to the Williams factory at Didcot, accompanied by Ginny and two nurses. He arrived unannounced. In the car park he was strapped into his wheelchair, propped up by a safety harness, and one of his nurses had to hold his head to stop it lolling sideways. As he and his entourage progressed towards the factory, the first mechanic to encounter his boss in this condition behaved as if he had seen a ghost. He turned round and sprinted back to the workshop without saying a word. But he must have spread the news of Frank's presence as within minutes a large crowd of Williams employees were congregating around the wheelchair, their reactions a combination of shock and smiles at the return of their owner.

One of Frank Williams's greatest achievements was that during the seven years since winning his first Grand Prix at Silverstone he had built a superb team. Williams Grand Prix Engineering (later renamed Williams F1) was not a one-man band, it was a highly professional motor racing business, so professional that it had won a succession of Grand Prix races in the three months since their supremo had been out of action. Yet as they looked at the thin, gaunt, paralysed body of Frank Williams on that afternoon of his first visit back to the factory, many members of the team must have feared that he would be out of action for ever.

Frank had no such fear, 'Luckily I was the majority owner of a business that could not sack me,' he says wryly. 'I knew I was coming back but I didn't know what hard work it was going to be. Soon after that first visit I began going into the factory for two or three afternoons each week, just doing a couple of hours at a time. My basic problem was that I don't have anything that works below my armpits. All I can move is my neck and shoulders and from them I can lift my arms. The muscles get overworked so that they ache and sting. Those difficulties didn't get in the way because I was surrounded by such a strong team, particularly Patrick Head and Sheridan Thynne who I could trust absolutely when my days in the office were quite short. But my brain was always fine and my dedication to motor racing never for one moment weakened.'

Given his iron dedication, it was only a matter of more time and more determination before Frank Williams was back at the helm of his company, travelling to Grand Prix races all over the world, carrying off many of the top prizes and championships. In the era since his accident, 1986–2006, the Williams team has seen many changes of drivers, many switches of sponsors, and many exits and entrances of manufacturers such as Honda, Renault and BMW. There have been nine wins of the Constructors' championship and seven of the Drivers' championship. These triumphs have occasionally been shadowed by tragedy, most poignantly the death of Ayrton Senna driving a Williams at the San Marino Grand Prix of 1994. There have been great years, good years and disappointing years. Yet for all the fortunes and misfortunes that go with the territory of the Grand Prix circuit, the unassailable fact remains that for well over a quarter of a century Frank Williams has been the dominant figure at the head of British motor racing and in the forefront of Formula 1 competitors across the world. For 20 of those 25-plus years he has been in a wheelchair as a quadriplegic.

Frank Williams is now in his sixty-fifth year. It is 40 years since he started his racing car business; 37 years since he became a Formula 1 team manager; and 20 years since he had the 'hooligan driving' accident that would have cut short the career of almost any other sporting hero. Looking back on these milestones does not interest him. As the 2006 Grand Prix season gets under way, there is no talk of nostalgia or retirement. As always, he is tightly focused on the coming races and on the long-term future of Williams F1. This future, he says, 'is as bright as ever', although he acknowledges that the last couple of seasons have been 'humbling'. By this he means a long run of disappointing race results and the loss of the partnership with BMW. This break-up was caused, according to Frank, by 'cultural differences', an elliptical comment which becomes slightly clearer when he adds, 'I am fiercely English.'

There are perhaps five 'fiercelys' in the life of Frank Williams. He is fiercely committed to motor racing. He is fiercely competitive within it. He is fiercely loyal to his team colleagues, his family and his friends. He is fiercely patriotic in an old-fashioned nationalistic way. Above all, he is, and always has been, fiercely determined. Paradoxically these elements do not combine to make him a fierce human being. For Frank Williams is a quiet man with outward manifestations of character that are gentle, genial and generous. Yet inwardly he is driven by a core of steel whose extraordinary strength has been forged in the white heat of suffering and stoicism. These qualities are worth analysing.

The commitment and competitiveness are self-evident. ' I want to prove we can do it again,' he says as his thirty-seventh season in Grand Prix racing opens. Experienced Williams watchers, mindful of how much he has proved in the past, will take this declaration seriously. Today Williams's F1 is a big business in fighting-fit shape. It employs over 500 people and has revenues of approximately £90 million a year, most of them coming from a new list of blue-chip sponsors Frank and his team have carefully wooed and won. These sponsors include the Royal Bank of Scotland, Budweiser, FedEx, Petrobras, Castrol and Reuters. Their resources put the team at the cutting edge of motor racing technology. This is vital because in Frank Williams's view the winning of Grand Prix races is much more of an engineering achievement than a driving achievement. He is excited by the wind tunnel tests on the new car the team has built, FW28, whose aerodynamics are showing great promise. Also looking good is his new V8 Cosworth engine, a redesigned descendant of the original Cosworths with which he started his career as an F1 manager. Yet for all the hoped-for superiority in engineering and technology, Williams F1 is a people business where loyalty plays a vital role in the team's success.

The bonds of loyalty between Frank Williams and his partner, the brilliant designer Patrick Head, have stood many tough tests. They own respectively 70 per cent and 30 per cent of the business. Since Williams F1 has been conservatively valued by City institutions at over £150 million, that makes Frank Williams's shares worth over £100 million and Patrick Head's shares worth just under £50 million. Are either of them sellers? 'Not yet. First I want to prove we can do it again. I'm sure Patrick feels the same way,' says Frank, 'and we are preparing for the long term. We have a successor management group in place consisting of the seven top people in the company which includes the two shareholders, Patrick and myself. Later on I see the company passing its shares on through an Employee Benefit Trust. I'll get a few bob out but I'll remain involved.'

Leadership through hands-on involvement is Frank Williams's style. He works at his desk in the factory, now located on a 50-acre site near Grove, Wantage, seven days a week. When the pressure is high he often sleeps on the premises in a small apartment just along the corridor from his office rather than returning to his 19-bedroom country house, Inholmes, New Hungerford. He bought it and the surrounding 1,300 acre estate in 1999, 'because I always wanted a bit of old England for my family'.

Family loyalty looms large in Frank Williams's world. Although he understates the emotions in his bonds with his nearest and dearest, there is no doubt of his paternal pride in his three children: Jonathan Piers (30), Claire (29) and Jamie (23). Jonathan and Claire work in the business and live on the Inholmes estate. Jamie 'the wild one', is a junior advertising executive with WWP in London. As for Frank's marriage to Ginny, this has been a rollercoaster ride. It began unilaterally with passion on her side and reluctance on his. During different stages of the ride he was wildly independent from her and then totally dependent on her, the accident being the watershed between the two situations. Once the adrenalin-filled battles of beating death and grappling with the early difficulties of quadriplegia were over, the situation changed. The couple's relationship deteriorated but survived. There was a high price to pay for the survival. The first instalment on the price was a separation. Ginny, who thought they had become two alienated people at loggerheads with each other, asked for it. 'If that's what you want to do, then that's what you have to do,' was her husband's laconic response to the request. On the day she moved out from their matrimonial home she was bewildered by his apparent lack of feeling. 'Don't you care, Frank?' she asked. 'Emotion is weak, Ginny,' he replied.

For 'weak' read 'under control'. All his life Frank Williams has kept an iron grip on the outward expression of his feelings. The grip tightened as he faced up to the grim reality of his physical condition. In the public arena of motor racing this required him to relinquish control over some areas of the business in which he had been absolute ruler. 'But he never had to be kicked into these adjustments' says his partner Patrick Head. 'He became surprisingly good at delegating even though he still can't quite understand that not everyone in Williams wants to work 7 days a week and 24 hours a day for the team like he does.'

In the private arena of his personal life Frank suppresses his emotions with equal vigour. On the surface his marriage to the semi-separated Ginny survives well, even to the point of him wishing her 'good luck' when she embarked on some of her new romantic involvements. Yet Frank can also allude to the darker side of these upheavals. 'The veneer looks nice but underneath there's been some unpleasant stuff,' is his laconic comment about their matrimonial dramas. The outward obliteration of the emotions he must feel about them has been another part of the price of survival.

Frank sometimes likes to claim that he has survived through ruthlessness and selfishness. Experienced Williams watchers tend to discount such sweeping descriptions of himself, saying that it is out of tune with his warm-hearted generosity when he says: 'I am an utterly selfish person . . . I can't see other peoples problems and emotions . . . being in a wheelchair like this has made me even more self-centred. That's just the way I am – single-minded and selfish.'

I know as well as anyone that these assertions are not the whole truth. For the 'selfish' Frank Williams would never have been such a kind and generous friend to me in the depths of my troubles. During my bankruptcy he helped to educate my children. While I was in prison he visited me twice, making long and for him physically difficult journeys to HMP Stanford Hill on the Isle of Sheppey. On the second of these visits he said to me, 'I reckon you will need a car when you come out of here. Can I lend you one on a long-term basis?' Later, the long-term loan turned into a gift. These are not the actions of a man who 'forgets to be caring' (according to Keke Rosberg's portrayal) or the man who in his own estimate is so self-centred that he 'can't see other people's problems'. There are many more complexities in Frank Williams than meet the eye once one gets behind his carefully cultivated image of stoicism and selfishness.

The complexities, though real, are peripheral to the two great driving forces of Frank Williams's life – surviving and winning. Everything else is controlled, channelled and directed to these purposes. He has suppressed life's sadnesses and put personal happiness on hold. He does not seem to rejoice much at times of joy. When he was honoured with a knighthood in the New Year's Honours List of 1999, Frank called it 'a bit of an embarrassment really – it was more of a recognition for the team than for me'. So heavily did he downplay it that he never mentioned it to his children or his wife. Ginny was left to hear that she had become Lady Williams from a radio news bulletin.

If there is one area of joy that brings the heart of Frank Williams out of its emotional deep freeze it is his unabashed patriotism. 'I am an immensely strong royalist and loyalist. I love England. I love to carry the flag,' he declares with passion. Until recently this nationalistic side of the Williams persona had to stay muted. As a multilingual leader of international motor sport, partnered by French and then German manufacturers, backed by multinational sponsors and operating across the world's continents, Frank had to recognize that his patriotic zeal might be bad for business. But with British-led sponsors, engines and technology powering FW28 in 2006, there is a feeling that he can take the mute off the trumpet, unfurl the Union Jack and wave it more vigorously than ever before.

This patriotic romanticism has its roots in the young Frank's education at St Joseph's, Dumfries. During his ten years at the school, its 320 pupils were evenly split between Scots boys and English boys. As a result of the division which affected team games, friendships, meals and every aspect of life, the young Frank 'developed a pride in my nationality that I'll never lose'. This bulldog 'England will show 'em' spirit of his teenage years in the 1950s seems likely to re-emerge on the Grand Prix circuit of 2006 now that the Williams team is for the first time for many years, strongly supported by national companies. 'I'd die for England, I really would,' says Frank in one of his flag-waving moods.

Such thoughts are purely metaphorical on the part of a man who has so spectacularly defeated his own death by sheer determination. What he lives for today is what he has always lived for – motor racing. 'F1 has given me my life, my motivation, my world – everything,' he says. His daily struggle to get up in the morning, eat, breathe, sit at his desk and then start making the decisions that run the huge Williams team and business empire is a daily demonstration of courage. That courage is a beacon of inspiration, not only to millions of motor racing fans and to hundreds of thousands of disabled people, but to countless individuals who see in Frank Williams the living proof of how the human spirit can triumph over adversity. If in the course of battling towards that triumph he has formed a few rough edges and suppressed some emotions, this does not diminish his courage or his record of outstanding achievement. He more than deserves his place of honour in this book of heroes and contemporaries.

CHAPTER 9

Michael Portillo

Michael Portillo is an enigma with many variations. As a young Cabinet minister, he looked the strongest and most successful Conservative politician of his generation. But when the Tory leadership seemed well within his grasp, he cut loose from his Thatcherite moorings and altered course from ascent to descent. Some of this navigation was involuntary because he lost his seat. More of it was a deliberate tack towards a reinvented personal image and political philosophy. In one sense the reinvention was successful for in his new guise as a liberal modernizer, Portillo was to prove a trailblazer for David Cameron. Yet having carved out the path for a softer and more sensitive Tory party to follow, Michael Portillo changed course again, this time on a quest for personal fulfilment outside the world of Westminster. Has he found it in his new role as a maker of TV documentaries and writer of newspaper columns? Who is the real Michael Portillo? What were the ingredients in his story that made it impossible for him to live happily ever after in politics? And why did he never become Leader of the Conservative party in the years when the crown was all but his?

There are mysteries here. They deepen, so far as the Tory leadership is concerned, with the realization that this is not so much a whodunnit or a whodunhimoutofit as a why-didn't-he-fight-harder-for-it detective story. To make it more intriguing, the clues to the mystery do not lie on the surface of political events. They are buried deep in the perplexities of Portillo's psyche and personality. Whether one regards him as one more loser in the list of Britain's ex-future Prime Ministers, or as the Conservative party Leader who never got to lead because he was ahead of his time; or as the most interesting nearly man of recent political history, or as a rising new star in the firmament of television documentaries, Michael Portillo is worth writing about from an insider's perspective.

I first came to know Michael Portillo in circumstances of adversarial Parliamentary combat. He had just joined the government, aged 34, on the lowest rank of the ladder as a junior whip. In that role he was put in charge of delivering the votes in the committee stage of the Channel Tunnel Bill. As this legislation began its journey in Committee Room 5 in the autumn of 1986 under the chairmanship of the future Speaker Betty Boothroyd, it soon became apparent that the Bill was in trouble. This was because the junior whip could not control his senior backbenchers. In committee, governments want obedient and punctual votes, not long-winded and unhelpful speeches. If they get filibusters, difficult amendments, questions exposing weaknesses in clauses, cross-party alliances formed on the floor of the committee and successful voting rebellions then the timetable flies out of the window, putting the entire Bill in jeopardy. This was the situation that soon faced the young Michael Portillo as his first committee began to look as if it might end in catastrophe.

Modesty compels me to admit that I was the instigator of the impending disaster. I was an opponent of the Bill, initially because of the damage it would do to the ferry ports of Dover and Ramsgate in my constituency. But as the committee deliberated, I soon detected structural weaknesses in the legislation, including lack of protection for the environment and for investors in the Channel Tunnel Corporation whose shares I predicted (correctly) would soon be worthless. These arguments won support on both sides of the committee. With the help of an articulate Labour MP, Nick Raynsford, an all-party coalition was formed. So many amendments and new clauses had to be debated at the behest of this coalition that the government began to lose control of the committee's progress.

Most junior whips would have lost their nerve in such a disintegrating situation. Michael Portillo kept his and showed more than a touch of steel. He never attempted to use any of the usual high-pressure tactics beloved of whips to stop me in my tracks. Instead he bided his time for weeks of filibustering and then counter-attacked. With a combination of charm and cunning, he cobbled together a counter-coalition of tired Labour MPs who could not be bothered to keep up their opposition and revived Tories whom he coaxed or cajoled into returning to the fold as supporters of the legislation. After a succession of all night or late night sessions the Bill was eventually railroaded through. Although so badly delayed that it had to be held over until the 1987 General Election, nevertheless it reached the statute book more or less intact. Portillo had achieved victory in his first serious war of attrition in a Commons committee. Moreover, he won it with tactics that were both fair and formidable. From that time onwards, I knew that he was a political contemporary to be reckoned with.

Portillo's next post in government was to be Under Secretary for Social Security. It was dismissively known as 'the letter-writing job' because of the huge volume of correspondence from MPs whose constituents had problems with the minutiae of Social Security regulations. Because my constituency contained the largest DSS office in South East, I was an almost daily writer of complaining letters to the new Minister, often raising specific queries in considerable detail.

I soon noticed that the quality of Portillo's Ministerial correspondence was in a different league to that of many of his colleagues. He replied to MPs' letters with a speed and attention to detail that was impressive. Often he showed a touch of personal courtesy by adding a handwritten PS along the lines of: 'I am so sorry we have been unable to help Mrs X after considering your representations carefully.'

Some months after he had been in this job I asked him if he would come down to my constituency, combining a political engagement with a Ministerial visit to the DSS office in Ramsgate where the administrative backlog was causing many problems. 'Done,' he said immediately, bringing his wife Carolyn to stay for the week-end at our family home overlooking the Channel at Sandwich Bay.

Portillo was just starting to attract the whiff of a 'rising star' reputation which brings in its wake a trickle of rumours. So I had already heard insinuations to the effect that he was 'too smooth', 'flashy', 'far too pleased with himself', and even that his marriage was 'in trouble'. It did not take long to see that these were canards invented by his detractors. Minister Portillo handled his far-from-easy tour of the DSS office with impressive gravitas and mastery of his brief. He talked to staff members, from managers to union representatives, with an openness and politeness which was much appreciated. Politician Portillo charmed the South Thanet Conservative Association with a speech and a sociability that won him many admirers. Off duty he and Carolyn seemed to be the strongest of married couples as well as the most delightful of guests. Later I discovered that the source of the negative rumours about their relationship stemmed from the fact that they were childless.

As we waved the Portillos goodbye at the end of their visit, I said to my wife: 'I wouldn't be surprised if Michael leads the party one day.' It was his combination of gravitas and levitas that caused me to make this prediction, coupled with my observation of the reserved element in his character. For Michael's outward persona of pleasant geniality concealed an inner aloofness and steeliness which gave him that touch of mystery which is so often an ingredient in the chemistry of leadership.

Portillo's rise continued inexorably through the middle ranks of government. He was in favour with Margaret Thatcher who promoted him to the Minister of State for Transport and then Minister of State for Local Government with special responsibility for the poll tax. Although he had his reservation about many details of the legislation which he did his best to correct, Portillo was loyal to the principle of the community charge and loyal to the Prime Minister who had appointed him to be its champion. When Margaret Thatcher was about to fall, the last and most impassioned fighter of the rearguard action to keep her at No. 10 was Michael Portillo. It was perhaps his finest hour. After a majority of her cabinet had sabotaged the Prime Minister's chances of survival, Portillo led a late night delegation of junior ministers and backbenchers urging her to stand and fight. When he was shown into her study, he found a tearful Margaret Thatcher: 'They tell me my support is evaporating,' she began.

'They are wrong,' replied Portillo with a strength of conviction that momentarily rallied the Prime Minister's spirits. As she related Portillo's intervention in her memoirs:

> He tried to convince me that the Cabinet were misreading the situation, that I was being misled, and that with a vigorous campaign it might still be possible to turn things around. With even a drop of this spirit in higher places it might, indeed, have been possible. But that was just not there.

Later that same evening, a few hours before Thatcher bowed to the betrayals of her Cabinet and announced her resignation, Portillo returned to No. 10 for a private farewell to his heroine. It was an emotional scene. He had arrived hoping to rouse her to a fight to the death but Denis Thatcher had already persuaded his wife to stand down and avoid the humiliation of public defeat. So it was all over bar the weeping.

At a time when many other junior ministers were already jostling for position with one or other of the contenders for Thatcher's crown, Michael Portillo's romantic, if hopeless, loyalty to her did him great credit. He remained aloof from the leadership contest, eventually voting for John Major with some reluctance only because Margaret Thatcher asked him to do so. In the first months of Major's premiership, Portillo became a key player in the middle ranks of government because he had mastered the technicalities of local government finance. In his role as legislative technician for the Department of the Environment, Portillo executed an adroit U-turn as the government dropped the poll tax and replaced it with a heavily subsidized council tax. Michael Heseltine as Secretary of State for the Environment took the credit for freeing the Conservative party from the poll tax millstone around its neck. However, it was Portillo who did the real work and steered the new Council Tax Bill on to the statute book with exemplary confidence and courtesy throughout a gruelling committee stage in which he was tested hard by a formidable Labour opposite number, David Blunkett.

Although Portillo saved the government's and Michael Heseltine's reputation by delivering an acceptable replacement to the poll tax, it was noticeable to insiders that the Secretary of State and the Minister of State at the Department of the Environment were not soulmates. There was a chilly formality in the relationship between Heseltine and Portillo, who were so divided on Europe and other issues that they resembled two distant snow-clad peaks at opposite ends of the political landscape. However, they moved closer together on one matter of personal style. Apparently impressed by the leonine locks so carefully sculptured on the head and shoulders of his boss, Portillo decided to dispense with his schoolboyish short back and sides. The catalyst for this change came from a lunch with his constituents at the 1991 Conservative party conference. The conversation turned to politicians hair-dos and Portillo's agent Malcolm Tyndall told him: 'You'll be in the cabinet soon. You can't carry on looking like a rugby player who's just come out of the shower.' This criticism set Portillo off to a hairdresser who provided his new customer with a most elaborate Heseltinian restyling. Its centrepiece consisted of two ornate quiffs twirling together like a pair of mating conch shells in the middle of his forehead. It was a cartoonist's dream but also the source of nightmarish mocking in the smoking room of the House of Commons. After his first glimpse of the newly coiffeured Minister of State for Local Government, the sharp-tongued Tory whip David Lightbown commented, 'Does Michael think he's a bridegroom on top of a wedding cake in that marzipan confection?'

Perhaps what the new hairstyle did show was that Michael Portillo was taking himself seriously enough to begin cultivating a new political image. Soon he had a new job to go with it. For after the unexpected Conservative victory in the General Election of 1992, John Major promoted the 40-year-old Michael Portillo into the Cabinet as Chief Secretary to the Treasury. He had arrived at the top table of politics.

Michael Portillo loved the job of Chief Secretary to the Treasury and was very good at it. He took control of all government expenditure at a time when the public sector borrowing requirement was already alarmingly high at £28 billion and rising. In harness with two strong but difficult Chancellors, Norman Lamont and Ken Clarke, both of whom had uneasy relationships with No. 10, Portillo brought in spending rounds that were tighter (i.e. lower) than forecast. The £3.5 billion underspend he achieved in the 1993 expenditure round surprised all his Cabinet colleagues including his Chancellor and Prime Minister. More importantly he had delivered real cuts without creating bad political fallout or bad feelings from ministers whose departmental budgets cut across every area of government. With his reputation rising in both the House of Commons and the country, Michael Portillo was becoming a political heavyweight.

It was during his Chief Secretaryship that I started to work closely with Michael Portillo because I was in his sights as one of the biggest spending ministers. My budget as Minister of State for Defence Procurement was nearly £10 billion. Could it safely be cut at a time when the threat from the Soviet Union appeared to be diminishing? I agreed it could, but not at the sharp end of vital equipment. Instead I worked out a deal with Portillo and senior Treasury officials. The terms were that the Ministry of Defence would conduct a Defence Costs Review under my chairmanship to cut the tail of administrative support, not the teeth of front-line equipment. The best part of the deal was that if the review resulted in greater savings than the Treasury's target figure of £1 billion, then 50 per cent of the administrative money saved could be spent on the new equipment the armed forces regarded as their highest priority.

This was creative thinking for a Chief Secretary of the Treasury and it worked, both for Michael Portillo and for me. Between us and with the help of an outstanding team of officials from the MoD and the Treasury, we achieved savings of over £2.8 billion, ploughing nearly a billion of it back into new ships, aircraft, tanks and cruise missiles. These achievements did not escape the notice of a former Chief Secretary to the Treasury, John Major. In his summer Ministerial reshuffle of 1994 he promoted Portillo to Secretary of State for Employment and brought me into the Cabinet as the new Chief Secretary to the Treasury.

As Portillo's successor, I saw his work from the inside and was impressed. In his new job as Secretary of State for Employment, he was a good colleague when it came to making effective reductions in his department's budget. He didn't 'go native' on becoming a spending minister. In Cabinet I found him a kindred spirit particularly on European issues. I was an admirer of his political speeches and lectures which were distinctive for their intellectual quality and their philosophical depth. So like most Portillo watchers at this time, I subscribed to the growing feeling in the party that he was likely to be an attractive standard bearer of the right in any future leadership election, a subject which was being increasingly discussed in the summer of 1994.

Although John Major's government was having a bumpy ride politically in the aftermath of the Exchange Rate Mechanism withdrawal and the Maastricht Treaty, there were many rumours but no serious prospects of a leadership election until the Prime Minister himself unexpectedly called one. The first Michael Portillo heard about this well-kept secret was on the afternoon of Thursday the 22 June when he received a pager message in the middle of a speech he was making in a Westminster hotel asking him to come round to No. 10 Downing Street urgently. 'John Major told me that he was going to give up the leadership of the party and stand for re-election,' recalls Portillo. 'So I thought to myself "Gosh, I've got a split second in which to say 'good luck, Prime Minister' or 'I'm sorry I'm going to oppose you.'" Whether it was a failure of nerve on my part or whether – and this is the explanation I gave myself – it was the right judgement, I thought a move to oppose him would be an incredible position for me. I'd been a member of his Cabinet, I'd been part and parcel of all the government's decisions – how could I credibly compete for the leadership when he wanted it? So I said "well good luck, Prime Minister", and that was that. Position sealed.'

In fact, cracks started to appear in this sealed position within 24 hours of his meeting with the Prime Minister when Portillo considered the likely scenario of the leadership election. In the past few months he had kept his ear close to the ground among dissident backbenchers in the 92 Group and other dining clubs of the right. He thought there were so many anti-Major MPs that the Prime Minister would not get the required two thirds majority on the first ballot even if a maverick stalking horse candidate was his opponent. So Portillo began pondering on, and preparing for, the second ballot.

Much of the ponderings and preparation were being done at

Chadacre Hall in Suffolk, the country house of David Hart. This intelligent, creative and lateral-thinking property tycoon had done the state some service in recent years, first as an informal adviser to Margaret Thatcher during the miners' strike of 1983 and then as special adviser to Malcolm Rifkind in the Ministry of Defence where Hart played a significant role, not least in making a success of the 1993–94 Defence Expenditure Review. I was a considerable admirer of David Hart whom I had known well since we were together in the same house at school. However, his campaign planning for Michael Portillo's leadership bid over the weekend of the 23–25 June 1995 was not his finest hour.

The tug of war between Portillo's political loyalties began to get unpleasant when Viscount Cranborne, Major's campaign manager and Leader of the House of Lords, telephoned the Secretary of State for Employment on the evening of Friday the 23 June. Robert Cranborne wanted to know why Michael Portillo was the only senior Cabinet colleague not to have publicly supported the Prime Minister in the 24 hours since the announcement of the leadership election. Irritated by Cranborne's tone, which he regarded as arrogant and peremptory, Portillo gave an evasive answer. Cranborne became more peremptory, advising Portillo not to make a fool of himself and not to renege on his promise of support for Major, but if he was hell-bent on both courses of action then to put his hat into the ring without delay and take the consequences. This bad-tempered phone call ended with Portillo saying he would support Major – but with an ambiguity of manner which gave Cranborne little confidence in the reliability of the support.

The ambiguities continued during the next 48 hours at Chadacre as Portillo agonized over his options. I was a fellow week-end guest of David Hart's but was excluded from most of the conversations between him and Portillo because they knew I was a loyal Cabinet supporter of John Major. However, it was easy to pick up what was happening. Hart argued that once Major faltered and a second ballot was held, then the leadership election would turn into a battle royal between the champions of the Tory Left and Right – Michael Heseltine and Michael Portillo, which the latter would narrowly win.

However, Portillo would win bigger and better if he was bold enough to challenge Major immediately.

Portillo accepted the first part of the Hart game plan but rejected the second. So he stuck to his original decision of supporting Major. This loyalty might have been taken at face value had Portillo not sounded so evasive in his telephone conversation with Cranborne. To make the evasiveness seem even more sinister, Portillo gave the nod to Hart's plans of logistical preparations for the second ballot. These included making arrangements for the Portillo campaign headquarters to be based in Greville Howard's house in Lord North Street, which was equipped with a battery of extra telephone lines. Unwisely the energetic Hart placed the order for these lines immediately and BT engineers began installing them the following day. Once Robert Cranborne got wind of this Portillo plot, he gleefully leaked it to the media who no less gleefully took photographs of the BT engineers starting work in Lord North Street. Within 24 hours Portillo had been portrayed as a treacherous figure, reviled for secretly setting up a well-equipped campaign headquarters from which to attack the Prime Minister to whom he had publicly given his loyalty. 'It was a complete disaster,' recalls Portillo with the wisdom of hindsight, 'I looked a wonderful combination of appearing both irresolute and disloyal.' The only person who did not seem to be unduly bothered about the disloyalty was John Major who made a good joke about the prematurely installed telephones in Prime Minister's Questions, describing them as 'a tribute to the new efficiency of British Telecom since privatization'. After he had won the leadership election by a convincing margin on the first ballot, Major showed further magnanimity by promoting Portillo higher in the Cabinet as Secretary of State for Defence.

Understanding that his stock had fallen within the party as a result of his confusing behaviour during the leadership election, Portillo was anxious to restore his reputation by making a rousing speech at the annual Conservative party conference in October 1994. Unfortunately he lowered his stock still further by another bad judgement. He attempted to wrap himself in the flag as a new Defence Secretary with a peroration about the fear that came into the hearts of Britain's enemies whenever they heard the three initials SAS. Instead of sounding proud and patriotic, Portillo's words seemed synthetic and self-serving. He was attacked for the bad taste of his speech by many commentators who saw it as a blatant attempt to use the armed forces for party-political advantage.

Chastened by these attacks, Portillo returned to the Ministry of Defence on the Monday morning after the conference and made amends for his mistake in an unexpected way. He asked the Chiefs of Staff to come to his office one by one and apologized to each of them personally. His contrite message was that he had made 'a complete balls up' of his speech and that he was 'awfully sorry' to have shown such discourtesy to the armed forces.

This apology won hearts and minds. The Chief of the Defence Staff, General Sir Charles Guthrie (a former SAS commander), said at the end of the conversation with his penitent political master: 'Well, I know this, Secretary of State, there is no previous holder of your office that I can think of who would have apologized in the way that you have just done.' This and other favourable reactions from the Chiefs to Portillo's repentance were stories that spread like wildfire through the Ministry of Defence and down the chain of command to the armed forces. The news was remarkably well received, so much so that within the military world Portillo's reputation and his relationship with his department were transformed. During his last 20 months as Secretary of State for Defence he became a popular departmental minister. A similar transformation took place in the political arena of Westminster. With the passage of time the bad memories of Portillo's blunders faded. His willingness to admit and learn from his mistakes was seen as an asset. So was his growing surefootedness as a platform speaker and Parliamentary debater. In the monochrome blur of the tired Tory Cabinet he stood out as a more colourful and energetic political figure than most of his colleagues. So as the General Election loomed in the spring of 1997, Michael Portillo was once again looking like a leader-in-waiting as the bookmakers' favourite to succeed John Major.

Although many were expecting the Tories to lose the 1997 Election, few predicted the devastating magnitude of their defeat. Portillo was prescient enough to be among the pessimists. He felt the size of the swing during the campaign and saw the trend confirmed by an opinion poll published by the *Observer* on the Sunday before the election which said that he was only 3 per cent ahead in his Enfield Southgate constituency. Although he was sitting on a massive majority of 15,700, Portillo thought that the publication of this poll was a serious blow to his prospects because it would encourage many Liberal supporters to vote tactically in order to get him out. That was exactly what happened.

At the beginning of election night Portillo was the Conservative party's spokesman on duty in the BBC's television studio commenting on the early election results. 'As soon as we got the exit poll I could see that the swing was so enormous that I realized I must have lost my seat,' he recalls. 'I was astonished that Jeremy Paxman didn't cotton on to this. He never thought to ask me if I was going to lose in my own constituency. As I travelled from the BBC in White City to Enfield Southgate I was pretty sure I had lost so I wasn't at all surprised when my agent called me from the count to say it was looking extremely bad.'

Portillo's defeat was another of his finest hours. He showed not only dignity but eloquent generosity of spirit to his opponents. His valedictory speech as the ousted MP surrounded by a hysterically hostile crowd of excitable enemies exulting over his humiliation was one of the highlights of the night's TV coverage. It was a seminal moment not only for Portillo but for the entire Tory party. They had lost not just the election but also the next Leader of the Opposition.

Curiously the thoughts of Michael Portillo when he made his exit as the Member of Parliament for Enfield Southgate were not nearly as negative as might have been expected. He did not see his defeat as a personal humiliation, for in neighbouring constituencies of North London there were even bigger swings against sitting Conservative MPs. Nor was he so devastated in terms of his political career as most people must have imagined.

'I don't say it wasn't difficult,' recalls Portillo, 'but on that election night I didn't really feel so very dejected. Even at the moment of defeat I felt a certain sense of relief. People find that hard to believe but I could see that the Tories were going to be in a hopeless minority so it wasn't going to be much fun being there in Parliament. Also I could see that I would be expected to run for the leadership but that the leadership itself would be a very dismal prospect. I also thought that the leadership contest would be extraordinarily unpleasant and I was kind of dreading it.'

In these private musings it is possible to see some of the ambivalences and insecurities within Michael Portillo which help to explain why he did not reach the top of the greasy pole. There was a touch of the young Lord Rosebery (although he did briefly become Prime Minister) in Portillo's distaste for the hard slog and rough passages of opposition. Of Rosebery it was said: 'He sought the palm without the dust.' A similar criticism can be levelled at Portillo at this stage of his career. He had spent 11 of his 13 years as an MP within the government. That made him a man of office rather than a Parliamentarian, which is a defect when it comes to leading and running Her Majesty's Opposition. Someone whose heart was devoted to politics would not have been 'relieved' by a defeat which denied him the leadership of the Conservative party, nor would the rough and tumble of an unpleasant contest for the top job have been a deterrent to any determined seeker of political power. Such fastidiousness in Michael Portillo was a weakness, perhaps his Achilles heel.

There was one other rather more surprising weakness that surfaced in Portillo's last hours as a government minister. It was his lack of understanding of the respect and popularity he had built up for himself after two years as Defence Secretary. He can be forgiven for this because the Ministry of Defence does not easily show admiration for its ministers. On the whole politicians are seen as temporary birds of passage among the sceptical military officers and civil servants who make up the defence establishment. So when, on the morning after his election defeat, Portillo went back to his office to say his farewells to his private secretaries and a handful of senior advisers, he was surprised to hear an announcement over the tannoy, 'Anyone who wants to say goodbye to the Secretary of State come to the South Concourse at 9.30.'

The South Concourse is the largest assembly hall in the MoD's Whitehall building. When Portillo came down there at 9.30 he was astonished to see it filled with well over 1,000 military and civilian personnel. The unexpected warmth and spontaneity of this gathering made it an emotional leave-taking, so much so that Portillo left the Ministry of Defence for the last time in tears.

Why was this leave taking a sign of weakness in Portillo? Not because of his tears but because of his failure to read the right message from the cheers. After a rocky start he had proved himself to be an exceptional minister to one of the most demanding constituencies in the world. The British military recognize a good leader and they reckoned they had found one in Portillo. They were genuinely sorry to see him go. Instead of being uplifted by their applause and recognizing that he had passed a difficult popularity test with flying colours, Portillo took a different psychological tack. He decided that he was a deeply unpopular public figure and that it was imperative for him to make a U-turn towards a completely different image. What drove him to such a dramatic decision? In his own words: 'I wasn't aware how disliked I was . . . I was obviously in need of personal rehabilitation . . . I was shaken by the joy over my defeat which was voted the third favourite moment of the century by the *Observer* newspaper . . . I lost quite a lot of my grit . . . Before 1997 I didn't mind a punch-up. After 1997 I didn't feel as pugnacious as I had before . . . I was also worried by the way I'd been boxed into a pigeon hole of being socially illiberal whereas in fact I was always pretty liberal . . . so I knew I had to change.'

Portillo's vehicle for change was making films. Within two weeks of clearing out his office at Westminster he started discussions with commissioning editors at Channel 4, and the BBC about presenting documentaries. He also dabbled in journalism. Over the next few months this new career was creating a new Portillo. His first foray into television was a three-part series for Channel 4, *Portillo's Progress*. The programmes were well received, not least because they contained no self-justification, plenty of soul-searching and a display of personal charm which sparkled through the series as he gently pleaded for the Tory party to come to terms with the changes in contemporary British society. This thesis-on-film was an extension of what Portillo believes was the best speech of his life to the October 1997 Conservative

conference in which he argued that Tory politics had become unbear-
able to the public and needed to undergo root-and-branch changes in
attitude and philosophy. Norman Tebbit denounced it as 'touchy-feely
pink pound politics', but the viewers of *Portillo's Progress* seemed to be
intrigued by the small screen version of the 'mea culpa – all change
here' manifesto presented to them.

Public perception of Michael Portillo changed still further when he
made his next programme which was a beautifully filmed travelogue
in the BBC series *Great Railway Journeys*. Portillo's journey was a
voyage round his father, Luis Portillo, shot on location in the places
which had transformed his paternal hero into the gentle pacifist,
idealist, and self-exiled opponent of Franco's fascist Spain. It was an
emotional essay in filial homage which won glowing reviews.

By now the world was waking up to the idea that Portillo was
reinventing himself. Some of his old right wing fans were uneasy
about his new political posture, among them Margaret Thatcher
who let slip her opinion that her former acolyte was 'getting
confused'. Yet if there was any confusion it was not about Portillo's
new attitudes but about his old ambitions. For there could be little
doubt that he had genuinely changed. His hard-nosed politics had
softened into beliefs that were more liberal, more private, more
creative and more compassionate. However, these qualities might
not be compatible with a return to the front rank of Conservative
politics. For as the twentieth century neared its end there were few,
if any, indications that the Tory party had begun to change direction
in the ways advocated by Portillo. If he was going to make a political
comeback there were bound to be tensions between the old and new
sides of his character.

I caught an interesting glimpse of the new Michael Portillo in the
summer of 1999 when he came to see me in prison. I do not believe
that the old Portillo would have bothered to make such visit. As
Cabinet colleagues we were friendly without being close friends, so I
had no expectation that he would want to make the long trek down to
HMP Standford Hill to see someone who could not possibly be the
slightest use to him or his future career. The only explanation was that
he was visiting me out of kindness, a quality that manifested itself

clearly during the one and a half hours that he spent in the prison. As I wrote in my diary a few hours after seeing him:

> Michael was the star of the visiting hall, not only in the way he talked to me but also in his reactions to other prisoners. Several of them came over to shake his hand including [my cell neighbour] Mickey Aguda whose son wanted his autograph. There are dimensions of empathy and sympathy in the new Portillo, which poured out of him as he responded with genuine warmth to these encounters. His rapport with even the most off-putting of cons reminded me for a moment of Princess Diana holding hands with AIDS patients. I felt his caring side myself when we said our goodbyes at the end of the visit. He really seemed to mean his 'I look forward to seeing you again when you come out of here.'

Within a few weeks of Portillo's prison visit to me, two events took place which had a great impact on his political career. The first came when he gave a profile interview to a reporter from *The Times* who in the course of it asked the question 'Did you ever have any homosexual experiences while at university?' 'Yes,' replied Portillo who had felt for sometime that he was fed up with dodging such journalistic enquiries. His one-word answer elicited no reaction or follow-up questions from *The Times* reporter. As a result, Portillo rather naively thought that his admission rated low in journalistic importance.

While the article was awaiting publication by *The Times*, the second event occurred. This was the death of Alan Clark MP. It created a by-election in the safe Conservative seat of Kensington and Chelsea. There was immediate speculation that Michael Portillo would be the front runner for the nomination.

With perfect journalistic timing, *The Times* ran its interview with Portillo, 48 hours after the death of Alan Clark. The admission of homosexual experiences at university featured prominently on the newspaper's front page. It was immediately followed by a noisy hue and cry in the rest of the press:

'I was so disappointed,' recalls Portillo, 'I could easily have avoided *The Times* question but I was fed up with the old rumours and by the hysterical past stories in the underground press full of unbelievable rubbish like I was molesting children, I was involved with Peter Lilley, etc. So I thought most people's reaction would be 'Oh well, now he's said this he's made a clean breast of it and that's that!' But that wasn't the media's attitude at all. The attitude was 'Ahaha! If that's come out, now what's the whole truth? How long did it go on? Who was involved? I guess I was very naive not to foresee all that, but it was my effort to get rid of the whole thing.'

To make matters worse, Portillo not only had to endure a spate of press stories about his youthful indiscretions: he was also under gay fire from another angle, namely charges of political hypocrisy made by Peter Tatchell and others.

The main thrust of the hypocrisy claim was that when he was Secretary of State for Defence, Portillo had upheld the long established ban on active homosexuals in the armed forces. Although the facts were true, the criticism was not fair. As I can confirm from my own time as a Defence Minister who had to steer the annual Discipline in the Armed Forces Order through a difficult debate in the House of Commons, the top brass in the military felt extremely strongly about the damage homosexual activity could do to comradeship and trust in the services. It would be a bold minister who overruled the united advice of the Chiefs of Staff on such a matter. Portillo, like all his predecessors, was not progressive enough to do so. He did not deserve vilification for declining to overturn his department's strong views on this issue on the basis of his personal feelings.

Unfortunately for Portillo he was getting vilification by the bucketful from the tabloids on almost every aspect of his decision to 'come out'. He had a miserable summer of hard pounding in the press which he did his best to ignore with dignity. However, the avalanche of negative publicity seemed likely to bury his chances of winning the nomination for Kensington and Chelsea.

In one of the earliest signals that attitudes were changing in the Tory party, the selectors and electors of Alan Clark's old seat took a different view from the media on the importance of Portillo's homosexual past. By November 1999 he was back in Parliament as the newly elected Member for the constituency, fired up with energy and idealism which he felt came from the recharging of his batteries during his past two and a half years out of the House of Commons. So Portillo re-entered Westminster with a spring in his step, full of optimism that a new chapter in his political career had begun.

The chapter turned out to be an unhappy one. Almost immediately Portillo came back into the spotlight as a leader-in-waiting. William Hague was doing badly in the opinion polls despite all his successes at Westminster as a Parliamentary debater. In the country, Portillo was seen as a more heavyweight politician. Some of this perception was due to one of Portillo's earlier television programmes, in which Hague had been the star interviewee. Portillo came across as a powerful television presence, looking fit, suntanned and totally in command of the screen. Hague by contrast was recovering from a virus. He looked peaky, sounded squeaky and seemed a smaller and inferior figure alongside his interrogator. These visual images, however unfair, were soon reinforced by columnists and cartoonists. One cartoon which captured the feeling of the period depicted Portillo the compassionate conservative as a leopard whose spots were changing into hearts. However, this likeable leopard was up in a tree lying alongside a trembling chimpanzee with the face of William Hague, who was clearly terrified of being gobbled up by the leopard.

Despite many such comparisons in the weeks after Portillo's return to Parliament, William Hague moved quickly to bring his alleged rival into the Shadow Cabinet. Hague's offer of Shadow Chancellor was gratefully accepted. As Portillo recalls the conversation: 'William said to me: "I can see us being a duumvirate. There'll not be a cigarette paper between us. We'll do things together. It'll be fantastic!" Now I was hugely enthusiastic about this proposition. I thought it would be marvellous. I was determined to make it work. I also thought that this was a way in which I could put behind me all that stuff about plotting against John Major behind his back. So I was committed to being loyal to William and really wanted to make our relationship succeed as if it was a two-headed thing.'

Unfortunately several other heads immediately began poking their noses into the duumvirate plan. The outgoing Shadow Chancellor Francis Maude, who was upset at being moved, had a first-class special adviser, Robin Gibb. He was moved out also at Hague's insistence, which did not bother Portillo who simply said when Hague mentioned the change, 'Fine, you're the leader.' But what seemed to be a minor matter became major newspaper headlines. The weekend after his appointment as Shadow Chancellor, lurid stories appeared in the Sunday papers saying that Portillo had been defeated and neutered by Hague as a result of the removal of Francis Maude's allegedly disloyal adviser. On discovering what they thought was strong evidence that these stories had emanated from briefings by Sebastian Coe and Amanda Platell, two key advisers in William Hague's office, Portillo and Maude became furious. As Portillo recalls the episode: 'Francis and I both went to William Hague and said, "We can't go on like this. We've got to quit. If your advisers are plotting against us, it's either the advisers or us." And William just said, "Well, I'm not getting rid of the advisers."'

Portillo and Maude seriously discussed resigning from the Shadow Cabinet at that point. Had they done so it would have been a declaration of war which would probably have brought down William Hague. But Portillo did not want to provoke a leadership election and decided to soldier on. Nevertheless the episode left an unpleasant odour which never quite disappeared.

'Trust was shattered from that first moment,' recalls Portillo, 'it is an important part of my personal story. I loathed it. I was so disillusioned. I loathed almost every moment of the next 16 months or so until the election came. I longed for it to come to an end. I just couldn't bear it.'

The passion with which Portillo speaks, to this day, about this incident is perplexing. Even if his account of the advisers' negative briefings against him is wholly accurate it is still in the category of what General de Gaulle once called *'une affaire des subalternes'*. A thick-skinned politician would surely have brushed it aside and got on with the most important issues. Was Portillo becoming too thin-skinned?

In the long winter of Tory discontent since his defeat in 1997, Portillo changed from a bruiser to a man who is easily bruised. He was struggling to come to terms with a number of sensitive issues, both political and personal. Many of them were to do with people's perceptions of him. Was he likeable or dislikeable? Gay or straight? Trustworthy or untrustworthy? Liberal or conservative in his attitudes to social policy? Confused or clear thinking in his political philosophy? Did his heart lie in his political career or in a new career as a filmmaker, writer and broadcaster? These are questions which are usually resolved in a man's life much earlier than the late forties and long before entering the frame as a serious competitor for the job of Prime Minister. As an individual, it was to Portillo's credit that he wanted to confront these issues even if it meant giving the impression that he was going through some sort of mid-life crisis. As a politician, his mixed signals created mixed opinions.

On his likeability, Portillo was often surprised by the number of people who said to him in his early years as a film-maker: 'Gosh, you're so much nicer in your documentaries than you were in politics.' Such comments accelerated his quest for what he called, 'my need for rehabilitation', but which may have been a much simpler and shallower desire to be liked. The premise on which this quest was based was arguable. For Portillo was never an objectionable or unattractive figure. Many politicians get caricatured at certain stages of their career but the idea that he was some sort of conservative 'Mr Nasty' is absurd. A bad booing on the night of an election defeat does not alter the reality that Michael Portillo always had plenty of charm, charisma, courtesy and character in his personality. He was well respected in all the Whitehall departments in which he served and exceptionally well regarded in some of them, particularly by the Treasury and the Ministry of Defence. The same can be said in broad terms of Portillo's reputation in the House of Commons. Ignoring these favourable judgements of his peers and allowing his self-confidence to be undermined by unfavourable vox pop opinions from the public in the aftermath of the 1997 Election debacle showed that Portillo was far less secure than he looked.

His insecurities can only have been increased by the artificial furore about his sexuality. He was unlucky in his timing. For most of the twentieth century, the Conservative party was at worst homophobic and at best hypocritical about MPs with gay histories. In 1999 Portillo was the first 'big fish' of Cabinet rank to make an open admission of his past homosexuality. The synthetic sensationalism that greeted his one word answer to *The Times* journalist's questions was the last gasp of overt homophobia among the chattering classes of conservatism. Five years later politicians with gay experiences in their lives are as routinely accepted as gays in any other walk of life. Portillo was the pioneer whose coming out made it possible for any other senior Tory politicians to come out with impunity. Seen with hindsight, he deserves credit for his honesty. At the time he must have wondered whether honesty had been the best policy, because his admission undoubtedly increased his bruises.

On the issue of trustworthiness, Portillo deserves a higher rating than the one he was given inside the Conservative party under the leaderships of John Major and William Hague. In this context an understanding of the Spanish side of Portillo's nature is helpful. For he is at heart a proud Castilian with an old-fashioned sense of honour. He becomes profoundly unhappy if he feels his honour is being tarnished, even and perhaps especially when he knows he has contributed to the tarnishing by his own mistakes. He accepted that he deserved to be criticized for plotting against John Major during the 1995 leadership election even though his deviousness consisted of nothing more serious than hesitation and hedging of bets in the middle of massive political turbulence. Before and after that leadership election I saw enough of him to know that Portillo was much more loyal than many members of the Cabinet to Major. He never deserved the Prime Minister's leaked private description of him as 'a bastard'. Nor did Portillo deserve the constant briefings against him by William Hague's aides, suggesting that he and unidentified 'Portillistas' were engaged on a constant campaign to seize the leadership of the Opposition at the earliest opportunity. Hague himself had more than a touch of paranoia about this possibility. Yet the truth was that Portillo never tried to undermine his Leader or to brief against him. What caused the relationship between these two outstandingly able men to deteriorate was Hague's constant blocking of Portillo's attempts to make headway in modernizing the Conservative party.

Portillo had first set out his stall on party modernization in an acclaimed lecture to the Conservative party conference in October 1997. He had warned his audience about the bad habits and images the party needed to discard. This unwanted baggage included 'disagreeable messages and thoughts . . . harshness . . . greed . . . being uncaring about unemployment, poverty, poor housing, disability and single parenthood . . . insensitivity, arrogance, and being out of touch'. The goals he wanted to champion were: 'compassion . . . dignity of choice in education and healthcare . . . opportunity to enter higher and further education . . . more decision-making at the local level . . . more support for voluntary organizations . . . tolerance as part of the Tory tradition . . . new attitudes to the personal relationships that people choose to enter . . . accepting the diversity of human nature . . . dealing with the world as it is now'.

In his role as Shadow Chancellor and de facto No. 2 in the party leadership, Portillo tried hard to make progress with this manifesto. Yet he became increasingly frustrated by Hague's unwillingness to move in the same direction. The Leader of the Opposition seemed stuck on what Portillo called 'the *Daily Mail's* agenda . . . and in the end we actually fought the election on tax cuts, Europe, and saving the pound sterling. Very depressing.'

Portillo tells a depressing story about one episode in the saga of the blocking of his modernization agenda by the Hague team. It happened in the spring forum of the Conservative party, in effect a mini-party conference held a few months before the 2001 General Election. In advance of the event, the Shadow Cabinet had agreed the principal modernization themes of the conference with key phrases such as 'Reaching Out', 'Connecting' and 'New Compassion'.

'So I wrote my press release and it contained all these phrases that we'd agreed, "Connecting"; "Reaching out", and so on,' recalls Portillo. 'I gave it to the party's press officer, Nick Wood, to release. He was a very hard-nosed Tory with a strong influence on William Hague. To my astonishment, Wood the press officer banned my statement. He refused point blank to release it. I tried to get Hague to overrule this decision but he could not be reached in time for the release to catch any deadlines. So the end result was the spring forum's modernization agenda never reached the press.'

With these kind of internal disputes going on, it was not surprising that the Conservatives were again routed at the polls. The margin of defeat was almost as bad as in 1997. Portillo was so demoralized by the result that his immediate private reaction was to decide that the coming Parliament would be his last as an MP. But in the days following the election when he was taking a break in his favourite hotel in Morocco, the Gazelle d'Or, he changed his mind and became a candidate for the leadership of the party. The speed of this strategic reversal suggests that Portillo was in a state of short-term emotional volatility, far removed from the determined tenacity that the long game of politics requires from its players. What happened was that as soon as William Hague made it clear that he was leaving, Portillo started receiving phone calls from Francis Maude and other supporters.

'These callers kept saying things like, "You've got to do it . . . it will be a shoe in . . . it will be an acclamation," and I believed them. I was pleased so I accepted their advice and ran,' he recalls.

Portillo ran on a modernization ticket. He talked in 2001 about many of the reforms that David Cameron is bringing to the Conservatives in 2006, such as changing the look of the party, changing the mix of MPs, bringing into Parliament more women and more people from ethnic backgrounds, and being representative of the country in attitudes and values.

'I wanted to make the Tory party quite different,' says Portillo, 'but it became clear that not enough of my fellow MPs shared the same view. I don't think my problem was getting the votes from Conservatives in the country. It was getting the votes from Conservatives in the House of Commons. I started my campaign with about 50 supporters there and I ended with the same number. I just didn't make any headway.'

There were several reasons for this lack of progress. The Tories had been reduced to an inward-looking rump of 170 MPs, many of them resigned to a long period of opposition. Old rifts and old factions divided them. They were not warm towards new ideas for modernization nor towards the candidate who was championing them. Portillo was neither likeable enough nor subtle enough to increase his votes among the uncommitted members of this strange, small electorate:

'I think my real problem was that I simply wasn't liked enough,' recalls Portillo. 'I was seen as too flash, half Spanish, and half gay as far as many of them were concerned. I was also campaigning on a programme equivalent to asking turkeys to vote for Christmas.'

Despite these real disadvantages it is probable that just enough turkeyish Tory MPs would have given Portillo the votes he needed to get into the final and, for him, far easier round of national party membership voting if only he had campaigned among his Parliamentary colleagues with greater skill and sensitivity. Instead he displayed an aloofness, at times an arrogance, as he presented his case for modernization in the most uncompromising of terms.

Portillo's tactics in the leadership election are said to have baffled one interested observer of the proceedings. This was Tony Blair who was reported to have made the comment: 'What's he doing? If he wants to change his party why doesn't he stay mum now and then do it after the election?'

Portillo would have no truck with such Blairite silence. Indeed there were moments when he seemed to be going out of his way to alienate his supporters. He was embarrassingly rude to one long-standing ally, Bernard Jenkin MP, who consequently switched his vote to Iain Duncan Smith. On the eve of the election, one of his likely supporters, Graham Brady MP, saw Portillo and said, 'You can have my vote if you promise you won't introduce women-only short lists.' Portillo had many options, as Cameron is now demonstrating, for bringing more Tory women into Parliament. But instead of discussing these with Brady, Portillo's answer was a curt: 'Thank you so much for coming to see me. I enjoyed talking to you.' As he failed to reach the final round of the leadership election by one vote, such stern unbending tactics look foolish in retrospect.

Portillo, however, had no regrets, 'I just felt such a strong will to get the leadership on my own terms with everything clear about what I was going to do that I knew I must get it that way or not do it at all,' he recalls, 'I don't repent that. In fact when the day of the ballot came round, to be honest about it, I was wanting to lose. I realised I wasn't going to get the big mandate I needed for modernization, which meant I wouldn't be able to get all the changes through. So when I was eliminated from the final round I gave a real Yahoo of joy!'

There could be no clearer evidence that Portillo had changed from being the professionally dedicated, highly ambitions politician of his Cabinet minister years. Yahooing with joy at being beaten into third place for the Tory leadership by Iain Duncan Smith and Ken Clarke is not the reaction of a serious contender for the job of Prime Minister. There is little doubt that Portillo could quite easily have become Leader of the Opposition, with a mandate to modernize the party, if he had fought the 2001 leadership election with greater determination. But like Lord Rosebery, 'He sought the palm without the dust.'

There was one other ingredient in Portillo's strange reluctance to do battle for the Tory crown with all his strengths and talents. Like another nearly man of history R. A. Butler (of whom Enoch Powell memorably commented in the 1963 leadership contest: 'Our cock won't fight'), Portillo was a man of government not a man of Parliament. As he himself puts it: 'I never had a particular love of the House of Commons. I very much enjoyed office, I enjoyed my constituency, but I wasn't good in the House of Commons. I found Opposition completely miserable and humiliating. I struggled for credibility as Shadow Chancellor and I found among my own colleagues both the disloyalty and the allegations of disloyalty against me very difficult to cope with.'

This self-portrait of Portillo as an unhappy Parliamentarian helps to explain his lack of hunger for the glittering prizes of political life. Moreover, because in his Ministerial days he seemed to personify what Disraeli called 'that indefinable air of fogs and grave statesmen which characterise English Conservatism', it was easy to miss the fey, artistic and sybaritic dimensions in Portillo's character which were his lighter hinterland. 'I am more laid back than I look,' he says, ' and I have always been determined to enjoy myself. So once I lost office I rather opportunistically used politics to move into other fields that gave me greater enjoyment.'

The opportunities for enjoyment came knocking in the form of more and more TV programme-making offers from the BBC, Channel 4 and ITV. The critical success of the *Great Railway Journeys* documentary about his father Luis led to Michael Portillo becoming a frequent presence on the nation's screens. In the last five years he has had a regular slot as co-host (with Andrew Neill and Diane Abbott MP) on *This Week*, BBC 1's political discussion show. He has hosted 26 editions of *Dinner with Portillo* and has made over 30 documentaries on musical, historical and environmental subjects of his choice, ranging from Wagner's Ring to Spanish wild life. So as a broadcaster he has carved out a formidable second career which he supplements with print journalism in the form of a weekly political column for the *Sunday Times* and being a theatre critic for the *New Statesman*. Some of his old political admirers saw most of these activities as lightweight ephemera compared to the serious business of a high-profile political career. However, in Portillo's new mood of detachment from the Tory front bench, it was difficult for the drudgery of Opposition to compete with the excitement of such well-recognized and well-rewarded creative success.

In his mind, Portillo returned to the plan that he formulated immediately after the 2001 General Election. He would quit the House of Commons at the end of the Parliament. However, there was one last unexpected development which might have lured him back towards the limelight and the leadership. This came in 2003 when a coup against Iain Duncan Smith suddenly erupted on the backbenches, and Michael Howard became Leader of the Opposition. Anxious to revive the Conservative fortunes by creating a Shadow Cabinet of all the talents, Howard offered Portillo a key appointment to the front bench.

There is a minor mystery about what exactly was on offer. It was widely reported that Howard wanted Portillo as Shadow Chancellor. However, Portillo has indicated that the new leader's first proposal to him was not a tempting one, 'I promised Michael I would never tell anyone what he offered me,' is all he will say about it. An improved offer of a Shadow Cabinet post was made but the invitation was declined. In a co-ordinated announcement, Portillo declared that he would be standing down as an MP at the next election. His political career was over.

There are mysteries that still cloud these events. If Portillo had accepted Michael Howard's offer and served in the Shadow Cabinet in some important role, surely he would have emerged after the 2005 election as the front runner in the race to become the leader of the Opposition. Would either David Davis (who had only been a middle ranking junior minister) or the unknown David Cameron have beaten a highly experienced Michael Portillo who had three Cabinet appointments, a Parliamentary fan club and plenty of media support behind him? Portillo himself finds this an implausible scenario. He does not believe that he could ever have won the Tory leadership in 2005 nor that the Conservatives can win the 2009 General Election. 'The prospect of hanging around in politics until 2013 hoping that I might be, say, Foreign Secretary at the age of 60 did not appeal to me,' he says.

Perhaps the attitudes behind these judgements reflect a shift in the values not just of Michael Portillo but in Britain as a whole. A career in politics has been downgraded to a position below a career in the media. It is better to be someone on the TV screen than to do something in the Cabinet. Fame and money are more exciting com- modities in our twenty-first century culture than political power and Parliamentary achievement. If that is the temper of our times, who can blame Michael Portillo for going with the flow.

Nevertheless it remains a puzzle why this gifted and dedicated politician (until the age of 50), who had at least two and arguably four golden opportunities in Tory leadership matches with the ball at this feet in the penalty area, should have hung up his boots at an early age without scoring. One explanation of this is that he lost his way and his will power on the more difficult stages of the road to No. 10 Downing Street. A simpler reason might be that he discovered his personal pref- erences lay towards life in the media rather than life in the House of

Commons. That may have disappointed the fans who believed he had the talent and the vision to be an outstanding British Prime Minister, but which of us should begrudge Michael Portillo the greater happiness he has found in his second career?

CHAPTER 10

Nicky Gumbel

'If I had to choose between being a cabinet minister, a millionaire or an evangelist I would now choose to be an evangelist. It is the evangelist who has the greatest capacity for doing good.'

These words, spoken by my great uncle, the first Lord Beaverbrook, are quoted in the opening chapter of this book. Perhaps it is an appropriate touch of author's symmetry to make my closing chapter a profile of the evangelist who has had a huge impact on my life. He is Nicky Gumbel, the world's most successful Christian evangelist of the twenty-first century. He himself would recoil with embarrassment at this description, but it is true. Not since Billy Graham in the 1950s or Pope John Paul II in the 1980s has any Christian communicator achieved the global influence and audience that Gumbel now reaches from his West London church, Holy Trinity Brompton (HTB), through the Alpha course.

What is Alpha and who is Gumbel? Only by answering the first question does the identity of this self-effacing 50-year old Church of England vicar emerge in a way that explains his importance as the pre-eminent leader of modern international evangelism.

Created in its contemporary form by Gumbel, Alpha is a ten-week Introduction to Christianity course subtitled *Explore The Meaning of Life*. Orthodox in its Biblical faithfulness yet unorthodox in its encouragement of questions from its participants, Alpha has been enthusiastically endorsed across a broad spectrum of denominations and doctrines, ranging from low-church Protestant evangelicals to high-church Anglicans and Roman Catholics. As a result of this unusual display of ecclesiastical unity towards Alpha, over 8 million people have now completed its courses in 160 countries under Gumbel's leadership. No other contemporary evangelist comes close to this range of global influence.

As Alpha's architect and principal teacher, Gumbel has crisscrossed the world during recent years in almost perpetual motion, launching the course in venues from Shanghai to Seattle, Moscow to Mombassa. His mission is deliberately made accessible to people who are not Christians. No-one quite understands why Alpha has been successful in reaching so many of these non-believers. Enthusiasts say that God must be using the course as his leading evangelistic tool in the present age. Opponents deride Alpha as a simplistic, although successful, evangelical cult. A neutral view might be that Gumbel has found an up-to-date and unthreatening formula for presenting Christianity to those who are normally lukewarm, ignorant or sceptical about matters of faith.

Whatever observers feel about the merits or demerits of Alpha, most would agree that it is not an ego trip for Nicky Gumbel. He designed the course not to compete against other churches but to complement them. Disliking personal publicity, he shies away from applause, accolades and all forms of self-aggrandizement. Yet for all his humility, there is a core of steel in Gumbel which gives him the cutting edge with which he is today driving Alpha and HTB towards ever-higher goals in accordance with what he believes are God's purposes. His visionary plans aim to get another 25 million people completing Alpha courses by 2020. Given his track record, and the current 1 million a year rate of individuals doing Alpha courses, Gumbel seems likely to hit his target. The story of the private man behind these public achievements is worth telling.

Nicky Gumbel was born just a few hundred yards along Knightsbridge from the church where he now is vicar, of unusual if not faintly eccentric parents in 1955. His father Walter was a German Jew from Stuttgart who left that city in the mid-1930s soon after having his licence to practise law withdrawn in one of the early Nazi purges. Walter emigrated to Britain and became a successful 'senior junior' at the English bar. After being briefly interned at the start of the war he spent the rest of it working in special operations for MI5. Returning to the law in 1945, this bustling bachelor remained single until the age of 49 when to everyone's surprise he married Muriel Glyn, a colourful young pupil in his chambers. Both parents were energetic to the point of being driven. Saving in order to educate their children was their principal drive. Walter worked legendary hours, even by barristers' standards. He never became a QC because in those days taking silk meant a drop in income for at least a year or two. Every penny counted in the Gumbel family as the redoubtable Muriel kept reminding them. She was a frugal lady with many of the instincts, political opinions and personality traits of a Margaret Thatcher. Believing in multiple sources of income and minimal outlets of expenditure, Muriel took in lodgers, gave lectures, practised law and offered investment advice. As a keen small investor, she played the stock market, at one time becoming chairman of the British Leyland minority shareholders committee even though she did not hold a driving licence. Effusively generous in her hospitality Mrs Gumbel could be over-zealous in her hoarding. 'Pieces of string too small to be useful' was the label on one of her boxes. 'Krugerrands and other small gold coins – in case of devaluation,' said another. When she was elected Mayor of the Royal Borough of Kensington, she saved the dress allowance given to her by Walter and bought her clothes from the charity shop instead. Such economies helped the Gumbels to educate their two children privately. At the age of 13 Nicky was sent to Eton where a contemporary remembers him as 'full of prodigious energy and dogged determination'. His lifelong friend Nicky Lee, who was in the same house recalls, 'There was always an affable ease of relationship with Nicky. He had no apparent ambition, no enthusiasm to know the right people, no agenda. He was a pleasant social sort of guy.'

Social life was a high priority for the young Nicky Gumbel. Lee recalls being amused by an early glimpse of him as a Cambridge undergraduate clasping a thick wad of engraved invitation cards in one hand, flicking through them at high speed with the other saying: 'yes . . . no . . . maybe . . . this one will be worth going up to London for . . .' and so on. However, Gumbel's enthusiasm for party invitations was matched by an aversion towards Christian invitations. During freshers' week at Cambridge when newly arriving students receive many approaches from local churches. Gumbel developed his own technique for keeping them at arm's length. 'If any of those Christians come and knock on your door, only open it an inch or two and talk to them through the crack,' he advised his fellow Trinity freshmen. 'If you let them come in they'll stay and bore you for hours.'

What began to soften Nicky Gumbel's aversion to Christians was the sudden decision of his friend and room neighbour at Trinity, Nicky Lee, to become one. Lee had been attending a series of mission evenings organized by the Cambridge Inter-Collegiate Christian Union (CICCU). On the last night of the week-long series he committed his life to Jesus Christ. Returning from this conversion experience on the night of Saturday the 14 February 1973 he found Gumbel in full swing at the Trinity St Valentine's Day ball. After the festivities wound down, the two Nickys exchanged reports on their respective evening's adventures, Lee with Jesus in church and Gumbel with girls on the dance floor. As they talked into the night, Lee realized that he could have a conflict of interest in his new life. For he had invited the CICCU missioner, who had converted him, the Revd David MacInnes, to lunch the next day without mentioning that he had a prior commitment to lunch with his girlfriend Sila. This double booking had the potential for double embarrassment. Lee was not sure whether new Christians were allowed to have girlfriends. Would the converter disapprove of his new convert's lifestyle? Listening to this, Gumbel thought his friend had gone mad and joined the Moonies. However, he offered a practical solution, suggesting that he should join them for lunch as well. This would defuse any possible embarrassment over Sila by safety in numbers.

The lunch with the Revd David MacInnes was a turning point in Gumbel's life. For the next two and a half hours he listened to the visiting missioner with growing interest, questioning him intensely about the idea of 'having a personal relationship with Jesus', which MacInnes said had transformed his own life, marriage and happiness. That night Nicky Gumbel began reading the Bible. He got through Mathew, Mark, Luke and half way through John's gospel, before falling into an exhausted sleep. When he woke up he finished John's

gospel and carried on through Acts, Romans, and 1 and 2 Corinth-
ians. 'I was completely gripped by what I read. I had read it before and
it meant nothing to me,' Gumbel recalled. 'This time it came alive and
I could not put it down. It had a ring of truth about it. I knew as I read
it that I had to respond because it spoke so powerfully to me.'

The next few weeks saw both Nickys on fire with their new-found
Christian fervour. Most of their spare time was spent attending
services and Bible study classes at the Round Church, the leading
centre of conservative evangelicalism in Cambridge. They became
prayer partners as well as friends, reading Ephesians, Philippians and
other letters of the New Testament together while also trying to
envangelize anyone else in their group of students who was willing to
listen to them.

'They really became an extraordinary couple,' said Nicky Lee's girlfriend Sila; 'within a week they were talking about getting ordained.
They even started growing beards to make themselves look like Jesus.'
Another young woman in their social circle, Pippa Hislop, had her
doubts about the mental equilibrium of Gumbel the convert. He had
not stopped going up to parties in London but his approach to girls
on the dance floor had become rather different. At one Chelsea soirée
Pippa was accosted by Nicky Gumbel who said: 'You look awful. You
really need Jesus.' If it was meant to be a joke it misfired badly. 'I
thought he had gone completely mad, he was so utterly different,' was
Pippa's recollection of this encounter. Her impressions were shared by
other observers of Gumbel at this time. 'He was completely OTT,' said
one contemporary, 'he went round with his pockets bulging out at the
sides because they were packed full of Christian tracts and booklets
which he would hand out to unsuspecting acquaintances in the pub
asking them if they would like to get to know Christ.' The smart set at
the Pitt Club in Cambridge soon made his behaviour a target for
gentle mockery. 'Here comes the divinely inspired Mr Nicholas
Gumbel!' was the sort of greeting he became used to receiving.

Gumbel may have seemed a little odd in these early days of his new
Christian zeal but he soon settled down to the disciplined life of being
both a hard-working student and a good Christian. The curate from
the Round Church, Jonathan Fletcher, was a key influence on him as

a personal and spiritual mentor. One of Fletcher's nostrums was: 'Christians going to heaven/Get to bed by eleven'. Gumbel more or less obeyed this ordinance, following a regime of hard work and early nights which helped him to get good marks for his essays in Economics and Law. At the same time he was seriously applying himself to Bible studies and courses organized by CICCU. Among the visiting preachers who made a great impact on Gumbel were John Stott and Dick Lucas. They were conservative evangelicals but Gumbel was beginning to take an interest in more adventurous Spirit-led churchgoing. With his two closest Christian friends at Cambridge, Nicky Lee and Ken Costa, he occasionally went to St Mathews, a charismatic church on the outskirts of the city. The trio also attended Christian teaching holiday camps at Iwerne Minister in Dorset led by the Revd E. G. H. 'Bash' Nash. Gradually the two Nickys and Ken Costa started to form their own distinctive view of the church and how it needed to change.

'In a way we were breaking new ground in what at that time was almost underground samizadat-type of spiritual territory,' recalls Ken Costa; 'we knew we were on to a different form of Christianity to that offered by the liberal college chaplains. But was it authentic? Were we just captured by an illusion of certainty? Led by Nicky Gumbel's highly discerning mind we pressed ourselves for the answers.'

Some of the answers flowed from their own bonding. These three musketeers – Gumbel, Lee and Costa – were reassuringly normal, cheerful, life-enhancing young students. Their friendship, which has remained close for over 30 years, was light years removed from asceticism, puritanism, fundamentalism or any other kind of religious-ism. Their confidence in tackling difficult questions came not only from their faith but also from their well-rounded, happy, undergraduate lives. All three were hospitable party-givers, enthusiastic games players, popular in the student community, secure in their relationships. They expected to have successful secular careers. They were all content to wait and see whether the God they believed in would call them to some aspect of his service and if so, how. It was in that frame of mind that their years at Cambridge came to an end in the summer of 1978.

In June Nicky Gumbel graduated with a respectable 2:1 degree in Law. One of his last parties at the University was the Trinity College Senior Ball. His date for the evening was the Chelsea girl who had at one time thought him 'completely mad', Pippa Hislop. Daughter of an army officer, Pippa had become a committed Christian through 'The Kitchen', a group of friends who cooked, prayed and ate together in and around a converted news garage in Kensington. Nicky and Pippa had been part of this set for two or three years. After the Trinity Summer Ball their relationship blossomed into love, engagement and finally marriage in 1978.

Although he had talked about ordination in the heady days immediately after his conversion experience during his second term at Cambridge, Nicky Gumbel put the idea of becoming a vicar on the back burner and settled down to the hard grind of becoming a barrister. Even after two years of reading law at university this required two years of further studies in London to pass the bar exams plus additional years of pupillage and eating dinners. Then he spent the next six years following in his father's footsteps, building up a common law practice that ranged from defending burglars to arguing complex commercial cases. By the early 1980s Nicky Gumbel was steadily climbing the ladder towards being a senior junior which would then have headed onwards and upwards to becoming a QC. It was exactly the career path his sister Elizabeth Anne Gumbel QC has followed, for she is now a leading silk with a successful practice in family law.

While his legal career was prospering in the world of Mammon, Gumbel did not neglect his relationship with God. After coming down from Cambridge in 1976 he became a regular worshipper at Holy Trinity Brompton in Knightsbridge. In the mid-1970s there were no clues that this might become a church which would revitalize Christianity across the world. In those days it was a somewhat staid ecclesiastical establishment with a robed choir, sung Matins from the 1662 Book of Common Prayer as its principal Sunday service, and sherry served immediately afterwards to its smartly dressed congregation of some 200 Kensington residents. However just below the surface of this outward formality, much was changing at HTB. This change was largely due to the arrival of a new young curate who was to exercise a powerful influence on the life of Nicky Gumbel and indeed on the life of the Church of England. He was the Revd Sandy Millar whose pre-ordination background of a career at the Bar, Trinity College Cambridge and Eton gave him an immediate rapport with Gumbel which ripened into a deep friendship.

Nicky and Pippa Gumbel, who were married at HTB in January 1978, threw themselves into the life of the church with passionate commitment. They headed up a pastorate group and a home group (both Millar's innovations), making a huge contribution to the rejuvenation and expansion of the congregation. This took a great step forward when it was decided to close the second church in the parish, St Paul's Onslow Square, and merge it with HTB. St Paul's had a younger, congregation, containing many students. The sudden mixture of college scarves and jeans with Savile Row suits and mink stoles in the pews of a much fuller HTB created a buzz in the church which began an era of energizing growth in which the Gumbels were attractive young leaders.

For Nicky and Pippa, the growth was personal as well as institutional. They deepened their prayer life and Bible studies, taking spiritual guidance from the new Vicar Canon John Collins, from his curate Sandy Millar, and from visiting speakers, of whom the American evangelist John Wimber had the most dramatic influence.

Gumbel was initially 'incredibly cynical' about Wimber who was a well-known pastor from the Vineyard church in Anaheim, California. A forceful speaker who combined charismatic preaching and Pentecostal Biblicism with a healing ministry, Wimber aroused strong anti-American prejudices in Gumbel. Those prejudices were deepened by the tone and context of Wimber's first Sunday evening sermon at HTB in the spring of 1982. Despite his cynicism, Gumbel came back the following Monday evening to listen to Wimber's talk to the church's home group members. Arriving late from a Crown Court where he had been appearing in formal barrister's attire, Gumbel, who described himself as 'looking incredibly pompous', had to take a seat embarrassingly close to the speaker at the front of the jam-packed hall.

Wimber's talk was about the power of the Holy Spirit to heal. He combined it by saying that he had some supernaturally inspired

'Words of Knowledge' to impart. The first such words were the statement: 'There are ten people in this room who have athlete's foot. Would they please stand up?' Nine people stood up. Nicky Gumbel, who did have athletes foot, sat firmly in his seat, determined not to draw attention to himself.

Pippa Gumbel had other ideas. She dug her elbow deep into her husband's ribs, saying 'That's you! Stand up!' These wifely nudges were the start of a life-changing experience. Gumbel stood up. An American member of John Wimber's ministry team came over and said 'Would you like me to pray for your athlete's foot?'

'No, thank you,' said Gumbel, desperately anxious to avoid further embarrassment. 'I am perfectly happy having athlete's foot. I find it quite satisfying being able to scratch it when it itches.' The American was persistent. 'Is there anything else we could pray for?' he asked. 'Well, what I would really like to pray for is an experience of the Holy Spirit,' replied Gumbel. 'Ok, we'll pray for that,' said the Wimber team member, opening up with a prayer which had, literally, earth-shaking effects.

'All I can say is that after he had been praying for about 30 seconds I experienced the power of God in a way that I had never experienced before,' recalls Gumbel. 'At that moment it was like 10,000 volts of electricity going through my body. I know that it does not happen like this for everyone but that was how it happened to me. In fact it was so powerful I really couldn't take it any more after a bit. I think this American must have only just joined the ministry team because basically he only had one prayer that he kept praying, 'More power, Lord!' And every time he prayed this prayer the power increased. So eventually I didn't know what to do so I decided the best thing to do was to pray against him. So I started praying, 'No more power, Lord!'

These conflicting prayers developed into something of a shouting match. It became such a noisy contest that it got everyone's attention. The whole room stopped praying as they watched what was happening in the front of the hall. John Wimber came over to the shaking Gumbel. 'Take that one out,' he commanded with the authority of a pastor who had seen manifestations of the Holy Spirit's power many times before. As the prostrate body of Nicky Gumbel was lifted off the ground and carried out through the French windows of Church House into the garden of Holy Trinity Brompton, John Wimber made an extraordinary comment: 'God is giving to that man the ability to tell people about Jesus.'

This comment struck home because it came at a time when Gumbel was revisiting the thoughts of ordination which had first stirred within him soon after his conversion experience at Cambridge nearly ten years earlier. Now with far greater intensity he again was asking: Did he have a call to serve God in the ordained ministry? He prayed and talked about it for many hours with Sandy Millar. One difficult sacrifice would be abandoning his life at the Bar, a move which would have horrified his agnostic and career-focused barrister father. But Walter Gumbel, who was revered by his only son, died in 1981 so was not around to argue differently. Instead, Sandy Millar advised Nicky to do some career futurology. He should imagine himself still at the Bar in ten years' time, assume he had achieved everything he hoped for, and then ask the question: 'Is that really where I want to be?' Millar said the most important question for Gumbel to ask himself was: 'Could the Holy Spirit be leading me in a quite different direction?'

With Sandy Millar's suggested course of action ringing in his ears, Nicky took Pippa away for a week-end to pray about this personalized issue of the law and the Spirit. Reading their Bible they drew inspiration from the book of the Old Testament prophet Nehemiah. Its early chapters tell the story of how Nehemiah prays to God and is divinely guided to start rebuilding the ruined city wall of Jerusalem. Despite many obstacles and considerable ridicule, God helps Nehemiah to succeed and the wall gets built. The message seemed clear to both Gumbels. Within days of coming back from their week-end, Nicky applied to become a candidate for ordination training.

Although his application was approved by the Church of England authorities, Nicky Gumbel soon encountered difficulties over his proposed change of career. He left the Bar despite strong opposition from members of his chambers and particularly from an all important figure there, Mr Alan Brewer the clerk of the chambers at 2 Hare Court. Then Gumbel discovered he could not get a place in the theological college he had chosen to do his training. This was Cranmer Hall, Durham. It was completely full for the academic year. The last available place had just been awarded to his great friend and Cambridge contemporary Nicky Lee. Faced with this 'no room at the inn' situation, Gumbel had to go back to the Bar for a year. This retracing of his steps did not get a good reaction from his chambers. Mr Alan Brewer, the clerk who controlled the flow of work, was understandably reluctant to pass briefs to a barrister who had become at best a bird of passage and at worst a lame duck. So Gumbel did not have a prosperous last year at the Bar as he waited to take up a place in a different theological college, Wycliffe Hall, Oxford.

Nicky Gumbel's three years of ordination training at Wycliffe, between 1983 and 1985, could appropriately be described as a 'curate's egg' experience. Parts of it were excellent but other parts disappointed him so much that there were times when he seriously doubted his vocation and considered a permanent return to the Bar.

One problem that cast a shadow over Gumbel's early months at Wycliffe was jaundice. He was diagnosed with the viral strain of hepatitis A within days of moving into his digs. As the virus is both debilitating and infectious, he had to stay away from lectures and was initially too tired to do all the required reading. Eventually he recovered, but the illness weakened him for months. It was not his only difficulty.

Wycliffe in 1983 was an evangelical theological college firmly rooted in traditions that were so formal and conservative that they bordered on stuffiness. By contrast Gumbel was an innovator, a charismatic, and a disciple of the John Wimber school of evangelism and miraculous healing. At 28 he was some five years older than most of his fellow students, married with two young children and with a background of professional experience as a barrister. 'Nicky seemed quite a bit different from the rest of us,' recalled his Wycliffe contemporary Graham Tomlin who shared tutorials with Gumbel; 'there were aspects of him that reflected an inner unhappiness which at times caused him to question whether or not there was a place, for him in the Church of England.'

One cause of this unhappiness was the curriculum of the Oxford school's course. This put so much emphasis on liberal theology and form criticism that the Biblically orthodox Gumbel had serious difficulties in reconciling the teachings of his tutors with the foundations of his faith. Another problem was an atmosphere of alienation which developed between members of the charismatic tendency at Wycliffe and the rest of the student body. Gumbel and his half dozen or so fellow charismatics slipped into a culture of separateness; sitting at their own table in hall, constantly chafing against the ecclesiastical staidness of the college.

Fortunately there was another side to Wycliffe. Some of it was supplied by a newly arrived 30-year-old lecturer of extraordinary talent and prodigious literary output. He was Alister McGrath, later to become Principal of the college, Oxford University Professor of Theology, and author of over 40 theological books. His lectures on Christian doctrine, reform theology, early church patristics and Martin Luther inspired Nicky Gumbel the ordinand. To this day many of Gumbel's talks at HTB, including the Alpha course sessions on the cross, are clearly derived from McGrath's teachings and writings. So too perhaps is Gumbel's emphasis on personal testimonies. For he is clearly a follower of that strand of Reformation theology enshrined in Melanchthon's famous dictum, 'to know Christ is to know his benefits'. To Gumbel real-life encounters with Christ are infinitely more important than academic-life writings about Christian doctrine. This may explain why Alpha has developed in a form that is acceptable to all denominations across a remarkable wide spectrum of Christian churches. Instead of concentrating on matters of doctrine, its strongest emphasis is on the authenticity of individual encounters with Jesus Christ.

One place where Nicky Gumbel encountered the transforming power of Jesus Christ while at Oxford was at Campsfield House, a Young Offenders' Institution in Kidlington, five miles north of the city. In the early 1980s the Home Secretary of the day, William Whitelaw, was endeavouring to impose the military culture of 'the glass house' and 'the short sharp shock' on teenage prisoners. Into this tough regime at Campsfield, Wycliffe sent Gumbel on a summer placement. 'It was an environment that brought out the best of Nicky's gifts. You could see so clearly that he was a real evangelist,' recalled Graham Tomlin who was doing the same placement at Campsfield; 'he was so good at communicating the gospel with real passion and simplicity. He had a natural rapport with people and an ability to bring them, without putting them under pressure, to the point where they wanted to make a commitment.'

As Nicky Gumbel came towards the end of his three-year BA degree course in the summer term of 1985, he was himself feeling under pressure on two fronts – to get a first and to get a job as a curate. The Oxford University examiners awarded him a Second, although his tutors and his contemporaries thought he deserved a First on grounds of both his intellect and his industry. If that result was a disappointment to him, it was a smaller one than his problem in finding a curacy. For of all the ordinands in his year at Wycliffe, Gumbel was the only one who went down from Oxford without being able to find an appointment anywhere in the Church of England. He was considered by nine parishes but none of his applications succeeded. Sometimes he was rejected, sometimes he himself felt he would not fit, and in one parish where everything seemed right on both sides the outgoing curate did not move out after all. By August 1985 Gumbel was getting so desperate that he signed on for the dole. He wondered whether God was signalling that he should serve in lay ministry rather than as an ordained priest. There were, however, other signs that his gifts as an evangelist might bring him to a place where God wanted him to be. Gumbel did a summer placement with an American Vineyard Church in Newport Beach, California, where his teaching skills won golden opinions and a flow of conversions. Then he led a house party, organized by the Stewards' Trust in Oxfordshire, where he had to give six one-hour talks on St Paul's letter to the Philippians. One of those present was Zilla Hawkins who remembers: 'I did not know Nicky all that well in those days but I was wowed by the brilliant way he taught the house party – so simply but so clearly. It's a big test to sustain a whole week of Bible teaching and he clearly had an extraordinary talent for it.' One other group of people who appreciated Gumbel's talent and wanted to make use of it were the leaders of HTB. 'I kept telling him in monosyllables that he must come here,' recalls his old friend Ken

Costa who by this time was a key figure on the Parochial Church Council. However, different monosyllables were being uttered by the Bishop of Kensington who maintained a rule in his diocese that newly ordained deacons should not return to the churches which had originally put them forward for ordination training. He reinforced it with the words 'over my dead body' when initially approached about allowing an exception in the case of Gumbel. The voice of the Bishop was met with the voice of rebellion. Ken Costa and his friends set off on a week-end of unusual spiritual activity at Ashburnham House in Sussex. Their mission was 'to pray against the Bishop's resistance'. Accompanied by some tough talking, the prayers worked. The combination of the iron determination of Ken Costa ('this was a battle that had to be fought and won') and the velvet diplomacy of Sandy Millar (by now the vicar) persuaded the Bishop to change his mind. In the autumn of 1986 the Revd Nicholas Gumbel joined HTB as a new curate. After a testing period in the wilderness he had come home.

In the first five years of his curacy Gumbel was engaged in general church duties shared by the HTB team of ordained ministers. It was a heady time of growth and renewal. During the 1980s HTB changed from being a quintessentially Anglican establishment into a Spirit-filled experimenting church with an extraordinary capacity for reaching out to young people. Some of its critics said 'HTB is going OTT', 'becoming more like a Pentecostal church' and 'catering for the over-excitable Hooray Henrys and Henriettas of South Ken'. None of these charges were true but nor were they completely false. Sandy Millar's deceptively vague style of collegiate leadership was tolerant enough to allow innovation but disciplined enough to stay within the boundaries of Anglicanism. Formal membership of the Church of England was not emphasised but not abandoned. Instead with an enormous confidence unshared by the majority of Anglican clergymen of the late twentieth century, the HTB team build a successful, thriving and dramatically growing church. It was based on a network of central London pastorates, home groups, church plants and Bible study conferences which brought more and more people, particularly young people, to a living faith.

Nicky Gumbel's speciality was the leading of pastorates and the evangelizing of younger people. His own youth, energy and charm enabled him to be particularly effective in small relational situations such as home groups. He was enjoying this form of ministry so much that he appeared far from pleased when in 1990 his role in the church changed and he was put in charge of Alpha. However, the appearance was not the whole story. 'Alpha was what he most wanted to do yet most dreaded doing,' said his wife Pippa. 'He knew it was his greatest challenge but at first he hesitated about taking it on because he was so overwhelmed with other work at the church.'

The Alpha course had been running for nearly ten years. It was an in-house teaching course for members of the congregation who wanted to strengthen their faith. It had been created in 1981 as a six-session seminar by Charles Marnham, a curate who thought that experienced Christians would appreciate an opportunity to ask questions about the deeper teachings of Jesus. It was developed by a successor curate, John Irvine, into a ten-week course for new Christians. Nicky Lee, who had preceded his friend Nicky Gumbel into ordination and a curacy at HTB in 1984, was the next Alpha leader but when he handed over the reins, the course was still predominantly for existing believers who were regular worshippers at the church.

During his first few months in charge of Alpha, Gumbel did not change a word of the course. Not only did he maintain its substance, he imitated his predecessor's style of delivery right down to inflexions of voice and timing of pauses. This was partly because Gumbel was simply too busy to review the entire project. Only after a member of the congregation told him he sounded 'too boring' did he begin to rethink and restructure the material. Gumbel's overhaul was radical. Instead of a course for new Christians, he was first to see the potential for using Alpha as a tool for a form of evangelism which would reach out to the unchurched far beyond the normal horizons of HTB.

Turning the potential into the reality was hard work. Blood, toil, sweat and tears (most of them Gumbel's) went into the remodelling of the Alpha course. At one level it was pitched in an unthreatening user-friendly way at uncommitted nominal believers who have vague leanings towards spiritual curiosity. On the other hand, the course was uncompromising in its orthodoxy and Biblical fidelity. Sources of theological inspiration included John Stott, Leslie Newbiggin, John Wimber on healing and the Holy Spirit, and the Pope's chaplain Father Raniero Cantalamessa on the forgiveness of sins. Whatever the mixture, it worked. When Gumbel took over the old Alpha it was the preserve of 100–200 local HTB adherents each year. The new Alpha has now been completed by 8 million people in 160 countries. What has caused this exponential growth and where is it heading?

The first sign that Gumbel's remodelled course might be a winner came within HTB when members of the congregation said in effect 'This is rather good'. They passed round invitations to their non-Christian friends. Those who came to it were relieved to find how 'unchurchy' Alpha was. Gumbel deliberately created a laid-back and casual atmosphere for Alpha evenings. Before the talk began the guests were given a meal at which no mention of God or religion were allowed. After the talk, groups were formed where no-holds-barred discussions were encouraged. It was a style that caught on. Other churches started to hear about Alpha and asked for material about it. A booklet was hastily published, tapes of Gumbel's talks were recorded, and in 1992 HTB put on its first ever Alpha conference. To general astonishment over 1,000 people attended, many from churches seeking a new form of evangelism. It proved popular. Within a couple of years several hundred churches in the UK were regularly offering Alpha courses in their local parishes and communities.

The next quantum leap forward for Alpha, both internationally and domestically, followed a bizarre episode which many HTB people are now too embarrassed to talk about. This was the summer of the Toronto Blessing in 1994.

HTB, for all its willingness to innovate and rejuvenate, had always been a well-run church filled with sensible Christian people. Suddenly it was hit by what Richard Chartres, the Bishop of London, calls 'one of those waves which create a moment when rational individuals can lose their moorings'. What happened was that two well-known supporters of the Alpha course came back from a visit to Canada and told the congregation of HTB about an extraordinary phenomenon they had experienced in a charismatic church near Toronto airport. The pastor of this church made a regular practice, as some charismatic pastors do, of calling down the Holy Spirit during the Sunday service. This would not have sounded all that unusual at HTB, for ever since the visit of John Wimber, appeals for the Holy Spirit to fill individual hearts had been a regular part of the Alpha course and the life of the church.

What was unusual about the calling down of the Holy Spirit at this church in Toronto was the reaction of the congregation. For Sunday after Sunday the call to the Holy Spirit, which became known as the Toronto Blessing, was accompanied by hundreds and hundreds of worshippers crashing to the floor in uncontrollable laughter. Whether this was due to mass hysteria, something in the air around this particular church in Toronto, or an extraordinary outpouring of sincere Spirit-led fervour, was a matter of speculation. The phenomenon itself was real, as many journalists and other outside visitors attested. But whatever was happening in Toronto, it was a safe bet that this 'blessing' could not conceivably be transplanted to a sensible Anglican church in central London with the same laughing, floor-crashing effects on a congregation of middle-class Kensington residents.

The safe bet would have been lost. For one Sunday evening at HTB when the congregation listened to an eyewitness account of the goings on in Toronto, the Revd Sandy Millar said to his congregation 'And now let us pray for the Holy Spirit to come and fill our hearts'. Whereupon, to most people's utter amazement, dozens and dozens of ordinary churchgoers fell to the floor in loud cries of laughter, moaning, and even occasionally dog-like barks. This astonishing behaviour was not a one-off event. For several weeks the 'rolling in the aisles' phenomenon became a regular feature of services and prayer meetings at HTB. The church had recently taken on a press officer, Mark Elsdon-Dew, a former foreign news editor of the *Sunday Express*. 'This was a press officer's nightmare,' he has recalled. 'Instead of doing my job of promoting a growing church run by respectable, Godly people I was dealing with the spectre of the same respectable people rolling around on the church floor.' An even more bemused witness of these startling activities was the Very Revd Ray Muller, the Archdeacon of Auckland, New Zealand. Arriving at HTB on time for his appointment, Archdeacon Muller asked for the Revd Nicky Gumbel, only to be told by a giggling receptionist, 'I'm afraid you'll have to wait. Nicky is crawling around on his hands and knees. He's having a Holy Spirit experience and he can't get off the floor.'

After a few more heady months of floor crawling and similar activities, the Toronto Blessing moved off the agenda at HTB. It stopped as mysteriously as it had started.

To this day opinions are divided on the merits or demerits of the Toronto Blessing's impact on HTB. One senior member of the congregation calls that period 'the unhappy time when Sandy Millar and Nickey Gumbel went off the rails'. The formidable Ken Costa disagrees: 'No, it put us on the rails. Our evangelism became more intense because of the Toronto Blessing.' The Bishop of London's studiously polite neutrality in describing it as 'one of those waves' represented the somewhat anxious view of the church establishment. On the whole, the members of the HTB congregation, both the ancient and modern, united in the view that their church was breaking experimental new ground in evangelism and that the pioneers of the experiment should be supported rather than scoffed at. Perhaps it should be recorded that the surprised Archdeacon of Auckland was not one of the scoffers. He came to regard these manifestations of the power of the Holy Spirit as 'totally authentic'. More importantly he took the Alpha course back to the churches and denominations of New Zealand with unparalleled effectiveness in terms of national coverage. For within the next seven years more New Zealanders per head of population (150,000 out of 3.3 million) completed the Alpha course than in any other country of the world.

International expansion did not come easily to either HTB or Alpha. Buoyed up by the course's success in the UK where over 5,000 churches were running it by 1995, Nicky Gumbel became an excited globalist when requests for information on how to start Alpha began arriving from countries all across the world. Sandy Millar, however, was more cautious. As vicar of HTB he did not want to see his church dominated by Alpha. For a time there was tension between the two close friends. It was resolved by prayer and mutual understanding. Nicky summoned up his reserves of patience and deferred obediently to his vicar. Sandy changed his mind and gave the green light to Alpha's international expansion, subject, however, to the somewhat bureaucratic proviso that the number of Alpha staff in the HTB office should always be equalled by the church staff. There was a touch of 'Yes, Minister' in this solution but it solved the problem.

At the height the frenetic global and UK growth that exploded in the mid-1990s for Alpha, Nicky Gumbel suffered an agonizing personal loss. One of his closest friends at HTB was Mick Hawkins, a 42-year-old Lloyds insurance broker. Both men were highly competitive in their regular games of squash. In July 1996, when 1500 members of HTB's congregation were enjoying an away week called 'Focus' at Pakefield holiday camp in East Suffolk, the two men went off to play at the nearby Kissingland squash club. In the third game of their match, Mick Hawkins had a massive heart attack and died on the court.

Nicky Gumbel was shattered to the core of his being. He could not understand how God could allow such a devastating tragedy. In his grief, in his efforts to comfort Mick's widow Zilla and their six fatherless children, and in his failure to build a bridge of comprehension between his faith and his loss, Gumbel passed through one of the worst periods of his life, equivalent to a long dark night of the soul.

There are those who believe that this terrible experience may have given Nicky Gumbel a more mature and a deeper spirituality based on the sharing of suffering. As he came through the dark valley of grief he gave wonderful pastoral care to the Hawkins family, holidaying with them annually and becoming a much-loved father figure to the bereaved children. He also threw himself into his Alpha work with even greater intensity. He analysed and published every word in the course, constantly adjusted its presentation, and was never satisfied with his own leadership of it. His obsessive attention to detail did not turn him into a proprietorial figure at Alpha. He was careful to emphasize that the course did not belong to him. He saw himself merely as its temporary custodian, equivalent to the borrower of a car.

The car was now travelling extremely fast. Alpha spread across the nation and the world because it filled a need and caught a mood. The need was for a new presentation of Christian evangelism that was relational, inclusive, unthreatening in its style yet Bibically faithful in its substance. The mood was for change: supported inside denominations and churches yet reaching outside to people, particularly younger people, whom the churches and denominations were failing to reach. It was a great mystery how Nicky Gumbel's became the evangelistic voice that was of such universal appeal that it could fill auditoriums and stadiums across the world with huge audiences of non-churchgoers, ranging from white Australians to black Zimbabweans and a melting pot of over 100 multiracial nationalities in between. This was no less a mystery to the man himself. 'We have watched with total astonishment as Alpha has spread through every major denomination in the world,' says Gumbel. 'What surprises us more than anything else is the way it seems to work in so many different cultures.'

One secular explanation for Alpha's success is good marketing. The course, now translated into 64 languages, is packaged and distributed worldwide on tapes and in booklets with exemplary efficiency. Another explanation is good speaking, with the lion's share of it being done by Gumbel himself on film, video tape and in person. In the last decade he has been an indefatigable traveller, at his best in the setting of what are called Alpha International Training Conferences. These are held in big cities for leaders who will themselves teach the course in their own parishes or denominational districts. In population centres as disparate as Washington DC, Melbourne, Singapore, Moscow, Lagos, Johannesburg, New York, Kuala Lumpur, Los Angeles, Tokyo and Shanghai, present and future leaders of the course flock in their hundreds, occasionally in their thousands, to listen to Gumbel's message which opens with a superbly effective address titled 'Principles of Alpha'.

This talk distils the essence of Alpha but also the essence of Nicky Gumbel. On display are the qualities that have made him such an outstanding evangelist. One is self-deprecation: 'I am *not* a natural evangelist,' he begins, going on to demonstrate with humour and humility how he has become exactly that. The humour is important. He has telling laugh lines such as 'We in the Anglican church are very keen on change, so long as nothing alters', and powerful anecdotes. Yet the core of his morning-long address (interspersed with coffee breaks) is the teaching of evangelistic principles. According to Gumbel: Evangelism is most effective through local churches. It is friendship based. It is a process of building trust. It must appeal to head, heart, conscience and will. It must go hand-in-hand with social action to transform society and it must be accompanied by a demonstration of the Spirit's power. The talk builds to a crescendo when Gumbel comes to his sixth and last principle of Alpha evangelism: 'Principle No. 6 – Effective evangelism requires the filling and refilling of the Holy Spirit. Please don't misunderstand what we are saying here. We are not talking about a second blessing. What we are talking about is experiencing God as Trinity: as Father, Son and Holy Spirit. And we believe that this experience should happen at the moment of conversion and continue in the life of the believer.'

Then Gumbel soars away on a romp through his heroes of spirit-filled evangelism. Peter on the day of Pentecost; John Wesley the founder of modern Methodism; Charles Finney; D. L. Moody; Billy Graham; and Father Raniero Cantalamessa, official preacher to the papal household of John Paul II. The talk concludes with the hilarious but powerful story of Gumbel's first experience of the Holy Spirit which ends with him being carried out through the French windows of Church House, HTB with John Wimber saying: 'God is giving to that man the ability to tell people about Jesus.'

At that point in his peroration, Nicky Gumbel drops his voice to quiet yet passionate intensity as he finishes: 'I have often looked back to that moment because what it has taught me is this: this experience of the Holy Spirit is not just for these great evangelists. It is for all of us. For ordinary people like me who are not natural evangelists and therefore it is for every single person who comes on an Alpha course. Our prayer is that they will come to know Christ. That they will be filled with his Spirit. That they will get excited about Jesus and they will go out and tell their friends.'

Nicky Gumbel must have delivered this 'Principles of Alpha' talk in well over 400 locations around the world. His international audiences of experienced church leaders are often initially resistant to the idea that a course created in an elite corner of the dear old Church of

England (memorably described by its then Archbishop of Canterbury to the Reader's Digest in 1991 as 'an old lady sitting in the corner mouthing ancient platitudes through toothless gums') could possibly be relevant and effective as a tool of worldwide evangelism. I well recall such audience scepticism at an Alpha Training Conference in Boston which I attended in 2001. Although many denominations from all over New England were represented, the preponderant element among the 1,500 church leaders present were Catholic clergymen from the Archdiocese of Boston. The group of these American clerics with whom I found myself sitting were openly sceptical about the value of what one of them called 'Protestant hot gospelling', explaining that they were only at the conference because their Bishop had ordered them to come. All this was before Nicky Gumbel had opened his mouth. After he finished his address it seemed as if the Holy Spirit had worked a miracle. For my neighbours had been transformed into Alpha enthusiasts, or at least into willing starters of Alpha courses in their own churches. I was amazed by their reactions, O me of little faith! Five years after that conference many Catholic Archdioceses in the USA are strong and successful supporters of Alpha's growth in their parishes, where over a million people have completed the course.

Perhaps I should not have been so amazed by the scepticism of those Catholic priests. For it is hard to imagine anyone who could have been more cynical about Alpha than I was on the evening of the 1 October 1997 when my friend Michael Alison physically escorted me into HTB on the first night of the autumn course.

As a somewhat nominal member of the church reticent wing of Anglicanism I was strongly resistant to what I thought Alpha involved: Happy clappies twanging electric guitars; 40 minute in-your-face sermons preached by wild curates; and cringe making sessions of group therapy in which a surfeit of religious cheese gets stuffed down the participants' throats by cheesy Christians. Although Michael Alison assured me these stereotypes would turn out to be wrong, I had read otherwise in magazine articles. In the end I only went along out of good manners to Michael (a former church warden of HTB and a retired MP) because he had been such a caring friend to me when my life was in freefall through the personal catastrophes of disgrace, defeat, divorce, bankruptcy and jail. Perhaps these breaking experiences gave me a greater willingness to take on some new listening experiences. So I said I was prepared to come and listen to Alpha – but only once.

My reactions to the first session of the Alpha course were personal relief followed by professional respect. Neither feeling was particularly spiritual.

The relief came from finding that no-one happied or clappied at me, nobody tried to stuff religion down my throat, and that the group I was assigned to consisted of normal, intelligent, congenial people who were extremely unlikely candidates for any sort of activity that might remotely resemble group therapy. In the discussion after the talk *Who is Jesus?* we all felt we had heard a well-argued case. 'You can tell he used to be good with juries,' someone said of the speaker. He was an athletic looking young man in his early forties coolly dressed in hipster-style jeans, wide-buckled belt and blue open-neck shirt which gave him the appearance of an in-vogue movie actor rather than an out of date clergyman. This was the first time I had heard of or listened to Nicky Gumbel. I remember being impressed by the depth of his historical research from sources like Tacitus and Josephus as well as by his skilful use of quotations from C. S. Lewis, Lord Hailsham and Josh McDowell. 'A good professional speaker,' I said to myself in a rather condescending way, simultaneously thinking that even though the evening had been much better than expected nevertheless I would not come back the following Wednesday for session No. 2 if I received any better invitation. It was, however, a time in my life when no invitations were coming through my letter box. So I stayed with the course for the next three or four sessions, becoming increasingly impressed by Gumbel's presentations but remaining resolutely semi-detached from God. This changed on the fifth talk which was given by a temporary replacement for Gumbel who had the visual advantage of being an attractive young woman in a mini-skirt. At the beginning of her talk I was much more interested in her mini-skirt than her message. However, as she warmed to her theme of *Why and how do I pray?* both the subject and speaker got to me. That night I went home and injected into my barren prayer life the Alpha course's suggestions on how to pray. They changed my prayer life and then my entire life. Soon I became conscious that I was travelling on a spiritual journey with a strange new momentum. It was strong enough to make me consider going to an event I would normally have run away from. This was the Alpha course's 'Holy Spirit weekend' whose importance had been heavily emphasized by Gumbel in his opening talks.

Nicky Gumbel's suggestion was that those of us doing the course under his leadership should set off in our groups for two nights at the Chatsworth Hotel in Worthing. During the week-end the Holy Spirit would be called down to fill our hearts. This was a concept far beyond the horizons of my imagination. Although I had been impressed and at times inspired by the teaching in the first eight sessions of the Alpha course, I was sure that this notion of the Holy Spirit appearing in the Chatsworth Hotel, Worthing was about as improbable an event as Marilyn Monroe's spirit making an appearance in Claridges Hotel, London. I was definitely a Spirit-sceptic.

Despite that scepticism I did have a powerful Holy Spirit experience during the Worthing week-end. As I have described it at length in an earlier book *Pride and Perjury* I will not repeat it here. It was not quite as spectacular as Nicky Gumbel's first Holy Spirit experience with John Wimber in 1982 but not all that far off it for my whole body was suffused by strange uncontrollable shakings, laughter and tears of joy. I could not believe these extraordinary phenomena were happening to me. Indeed, I might well have pretended to disbelieve them immediately afterwards but for the fact that my immediate companions praying over me at the time were two successful lawyers, Tom Adam, a tax barrister and Bruce Streather, the founding partner of Streathers, a well-known firm of solicitors. In these circumstances there could be no doubt, especially in the presence of such good legal witnesses, that I had received a genuine manifestation of the power of the Holy Spirit. A little later when I had calmed down I talked to Nicky Gumbel about what had happened. 'This will be a turning point for you,' he said. 'Everything in your life could change.'

Everything in my life did change – dramatically for the worse so far as anyone's outward eye could see. Eighteen months later I was in jail having pleaded guilty to perjury committed in my libel case against the *Guardian*. One of my first visitors in HMP Belmarsh was Nicky Gumbel. For a moment I almost failed to recognize him. So relaxed is his usual style of dress at Alpha events that I had never seen him wearing anything formal, let alone clerical. But under some curious Belmarsh rule, all ordained ministers entering the prison were required to dress like Victorian vicars. The sight of Nicky in his unaccustomed garb amused me: 'Wearing a dog collar! Now I really believe in miracles,' I said.

For all his outward geniality, Nicky Gumbel is inwardly a shy man. He has trained himself to overcome this difficulty when addressing large audiences. In one-on-one pastoral situations his shyness can return, as it did at the start of our encounter in HMP Belmarsh. Yet he also has the gift of communicating compassion perhaps because of what in his schoolboy years his friends saw as 'an ease of relationship'. This ease, combined with a natural empathy and sympathy for someone in trouble, soon turned his prison visit to me into a loving meeting of hearts, minds and prayers.

There was, however, one surreal note struck by Gumbel as we talked in the afternoon sunshine streaming through the iron-barred windows of Belmarsh. This came when he said: 'You must speak about repentance when you come out of prison. Many people will want to listen to you. You could have a powerful impact as a witness for Christ.' This seemed such a ridiculous idea that I laughed. In the days after my sentence I was so vilified as a media hate-figure that the idea of doing any sort of public speaking seemed impossible. This was not false modesty on my part. It was an utterly realistic assessment not only from my perspective as a prisoner but also, I suspect, from the perspective of 99 per cent of the newspaper-reading public. So I dismissed the suggestion, saying that no-one would want to listen to me.

In the six years since Nicky Gumbel's visit conversation with me in Belmarsh prison our friendship has deepened and his prediction has come true. For I now fulfil about a hundred Christian speaking engagements a year, many of them at Alpha suppers or in Alpha courses. In the beginning my reluctance to take on this role was almost as great as my reluctance to attend my first-ever Alpha session in October 1997. But there is a passive verb in the vocabulary of HTB – 'To be Gumbeled'. It means to be gently persuaded by Nicky's charm into doing something you would rather not take on, or feel inadequate to take on, for all manner of good reasons which he persuades you to ignore. Like many others, I have been well and truly Gumbeled, particularly since the summer of 2005 when he was installed as Vicar of HTB after Sandy Miller's retirement.

Although Alpha courses continue around the world in record-breaking numbers under his leadership, Vicar Gumbel is moving on from Alpha chaplain Gumbel in his evangelistic vision. This is becoming far wider and deeper with a surge of confident global expansionism. From his vicarage he has just launched a new initiative, the Alpha International Campus. In physical terms it will end up as a £20 million development of the property in and around St Paul's Onslow Square, the second church in the HTB parish which has been unused as a place of worship for over 20 years. However, the spiritual development from the site is infinitely more important that the bricks and mortar development of the site.

Nicky Gumbel's vision is to build Alpha into a much larger Holy Spirit-filled international evangelistic ministry that will transform tens of millions of lives in London and in other cities and nations across the world. To unbelieving sceptics this will seem a preposterous fantasy. To evangelical enthusiasts it will seem a project, dedicated to the glory of God, which is rooted in realism as well as believism. For Gumbel's target of 25 million people doing Alpha in the next 15 years starts from the firm track record of 8 million people having completed the course in the last ten years. The previous decade's growth of Alpha, which began in the second half of the 1990s, was achieved by old-fashioned methods of communication (word of mouth, printed booklets, announcements from pulpits) and administration. With modern communications and far stronger support mechanisms in place, a three-fold increase in Alpha before 2025 is surely achievable, says Gumbel, always adding his all important rider about the power of the Holy Spirit.

The practicalities of Gumbel's new vision for Alpha requires the transformation of the St Paul's Onslow Square site into a multipurpose facility which includes a 1,400 seat auditorium for London Alpha goers; a state-of-the-art broadcasting facility to transmit Alpha talks and training sessions live across the world; a Family centre for the teaching of courses on Christian family values; a Social Action centre for the work of Alpha in Prisons, Caring for Ex-Offenders, Alpha in the Armed Forces and other similar HTB offshoots which require practical back-up; and a new teaching centre, whose recently appointed principal says it will become 'the best theological college in the world'.

This ambitious new principal of what is called the St Paul's Theological Training College is Nicky Gumbel's old classmate and tutorial-sharer from Oxford days, the Revd Dr Graham Tomlin, until recently the Vice Principal of Wycliffe Hall. Anyone who knows Graham Tomlin's scholarship, teaching gifts and leadership skills (I experienced them at first hand during my two years of reading theology under him as a Wycliffe student) will know that his desire to create 'the best theological college in the world' is unlikely to prove an empty boast. Already Tomlin and Gumbel have signed up a remarkable range of theological teachers and lecturers (including Rowan Williams the Archbishop of Canterbury) who are attracted by the chance to play their part in Alpha's transformation of the worldwide church. So theology is going to play a key part in the Gumbel vision during the coming years.

Some pessimists worry that this vision is just too big, even for HTB with all its contacts, resources and global reach through Alpha. For the Alpha International Centre is in material terms a huge project and in spiritual terms far huger. But optimists point out that the project is already backed by highly influential believers, including supporters of great wealth, growing churches across the usual denominatial divides, and important religious leaders. In the last category is the Rt Revd Richard Charles Bishop of London who says, 'Nicky Gumbel has the energy and the leadership gifts to make this extraordinary development succeed. I believe he will achieve nothing less than the reconnection of the people of London with God.'

In some ways, Nicky Gumbel's thoughts are greater than those of his Bishop. For to Alpha and HTB the field is not just London but the world. Yet London has become such a multi-national, cosmopolitan crossroads for meetings between Christians from America, Africa, Asia, Australasia, Europe and Britain that it may well be the most suitable international capital to be the launching pad for Gumbel's new vision.

This vision is so astonishing that it would be easy to ridicule were it not for the past achievements of HTB and Alpha. So when Gumbel speaks futuristically of 25 million people around the world being enabled to do Alpha with the help of new broadcast studios, a theological college and a campus of supporting ministries, his words deserve to be treated realistically. For he is a practical as well as a visionary evangelist with a track record that tells its own story. That story shows that Nicky Gumbel is first and last a true servant to God; faithful to the Biblical word and confident that he and his church have been empowered by the Holy Spirit. If that power achieves in the first two decades of the twenty-first century even more than it achieved in the last 20 years with Alpha and HTB, then the world will be learning and knowing a great deal more about Nicky Gumbel.

Source Notes

Chapter 1
Author's diaries, letters, interviews and recollections
Janet Aitken Kidd: *The Beaverbrook Girl* (Collins, 1987)
Lord Beaverbrook: *The Decline and Fall of Lloyd George* (Collins, 1963)
—— *The Divine Propagandist* (Heinemann, 1963)
—— *Don't Trust to Luck* (Stanley Paul, 1921)
Anne Chisholm and Michael Davie: *Beaverbrook: A Life* (Hutchinson, 1992)
David Farrer: *G for God Almighty* (Weidenfeld & Nicolson, 1969)
A. J. P. Taylor: *Beaverbrook* (Hamish Hamilton, 1972)
C. M. Vines: *A Little Nut Brown Man* (Leslie Frewin, 1969)

Chapter 2
Author's diaries, letters, interviews and recollections
Martin Gilbert: *The Churchill Biography: Volume VIII: 'Never Despair' 1945–1965* (Heinemann, 1984)

Chapter 3
Author's personal diaries, letters, interviews and recollections
Randolph S. Churchill: *The Fight for the Tory Leadership* (Heinemann, 1964)
Winston S. Churchill: *His Father's Son* (HarperCollins, 1996)

Martin Gilbert: *In Search of Churchill* (HarperCollins, 1993)
Kay Halle: *Randolph Churchill, The Young Unpretender* (Heinemann, 1971)

Chapter 4
Author's diaries, letters, interviews and recollections
Jonathan Aitken: *Porridge and Passion* (Continuum, 2005)
Lord Longford: *Five Lives* (Hutchinson, 1964)
—— *Pornography: the Longford Report* (Coronet, 1964)
—— *Nixon: a Study of Extremes of Fortune* (Weidenfeld, 1980)
—— *Avowed Intent* (Little Brown, 1994)
—— *Lord Longford's Prison Diary* (Lion, 2000)
Frank Pakenham: *Born to Believe* (Cape, 1953)
—— *The Idea of Punishment* (Geoffrey Chapman, 1961)
—— *Causes of Crime*, with Roger Opie (Weidenfeld, 1958)
Peter Stanford: *The Outcasts' Outcast* (Sutton, 2003)
Peter Wildeblood: *Against the Law* (Weidenfeld, 1955)

Chapter 5
Author's diaries, letters, interviews and recollections
Jonathan Aitken: *Nixon: A Life* (Weidenfeld, 1993)
James Callaghan: *Time and Chance* (Collins, 1987)
Paul Foot: *The Politics of Harold Wilson* (Penguin, 1968)
Tom Mangold: *Cold War Warrior, James Jesus Angleton* (Simon & Schuster, 1991)
Ben Pimlott: *Harold Wilson* (HarperCollins, 1992)
Harold Wilson: *The Making of a Prime Minister 1916–1964* (Weidenfeld, 1986)
—— *Final Term 1974–76* (Weidenfeld, 1979)
—— *The Governance of Britain* (Weidenfeld, 1979)

Chapter 6
Author's diaries, letters, interviews and recollections
Jonathan Aitken: *Pride and Perjury* (HarperCollins, 2000)
Mark Hollingsworth and Paul Halloran: *Thatcher's Fortunes* (Mainstream, 2005)

Carol Thatcher: *Below the Parapet* (HarperCollins, 1996)
Margaret Thatcher: *The Downing Street Years* (HarperCollins, 1993)
—— *The Path to Power* (HarperCollins, 1995)
Hugo Young: *One of Us* (Macmillan, 1989)

Chapter 7
Author's diaries, letters, interviews and personal recollections
Jonathan Aitken: *The Young Meteors* (Secker and Warburg, 1966)
Aspinall, John: *The Best of Friends* (Macmillan, 1976)
—— *Some Aspects of Gorilla Behaviour* (Hanover, 1982)
Ivan Fallon: *Billionaire* (Hutchinson, 1991)
Annabel Goldsmith: *Annabel* (Weidenfeld, 2004)
Richard Ingrams: *Goldenballs* (Deutsch, 1979)
John Major: *The Autobiography* (HarperCollins, 1999)
Brian Masters: *The Passion of John Aspinall* (Cape, 1968)
John Pearson: *The Gamblers* (Century, 2005)
Taki Theodoracopulos: *Princes, Playboys and High Class Tarts* (Karz-Cohl, 1984)
Geoffrey Wansell: *Tycoon, the Life of James Goldsmith* (Grafton, 1987)

Chapter 8
Author's diaries, letters, interviews and recollections
Adam Cooper: *Piers Courage* (Haynes Publishing, 2003)
Maurice Hamilton: *Frank Williams* (Macmillan, 1998)
Doug Nye: *Racers* (Arthur Barker, 1982)
Virginia Williams: *A Different Kind of Life* (Doubleday, 1991)

Chapter 9
Author's diaries, letters, interviews and recollections
Michael Gove: *Michael Portillo, The Future of the Right* (Fourth Estate, 1995)
Margaret Thatcher: *The Downing Street Years* (HarperCollins, 1993)

Chapter 10
Author's diaries, letters, interviews and recollections
Jonathan Aitken: *Pride and Perjury* (HarperCollins, 2000)
—— *Porridge and Passion* (Continuum, 2005)
Nicky Gumbel: *Questions of Life* (Hodder & Stoughton, 2001)